ADVANCES IN ECONOMETRICS AND MODELLING

**ADVANCED STUDIES IN THEORETICAL AND APPLIED ECONOMETRICS
VOLUME 15**

For a complete list of volumes in this series see final page of this volume.

Advances in Econometrics and Modelling

edited by

Baldev Raj
Wilfrid Laurier University, Waterloo, Canada

KLUWER ACADEMIC PUBLISHERS
DORDRECHT / BOSTON / LONDON

Library of Congress Cataloging in Publication Data

Advances in econometrics and modelling / edited by Baldev Raj.
       p.   cm. -- (Advanced studies in theoretical and applied
    econometrics ; v. 15)
      Papers based on presentations at conferences held by the Canadian
    Econometric Study Group.
      Includes bibliographies and index.
      ISBN 0-7923-0299-0 (U.S.)
      1. Econometrics--Congresses. 2. Econometric models--Congresses.
    I. Raj, Baldev, 1941-   . II. Canadian Econometric Study Group.
    HB139.A34   1989
  · 330'.01'5195--dc20   89-8190
                                                                  CIP

ISBN 0-7923-0299-0

Published by Kluwer Academic Publishers,
P.O. Box 17, 3300 AA Dordrecht, The Netherlands.

Kluwer Academic Publishers incorporates
the publishing programmes of
D. Reidel, Martinus Nijhoff, Dr W. Junk and MTP Press.

Sold and distributed in the U.S.A. and Canada
by Kluwer Academic Publishers,
101 Philip Drive, Norwell, MA 02061, U.S.A.

In all other countries, sold and distributed
by Kluwer Academic Publishers Group,
P.O. Box 322, 3300 AH Dordrecht, The Netherlands.

printed on acid free paper

Printed in The Netherlands

Dedication

Canadian Econometric Study Group

and

Wilfrid Laurier University

Contents

Preface

During 1985-86, the acquisition editor for the humanities and social sciences division of Kluwer Academic Publishers in the Netherlands visited the University of Florida (where I was also visiting while on sabbatical leave from Wilfrid Laurier University as the McKethan-Matherly Senior Research Fellow) to discuss publishing plans of the faculty. He expressed a keen interest in publishing the proceedings of the conference of the Canadian Econometric Study Group (CESG) that was to be held the following year at WLU. This volume is the end product of his interest, endurance, and persistence. But for his persistence I would have given up on the project.

Most of the papers (though not all) included in this volume are based on presentations at CESG conferences. In some cases scholars were invited to contribute to this volume where their research complimented those presented at these conferences even though they were not conference participants. Since papers selected for presentation at the CESG conferences are generally the finished product of scholarly research and often under submission to refereed journals, it was not possible to publish the conference proceedings in their entirety. Accordingly it was decided, in consultation with the publisher, to invite a select list of authors to submit significant extensions of the papers they presented at the CESG conferences for inclusion in this volume.

The editor wishes to express gratitude to all those authors who submitted their papers for evaluation by anonymous referees and for making revisions to conform to our editorial process. In some cases where papers would have required substantial revision before being accepted, it was decided to exclude them from the volume due to tight deadlines imposed by the publisher. The editor expresses sincere regrets to those whose papers could not be included. The co-operation, participation, and encouragement of all participants is sincerely appreciated.

It is with great pleasure and gratitude that the editor acknowledges the help of referees. The referees did a fine job despite the tight time constraint on them for their reports. Their names are recorded in alphabetical order following this preface. In most cases their help improved the papers.

The help from Pierre L. Siklos in making local arrangements for the conference at Laurier is also acknowledged. Of course the able assistance of Ann-Marie Arndt in these matters made matters quite straightforward for both of us.

The CESG meetings have been regularly funded in part by grants from the Social Sciences and Humanities Research Council of Canada (SSHRCC). This financial support is acknowledged. Substantial support for the CESG Conference at Laurier was also received from the Research Director, Wilfrid Laurier University, the Dean of the School of Business and Economics, and the Chairman, Department of Economics. The NSERC grant no. OGP007999 to the editor as a general research support in the form of an operating grant is also gratefully acknowledged. Funding for the camera-ready copy was graciously provided by the Research Grants Committee of Wilfrid Laurier University in the form of a Book Preparation Grant. The general encouragement and financial support from Barry B. McPherson and other members of the Research Grants Committee is acknowledged.

Charles Beach of Queen's University, in his capacity both as a member of the program committee as well as the Secretary of the CESG, has implicitly contributed to the success of this volume. His efforts are gratefully acknowledged. Helpful advice or encouragement of Aman Ullah, Peter Phillips, Alice Nakamura, Frank Diebold and Chris Nicol is also appreciated.

The expert typing of the essays for a camera-ready copy was done by Trudy Trudel and Elsie Grogan. Dave Kroeker copy-edited the manuscript. I thank them all for their fine efforts.

The editor also wishes to thank his colleagues, particularly Frank Millerd, John Finlay, Alex Murray and John Weir for their continuing encouragement and support for his research efforts of which this volume is a part.

Last but not least thanks to my wife Bobbie and son Rahul for their affection and for putting up with the inconveniences such duties entail.

Baldev Raj
Wilfrid Laurier University

Contributors

Jeffrey I. Bernstein
Carleton University
Department of Economics
Ottawa, Ontario
Canada   K1S 5B6

John S. Chipman
University of Minnesota
Minneapolis, Minnesota 55455
U.S.A.

Francis X. Diebold
Board of Governors
Federal Reserve System
Division of Research and Statistics
20th and Constitution Avenue, N.W.
Washington, D.C. 20551
U.S.A.

Walter Krämer
University of Dortmund
Department of Statistics
D-4600 Dortmund 50
West Germany

K. Kontrus
Institute for Advanced Studies
A-1060 Wien
Austria

John McMillan
University of California
Department of Economics
San Diego, California 92037
U.S.A.

M. Ishaq Nadiri
New York University
Department of Economics
New York, New York 10003
U.S.A.

Alice Nakamura
University of Alberta
Faculty of Business
Edmonton, Alberta
Canada   T6G 2R6

Masao Nakamura
University of Alberta
Faculty of Business
Edmonton, Alberta
Canada   T6G 2R6

Christopher J. Nicol
University of Regina
Department of Economics
Regina, Saskatchewan
Canada   S4S 0A2

Sam Ouliaris
University of Maryland
Department of Economics
College Park, Maryland 20742
U.S.A.

Joon Y. Park
Cornell University
Department of Economics
Ithaca, N.Y. 14853
U.S.A

Pierre Perron
Princeton University
Department of Economics
Princeton, New Jersey 08544
U.S.A.

Peter C. B. Phillips
Yale University
Cowles Foundation for Research
New Haven, Connecticut 06520-2125
U.S.A.

W. Ploberger
Technische Universtät Wien
Institut für Ökonometrie
A-1040 Wien
Austria

Radhey S. Singh
University of Guelph
Department of Math. & Statistics
Guelph, Ontario
Canada   N1G 2W1

Guoqiang Tian
Texas A & M University
Department of Economics
College Station, Texas 77843-4228
U.S.A.

Aman Ullah
University of Western Ontario
Department of Economics
London, Ontario
Canada   N6A 5C2

H. D. Vinod
Fordham University
Department of Economics
Bronx, New York 10458-5158
U.S.A.

Referees

Gordon Anderson	University of Toronto and The Australian National University
Anil K. Bera	University of Illinois at Urbana-Champaign
Jeffrey I. Bernstein	Carleton University
Francis X. Diebold	Federal Reserve System, Washington
Walter Krämer	Universität Dortmund
Lonnie Magee	McMaster University
Pierre Mohnen	Universite du Quebec a Montreal
Christopher J. Nicol	University of Regina
Harry J. Paarsch	University of British Columbia
Pierre Perron	Princeton University
Peter C. B. Phillips	Yale University
Baldev Raj	Wilfrid Laurier University
Paul Rilstone	Laval University
Andrew K. Rose	University of California at Berkeley
Gary S. Shea	Pennsylvania State University
William Veloce	Brock University
H. D. Vinod	Fordham University, New York

PREAMBLE

INTRODUCTION

BALDEV RAJ*
Department of Economics
Wilfrid Laurier University
75 University Ave.
Waterloo, Ontario
Canada N2L 3C5

Econometrics and modelling in economics are carried out under a set of simplifying assumptions in order to achieve generality through simplicity. As long as the results from these models are not considered overly sensitive to violations of these assumptions the results still perform a useful function. However, when these results fail to be robust, provide unsatisfactory explanations for a newly observed phenomenon, or yield inaccurate predictions, then the justification for the simplifying assumptions becomes suspect. This leads to a need for models which use assumptions that are less restrictive and whose logical and empirical underpinnings are more firmly embedded in economic theory than those previously used.

This volume contains eleven essays which focus on a selection of recent advances in econometrics and modelling. The first area examined is testing for unit roots in univariate time series (an analytic step that precedes estimation); this has become an important area of research after the seminal study by Nelson and Plosser (1982). Nelson and Plosser, using Dickey-Fuller's (1979) statistical methodology, found that most of the fourteen macroeconomic variables they studied could be characterized as a univariate time series with a unit root. Many analysts now believe that almost all macroeconomic series are characterized by a unit root or have a stochastic trend instead of a deterministic trend. The first three essays deal with testing for unit roots, fractional integration, and a random walk in a univariate time series.

The essay by Sam Ouliaris, Joon Park and Peter Phillips develops tests for detecting a unit root that allow for higher-order trends and other general components under the maintained hypothesis. An important feature of these tests is that they permit weak dependance and heterogeneity in the stochastic process. This result is achieved by using the invariance principle employed in Phillips (1987). The authors also develop diagnostic procedures for detecting whether a time series is stationary. These procedures are based on the idea that a stationary time series, if over-differenced, possesses a moving average representation with a (negative) unit root. Unlike conventional unit root tests, these procedures allow, in a straightforward fashion, for deterministic nonstationarity of an arbitrary, but known, form.

Frank Diebold's paper is concerned with the important issue of whether a researcher can, using conventional tests, detect deviation from unit root behavior in a particular time series if the time series has a long memory instead of a unit root. The paper stresses that conventional unit root tests may not have good power against the long memory hypothesis and presents finite sample fractiles for a fractional-integration test in a time series.

Pierre Perron's essay focuses on the power comparison of various tests of the random walk hypothesis against the stationary first-order autoregressive process when the sampling interval is allowed to vary. His analysis shows that in a time series context the notion that more information is desirable (i.e., more data would be good) may not always be correct in that the power of the test depends both on the time interval between each observation as well as the specification of the null and alternative hypotheses.

These essays introduce new results in this fast-growing research area. They also provide an overview of the issues involved in unit root testing. Readers interested in further elaboration and exposition of unit root tests should consult expositional essays by Dickey, Bell, and Miller (1986) and Stock and Watson (1988). A selective survey of the unit root literature is provided by Diebold and Nerlove (1989). Raj and Siklos (1989) provide a selective survey of the adequacy of simple filters and transformations.

Essays four and five focus on the theory and application of Kernel estimation, a popular nonparametric econometric estimation technique. The nonparametric methods are claimed to be robust to misspecification of functional form and/or modest levels of data inconsistency. In this sense these methods are improvements over commonly used parametric methods in econometrics which use restrictive assumptions about the functional form. The loss of interpretability and efficiency both cause some concern in using these methods, and some econometricians favor using semiparametric methods, where only the stochastic part of the model is nonparametrically specified. The Kernel estimation method and its competitors can be quite useful as "exploratory" and "confirmatory" analytical tools in the social sciences. Aman Ullah and Radley Singh present a class of Kernel estimators that are asymptotically unbiased and consistent. They illustrate the use of these methods with the help of a variety of economic examples using real world data. John McMillan, Aman Ullah, and Rick Vinod apply the Kernel estimation approach by estimating the shape of the demand curve. Their objective is to examine if Marshall's Law of the elasticities of demand—that is, the elasticity of income increases with price, is supported by the data.

A good account of both the Kernel and related nonparametric regression methods can be found in Eubank (1988). The technical literature on Kernel estimation is reviewed by Prakasa Rao (1983), and Silverman (1986). Nonparametric estimation methods continue to be a popular area of research. Surveys of Kernel methods for estimating economic functionals are provided by Bierens (1987), Ullah (1988), and others. Various applications of semiparametric and nonparametric methods are discussed in a special double issue of *Empirical Economics* (1988).

Essays six, seven, and eight focus on various econometric and modelling issues in demand systems analysis. Guoqiang Tian and John Chipman's essay considers a fairly general class of dynamic demand systems. For this class of demand systems they obtain a closed-form solution for optimal decision functions in a dynamic setting, that is, they derive the aggregate consumption and savings functions, and demand functions. An attractive feature of the closed-form solution is that it can be used directly in empirical studies. Chris Nicol considers the implicit restrictions associated with the Almost Ideal Demand System. He goes on to reinterpret this demand system as a third-order translog model and undertakes a testing of these restrictions. Finally, Chipman and Tian point out that commonly used stochastic specifications in the linear expenditure system are somewhat flawed. They show a way to deal with this deficiency. They consider Maximum-Likelihood estimation of the linear expenditure system by assuming that the minimum required quantities for the commodities have a three-parameter multivariate lognormal distribution. A review of some other econometric issues of demand systems is provided by Theil (1987). Raj and Taylor (1989) give some empirical evidence from testing demand homogeneity by showing that a bootstrap testing procedure using an asymptotic test statistic can provide significance levels equivalent to an exact test.

The last three essays are concerned with some important modelling issues. Alice and Masao Nakamura provide a resolution of certain problems associated with specific properties of Heckman's two-step estimation method for censored regression models and provide an application of their improved method to the analysis of income dynamics using panel data.[1] They also provide an extensive bibliography on this literature. Krämer, Ploberger, and Kontrus provide a comparison of alternative pure significance tests for structural changes in the linear regression when both the timing and number of structural breaks are assumed to be unknown. They show that the test they proposed in an earlier paper is better in some respects than an alternative test of structural breaks.[2] The final essay by Jeff Bernstein and Ishaq Nadiri examines the nature of factor substitution possibilities in dynamic settings between factor inputs such as labor, physical capital, and R&D capital. They also examine the extent to which adjustment costs associated with some factors being quasi-fixed can affect factor demands.

Notes

* Helpful comments from John Chipman, Frank Diebold, Chris Nicol, and Sam Ouliaris are gratefully acknowledged.

1. An excellent review of earlier literature on this topic is given by Maddala (1983).

2. Some recent developments in Structural Stability Analysis are discussed in a special issue of *Empirical Economics* (1989).

References

Bierens, H.: 1987, 'Kernel Estimation of Regression Functions', in T. F. Bewley (ed), *Advances in Econometrics*, Cambridge University Press, New York, New York, U.S.A., pp. 99-144.

Dickey, D. A., and W. A. Fuller: 1979, 'Distribution of the Estimators for Autoregressive Time Series with a Unit Root', *Journal of the American Statistical Association*, **74**, 427-431.

Dickey, D. A., and W. A. Fuller: 1981, 'Likelihood Ratio Statistics for Autoregressive Time Series with Unit Root', *Econometrica*, **49**, 1057-1072.

Dickey, D. A., W. R. Bell, and R. B. Miller: 1986, 'Unit Roots in Time Series Models: Tests and Implications', *The American Statistician*, **40**, 12-26.

Diebold, F. X., and M. Nerlove: 1989, 'Unit Roots in Economic Time Series: A Selective Survey', in T. B. Fomby and G. F. Rhodes (eds), *Advances in Econometrics: Co-Integration, Spurious Regressions, and Unit Roots*, JAI Press, Greenwhich, Conneticut, U.S.A., forthcoming.

Empirical Economics, 1988, Special Double Issue on *Semiparametric and Nonparametric Econometrics*, guest editor: Aman Ullah.

Empirical Economics, 1989, Special Issue on *Estimation of Structural Change*, guest editor: Walter Krämer.

Eubank, R. L. C.: 1988 'Spline Smoothing and Nonparametric Regression', Marcel Dekker, Inc., New York, New York, U.S.A.

Maddala, G. S.: 1983, *Limited Dependent and Qualitative Variables in Econometrics*, Cambridge University Press, Cambridge, Massachusetts, U.S.A.

Nelson, C. R., and C. I. Plosser: 1982, 'Trends and Random Walks in Macroeconomic Time Series', *Journal of Monetary Economics*, **10**, 139-162.

Phillips, P. C. B.: 1987, 'Time Series Regression with Unit Roots', *Econometrica*, **55** (2), 277-302.

Prakasa Rao, B. L. S: 1983, *Nonparametric Functional Estimation*, Academic Press, Orlando, Florida, U.S.A.

Raj, B., and P. L. Siklos: 1989, 'The Adequacy of Simple Filters and Transformations: A Brief Survey and Some Practical Suggestions', *Belgian Journal of Operations Research, Statistics, and Computer Science*, in press.

Raj, B., and T. G. Taylor: 1989, 'Do Bootstrap Tests Using an Asymptotic Test Statistic Provide Significance Levels Equivalent to an Exact Test?', *Journal of Quantitative Economics*, in press.

Silverman, B. W.: 1986, *Density Estimation for Estimation and Data Analysis*, Chapman and Hall, New York, New York, U.S.A.

Stock, J. H., and M. W. Watson: 1988, 'Variable Trends in Economic Time Series', *Economic Perspective*, **2**, 147-174.

Theil, H.: 1987, 'The Econometrics of Demand Systems', Chapter 3 in H. Theil and K. W. Clements, *Applied Demand Analysis: Results from System-Wide Approaches*, Ballinger Publishing Co., Cambridge, Massachusetts, U.S.A.

Ullah, A.: 1988: 'Nonparametric Estimation of Econometric Functions', *Canadian Journal of Economics*, **21**, 625-658.

PART ONE

UNIT ROOT AND FRACTIONAL INTEGRATION

CHAPTER 1

TESTING FOR A UNIT ROOT IN THE PRESENCE OF A MAINTAINED TREND

SAM OULIARIS*
Univ. of Maryland
Department of Economics
College Park, Maryland

JOON Y. PARK
Cornell University
Department of Economics
Ithaca, New York

PETER C. B. PHILLIPS
Yale University
Cowles Foundation for Research
Yale Station
New Haven, Connecticut

ABSTRACT. This paper develops statistics for detecting the presence of a unit root in time series data against the alternative of stationarity. Unlike most existing procedures, the new tests allow for deterministic trend polynomials in the maintained hypothesis. They may be used to discriminate between unit root nonstationarity and processes which are stationary around a deterministic polynomial trend. The tests allow for both forms of nonstationarity under the null hypothesis. Moreover, the tests allow for a wide class of weakly dependent and possibly heterogenously distributed errors. We illustrate the use of the new tests by applying them to a number of models of macroeconomic behavior.

1. Introduction

The purpose of this paper is to extend some existing statistical procedures for detecting a unit root in time series data. In the tests of Dickey and Fuller (1979) and Phillips and Perron (1988), the maintained hypothesis is that the time series is integrated with drift but with no trend. This paper extends these tests to allow explicitly for a deterministic polynomial time trend in the maintained hypothesis. An important feature of the new procedures is their invariance to the presence of drift and polynomial trend in the true data generation process. They should therefore be helpful in discriminating between the difference stationary and trend stationary specification. Our analysis is motivated in part by recent work by Bhargava (1986) which emphasizes the importance of developing tests of the unit root hypothesis that explicitly allow for trend in the maintained hypothesis. It is also motivated by the view that the linear time trend hypothesis is inappropriate for modelling the deterministic component of an economic time series. Perron (1987) has recently demonstrated the importance of using a flexible specification for the deterministic component. He shows that the results of Nelson and Plosser (1982), which provide support for the unit root hypothesis, may be reversed by using unit root tests which allow for a structural break in the deterministic component of a time series.

The issue of trend stationarity versus difference stationarity is critical in the ongoing debate on the nature of the business cycle. Most macroeconomic time series exhibit nonstationarity through the presence of a secular growth component. If a macroeconomic variable is trend stationary, then short-term shocks (such as those arising from variations in government policy) have only a temporary impact on the long-run evolution of the series. This behavior is consistent with traditional theories of the business cycle. However, if a macroeconomic variable is difference stationary, then short-run shocks affect the level of the variable permanently. This is more compatible with real business cycle models of equilibrium output.

Prior to the work of Nelson and Plosser (1982) the prevailing view was that the secular component of macroeconomic time series was trend stationary and that the long-term trend had little to do with the year-to-year variations in economic conditions. This led to the routine practice of detrending macroeconomic series in order to identify the cyclical component that was to be explained by business cycle theory. However, using the Dickey-Fuller (1979, 1981) procedures for detecting a unit root in time series models, Nelson and Plosser (1982) found strong evidence against the trend stationary model. Nelson and Plosser tested the null hypothesis of a unit root (with drift) for 14 macroeconomic time series and could not reject the unit root hypothesis in 13 cases. Perron (1986) has recently confirmed the findings of Nelson and Plosser using the statistical procedures developed in Phillips (1987) and Phillips and Perron (1988). Unlike the Dickey-Fuller statistics, these procedures allow for quite general weakly dependent innovation sequences. From the point of view of business cycle theory, the Nelson and Plosser results are more consistent with the implications of real business cycle theories since innovations in the stochastic trend apparently account for a significant portion of the short- as well as the long-run variation in the time series. The interested reader is referred to Campbell and Mankiw (1987) for further discussion on the implications of the unit root hypothesis for modelling macroeconomic behavior.

The appropriate representation of nonstationarity in macroeconomic time series is also a vital issue from an econometric perspective. Durlauf and Phillips (1987) show that misspecification of a random walk as a stationary process evolving around a deterministic trend has major effects on the statistical analysis of the data. For example, it is well known that inappropriate detrending of a random walk produces spurious periodic behavior at long lags, and this gives a misleading impression of persistence and high variance in the business cycle (Nelson and Kang, 1982, and Chan, Hung and Ord, 1977). In addition, the theory of cointegration has emphasized the need to pre-test time series for unit roots. A cointegrated process is a linear combination of integrated variables which are stationary. In practical applications it is important to determine whether each series (once purged of its deterministic part) possesses a unit root. Pretesting guards against inadvertently mixing processes which are integrated of different orders (such as $I(1)$ and $I(0)$ processes, where the notation $I(k)$ signifies a process whose kth difference is stationary) since such processes are trivially cointegrated. Finally, a null hypothesis of no cointegration may itself be tested by applying unit root procedures to the residuals of the cointegrating regression (see Phillips and Ouliaris, 1987).

The organization of this paper is as follows. Section 2 develops Wald statistics for the null hypothesis that a time series has a unit root and possibly trend polynomials of an arbitrary order. The statistics are developed using the methodology in Phillips (1987). In Section 3 we show how to incorporate a general polynomial time trend in the maintained hypothesis when the bounds procedure of Phillips and Ouliaris (1988) is applied. The new procedures are then applied to empirical models in the cointegration literature to see whether the original data stands up to the null hypothesis of a unit root.

2. Unit Root Tests with Deterministic Trend

Following the methodology in Phillips (1987), we begin by letting $\{y_t\}_0^\infty$ be a time series generated according to:

$$y_t = \sum_0^{P-1} \beta_k t^k + y_{t-1} + \xi_t, \quad \beta_k \in R. \tag{1}$$

y_0 = random with a distribution that is independent of n, the sample size.

Model (1) allows y_t to be an integrated process with a pth order deterministic time polynomial in the null hypothesis. It encompasses most of the unit root models considered previously in the literature as special cases. [1] For example, Phillips (1987) considers (1) under the assumption that $p = 0$ while Phillips and Perron (1988) allow $p = 1$.

In what follows, we assume that $\{\xi_t\}_0^{\infty}$ is a weakly stationary, zero mean innovation sequence with spectral density $f_\xi(\lambda)$. The partial sum process $X_n(r) = n^{-1/2} S_{[nr]} = n^{-1/2} \sum_1^{[nr]} \xi_t$, for $r \in [0, 1]$, is required to satisfy an invariance principle for partial sums of weakly dependent innovations. Specifically, we require

$$X_n(r) \overset{D}{\to} B(r) \text{ as } n \to \infty. \tag{2}$$

The symbol '$\overset{D}{\to}$' here signifies weak convergence of the associated probability measure, while $B(r)$ is scalar Brownian motion with long-run variance

$$\omega^2 = \lim_{n \to \infty} \frac{1}{n} E(S_n^2) = 2\pi f_\xi(0) = \sigma^2 + 2\lambda$$

where $\sigma^2 = E(\xi_1^2)$, $\lambda = \sum_{j=2}^{\infty} E(\xi_1 \xi_j)$. We let $B(r) = \omega W(r)$ so that $W(r)$ is the standard Brownian motion. We refer to ω^2 as the long run variance because

$$n^{-1/2} \sum_1^{N} \xi_t = X_n(1) \overset{D}{\to} B(1) \equiv N(0, \omega^2).$$

In what follows we represent $B(r)$ by B and $W(r)$ by W to simplify the presentation of the results.

Invariance principles such as (2) have been used extensively to analyze time series models with general integrated processes. They are known to apply for a very wide class of random sequences which are weakly dependent and possibily heterogeneous. In particular, following Hall and Heyde (1980), it may be shown that the invariance principle applies to all stationary and invertible ARMA models. Thus the maintained hypothesis given as (1) encompasses a very broad class of time series models.

Consider the least squares regression:

$$y_t = \sum_0^{P} \hat{\beta}_k t^k + \hat{\alpha} y_{t-1} + \hat{\xi}_t. \tag{3}$$

The hypotheses we are interested in testing are:

(I) $\alpha = 1$,

(II) $\alpha = 1$, and $\beta_p = 0$.

Let $h_p(\hat{\alpha}) = n(\hat{\alpha} - 1)$ represent the test statistic for (I) based on the estimated parameter for α derived from least squares estimation of (3). Similarly, let $t_p(\hat{\alpha})$ and $F_p(\hat{\alpha}, \hat{\beta}_p)$ denote the t and Wald statistics for (I) and (II), respectively. We assume $\beta_p = 0$ in (3) when the null hypothesis is true. If $\alpha < 1$ under the alternative, however, β_p may not be zero. We therefore maintain a pth order polynomial trend both under the null and the alternative. The statistics are invariant with respect to β_k, $k = 0, \ldots, p-1$.

Note that one must include a pth order time polynomial in the fitted regression in order to test (*I*) and (*II*) satisfactorily. A regression model without this term would not discriminate between the trend/difference stationary specification since the regressor y_{t-1} in (3) would contain an unexplained time trend t^p which clearly dominates all the other components. In fact, the asymptotic power of t-type statistics for the null hypothesis $\alpha = 1$ using (3) without t^p would be zero. (See Perron, 1988 for a formal proof of this statement when $p = 1$).

The asymptotic distributions of the above statistics may be represented succinctly in terms of standardized Brownian motion. To facilitate the representation of the distributions, we define $W_k(r)$ to be the stochastic process on [0, 1] such that $W_k(r)$ is the projection residual of a Brownian motion $W(r)$ on the subspace generated by the polynomial functions $1, r, \ldots, r^k$ in $L^2[0, 1]$. Here, $L^2[0, 1]$ denotes the Hilbert space of square integrable functions on [0, 1] with the inner product $(f, g) = \int_0^1 fg$ for $f, g \in L^2[0, 1]$. For explicit representations of W_k, $k = 0, 1$, see Park and Phillips (1988) and the review paper of Phillips (1988a). We also define r_p to be the projection of r^p on the space spanned by the polynomials $1, r, \ldots, r^{p-1}$.

Theorem 1 represents the asymptotic distributions of these statistics in terms of the above notation.

Theorem 1: *Assume the time series $\{y_t\}$ is generated by (1). Then*

(a) $h_p(\hat{\alpha}) \xrightarrow{D} (\omega^2 \int_0^1 W_p dW + \lambda) (\omega^2 \int_0^1 W_p^2)^{-1}$,

(b) $t^p(\hat{\alpha}) \xrightarrow{D} (1/\sigma) (\omega^2 \int_0^1 W_p dW + \lambda) (\omega^2 \int_0^1 W_p^2)^{-1/2}$,

(c) $F^p(\hat{\alpha}, \hat{\beta}) \xrightarrow{D} \dfrac{1}{\sigma^2} \left[(\omega^2 \int_0^1 W_p dW + \lambda)^2 (\omega^2 \int_0^1 W_p^2)^{-1} + (\omega \int_0^1 dW)^2 (\int_0^1 r_p^2)^{-1} \right]$.

The limiting distributions of the statistics are nonstandard. They depend on nuisance parameters through the presence of λ and ω^2. This hinders hypothesis testing, making the selection of appropriate critical values for statistical inference extremely difficult. However, we may define transformations of the statistics that eliminate the nuisance parameters asymptotically. In particular, we define:

$$K_p(\hat{\alpha}) = n(\hat{\alpha} - 1) - \frac{n^2(\hat{\omega}^2 - \hat{\sigma}^2)}{2s_0^2} ,$$

$$S_p(\hat{\alpha}) = \frac{\hat{\sigma}}{\hat{\omega}} t(\hat{\alpha}) - \frac{n(\hat{\omega}^2 - \hat{\sigma}^2)}{2\hat{\omega}s_0} , \text{ and}$$

$$G^p(\hat{\alpha}, \hat{\beta}_p) = (\hat{\sigma}^2/\hat{\omega}^2)F_1 + \frac{n^2(\hat{\omega}^2 - \hat{\sigma}^2)^2}{4\hat{\omega}^2 s_0^2} - n(\hat{\alpha} - 1)(1 - [\hat{\sigma}/\hat{\omega}]^2)$$

where

s_0^2 = residual sum of squares from the regression of y_{t-1} on $1, t, \ldots, t^p$, and

$\hat{\omega}^2$ = any consistent estimator of ω^2 obtained from the estimated residuals in (3), $\hat{\xi}$.

The asymptotic distributions of these statistics are presented in the following theorem.

Theorem 2: *Assume the time series $\{y_t\}$ is generated by (1). Then*

$$K^p(\hat{\alpha}) \xrightarrow{D} (\int_0^1 W_p dW)(\int_0^1 W_p^2)^{-1},$$

$$S_p(\hat{\alpha}) \xrightarrow{D} (\int_0^1 W_p dW)(\int_0^1 W_p^2)^{-1/2}, \text{ and}$$

$$G_p(\hat{\alpha}, \hat{\beta}_p) \xrightarrow{D} \left[(\int_0^1 W_p dW)^2 (\int_0^1 W_p^2)^{-1} + (\int_0^1 r_p dW)^2 (\int_0^1 r_p^2)^{-1} \right].$$

These distributions are free of the nuisance parameters λ and ω^2. Monte-Carlo techniques can be used to simulate the distributions and thereby provide critical values for the purpose of hypothesis testing. The asymptotic distributions of the statistics are tabulated in Appendix 2 for $p = 2, 3, 4, 5$. Monte-Carlo evidence on the perfomance of the statistics for $p = 2$ is presented in Appendix 3.

In order to make the new procedures fully operational, we require a consistent estimator for the long-run variance ω^2. It may be consistently estimated in a number of ways. Newey and West (1987) and Phillips (1987) recommend a class of estimators which can be written as

$$\omega^2 = \frac{1}{n}\sum_1^n \xi_t^2 + \frac{2}{n}\sum_{k=1}^l w_l(k) \sum_{t=k+1}^n \xi_t \xi_{t-k}$$

for a suitable weight function $w_l(k)$ which depends explicitly on the lag truncation parameter l.

Since $\omega^2 = 2\pi f(0)$, the asymptotic variance may also be estimated by obtaining a consistent estimate of the spectrum at frequency zero. Let

$$I_n(v_j) = n^{-1} \mid \sum_1^n \xi_t e^{-it} v_j \mid^2$$

represent the periodogram of ξ_t evaluated at the frequencies, $v_j = \dfrac{2\pi j}{n} \in [-\pi, \pi]$. Estimates of ω^2 may be formed by smoothing the periodogram ordinates around frequency zero, namely:

$$\hat{\omega}^2 = \sum_{-k}^{+k} W_n(j) I\left(\frac{2\pi j}{n}\right), \quad \mid j \mid \le k,$$

where

$$\sum_{-k}^{+k} W_n(j) = 1, \quad W_n(j) \ge 0 \text{ for all } j,$$

and k grows with n such that $k/n \to 0$ and $\sum_{-k}^{+k} W_n^2(j) \to 0$. The latter condition is required in order to ensure that the estimator is consistent for ω^2.

Note that there is always a tradeoff between bias and variance in choosing a weight function. A weight function which assigns equal weights to a very broad band of frequencies will produce an estimate of $f_\xi(0)$ which may have a large bias because the estimate depends on values of the periodogram at frequencies which are distant from zero. On the other hand, a weight function which assigns most of its weight to a narrow frequency band centered at zero will yield an estimator of the spectrum with a relatively small bias, but a large variance.

The bias can be controlled by prewhitening the series prior to estimating the spectrum. Prewhitening serves to equalize the periodogram ordinates over a broad band of frequencies, thereby minimizing the role of the weight function. For example, suppose we fit the following ARMA(p, q) model to ξ_t:

$$\phi(L)\xi_t = \Psi(L)v_t$$

where

$$\phi(L) = 1 - \phi_1 L - \phi_2 L^2 - \phi_3 L^3 - \cdots - \phi_p L^p,$$

$$\Psi(L) = 1 - \psi_1 L - \psi_2 L^2 - \psi_3 L^3 - \cdots - \psi_q L^q,$$

and v_t is a weakly stationary process with spectrum $f_v(\kappa_j)$. (All the roots of $\phi(L)$ are assumed to be outside the unit circle.) Then the spectrum of ξ_t at frequency κ_j is given by

$$f_\xi(\kappa_j) = f_v(\kappa_j) \frac{\mid 1 - \sum_1^q \phi_j e^{-ij\kappa_j} \mid^2}{\mid 1 - \sum_1^p \psi_j e^{-ij\kappa_j} \mid^2}.$$

Thus, for $\kappa_j = 0$

$$\hat{f}_\xi(0) = \hat{f}_v(0) \frac{\mid 1 - \sum_1^q \hat{\phi}_j \mid^2}{\mid 1 - \sum_1^p \hat{\psi}_j \mid^2}$$

where $\hat{\phi}_j$ and $\hat{\psi}_j$ are consistent estimates of ϕ_j and ψ_j respectively.

The results presented in this paper are based on the Daniell estimator for $f_\xi(0)$. The Daniell estimator uses equal weights to smooth the periodogram. Thus $W(k) = (2k)^{-1}$ and

$$\hat{\omega}_D^2 = \frac{1}{k} \sum_1^k Re\left[I(\frac{2\pi j}{n}) \right]. \tag{4}$$

Since the Daniell estimator is best suited to models with 'flat' periodogram values around frequency zero, the prewhitening technique will be used in order to minimize the distortion arising from large periodogram ordinates distant from zero.

Finally, a word of caution must be given with regard to the estimation of the long-run variance ω^2 used to construct the statistics. It is important to use the residuals from the regression (3) and not to incorporate the hypothesis $\beta = 1$ when estimating ω^2. Failing to do so has substantial effects on the power of tests and may result in the procedure being inconsistent. This problem has recently been pointed out by Phillips and Ouliaris (1987) in a related context of the residual-based tests for cointegration. To look at the problem more closely, consider the simplest case of $p = 0$. The tests are therefore based on the regression,

$$y_t = \hat{\alpha} y_{t-1} + \hat{\xi}_t. \tag{5}$$

Under the assumption of integration we may estimate ω^2 using $\{\Delta y_t\}$ or $\{\hat{\xi}_t\}$ from (5). This would not affect the result since $\hat{\alpha} = 1 + O_p(n^{-1})$ under the null hypothesis. The two estimators, however, behave rather differently under the alternative hypothesis of no unit root. This occurs because $\{\Delta y_t\}$ has a moving average representation with a unit root when $\{y_t\}$ is stationary. If the estimation is based on $\{\Delta y_t\}$, then $\hat{\omega}^2 \xrightarrow{p} 0$. Furthermore, if some estimators such as a smoothed spectrum are used, we have $\hat{\omega}^2 = O_p(n^{-1})$ and the test becomes inconsistent (see Phillips and Ouliaris, 1987). Loosely put, the inconsistency is due to the fact that the behavior of the correction term mimics that of the leading term too closely when $\hat{\omega}^2$ is negligible. The proof is essentially the same as the one in Phillips and Ouliaris (1987) and will not be repeated here. The problem of inconsistency does not arise if the estimation of ω^2 is based on the regression residual in (5).

3. Testing for Unit Roots with General Deterministic Trends

The statistical procedures developed in the previous section enable us to detect a unit root in models with a deterministic time polynomial of an arbitrary order. However, they cannot immediately deal with more general trend cycle models of the form:

$$y_t = \mu + \phi(t, \theta) + u_t \tag{6}$$

where $\phi(t, \theta)$ is a deterministic function of time with parameter θ. Although it is in general possible to modify Wald statistics to account for general deterministic trends such as (6), the critical values of these statistics depend on the form of $\phi(t, \theta)$. This is, of course, already clear from Theorem 1 (a) - (c) where these limit distributions depend on the projection of $W(r)$ on the orthogonal complement of the polynomial trend of order p, namely $W_P(r)$.

Equation (6) embodies a broad spectrum of stationary data generation processes and yields a very general alternative to the difference stationary specification. It is therefore desirable to have a method for directly testing (6) against a unit root specification. We now develop a nonparametric method for doing this. Our approach is based on the univariate bounds procedure for no cointegration developed in Phillips and Ouliaris (1988). This procedure exploits the fact that differencing a stationary series induces a negative unit root in its MA representation, resulting in a zero spectrum at the zero frequency. The bounds procedure provides a diagnostic for assessing whether or not the estimated spectrum at the zero frequency is sufficiently small to be negligible. It can easily be modified to deal with models such as (6).

The general approach is best introduced by way of example. Let $p = 0$ and

$$\xi_t = \Delta y_t = y_t - y_{t-1} .$$

Under the null hypothesis of a unit root, $\{\xi_t\}$ is a stationary process having positive asymptotic variance. If, however, $\{y_t\}$ is stationary under the alternative, then $\{\xi_t\}$ has an MA(1) representation with a unit root and its spectrum will be zero at the zero frequency. Moreover, if the smoothed spectrum estimator is used to estimate $\omega^2 = 0$, the results in Phillips and Ouliaris (1987) imply that $\hat{\omega}^2$ is $O_p(n^{-1})$. This means that we may obtain diagnostic evidence in favor of the trend stationary specification by showing that the estimated spectrum at the zero frequency is negligible and thus consistent with the alternative hypothesis of $\omega^2 = 0$. This in turn may be done using the unit-free (scalar) bounds procedure of Phillips and Ouliaris (1988).

To explain this procedure, let $\rho^2 = (\omega/\sigma)^2$, and $\hat{r}^2 = (\hat{\omega}/\hat{\sigma})^2$, be any consistent estimator of ρ^2. Also, we assume ω^2 is estimated by (4). We are therefore interested in the alternative hypothesis:

$$H_a = \rho^2 = \frac{\omega^2}{\sigma^2} = 0 .$$

According to the univariate bounds test, H_a is accepted if the upper limit for the true ρ^2 is 'sufficiently' small. Phillips and Ouliaris (1988) point out that under the null hypothesis that $\rho^2 > 0$, $\hat{r}^2$ has an asymptotic normal distribution with mean ρ^2 and variance $\rho^2 \left[\sum_{-k}^{+k} W_t(j)^2 \right]$. Thus for the Daniell estimator given by (4) we have

$$k^{1/2}(\hat{r}^2 - \rho^2)/\rho^2 \xrightarrow{d} N(0, 1) \tag{7}$$

with a corresponding confidence interval for ρ^2 of:

$$\hat{r}^2/(1 + (z_\alpha/k^{1/2})) \leq \rho^2 \leq \hat{r}^2/(1 - (z_\alpha/k^{1/2})) \tag{8}$$

where z_α is the $(1 - \alpha)$ percentage point of the standard normal distribution. Similarily, H_a is rejected if the lower limit is above a preassigned level.

A maintained polynomial trend may be allowed for in a straightforward fashion. That is, when $p \geq 1$ we simply compute the regression residuals $\hat{\xi}_t$ from:

$$\Delta y_t = \sum_0^{p-1} \hat{\beta}_j t^j + \hat{\xi}_t$$

and mount the bounds test using $\hat{\xi}_t$. Of course, this approach can be generalized to allow for any form of deterministic trend in the maintained hypothesis, such as $\phi(t, \theta)$ for example. For a given ϕ the null hypothesis is specified as:

$$y_t = \mu + \phi(t, \theta) + y_{t-1} + \xi_t$$

and the test is mounted using the least squares residuals $\hat{\xi}_t$ from the regression:

$$\Delta y_t = \hat{\mu} + \phi(t, \hat{\theta}) + \hat{\xi}_t .$$

Again, we need to test whether ξ_t has an MA(1) representation with a unit root. Since the least squares estimators of $\hat{\mu}$ and $\hat{\theta}$ will be $O_p(n^{1/2})$ consistent under the null, we do not need to make any adjustments to the procedure.[2]

In order to make the diagnostic procedure operational, guidelines must be set as to what constitutes a 'sufficiently' small estimate for the upper bound. It is also necessary to set criteria for deciding when the lower bound is too large to accept the alternative hypothesis of $\rho^2 = 0$. These issues are complicated by the fact that the limit distribution (7) for $\hat{r}^2$ does not hold when $\rho^2 = 0$. Moreover, since our estimate of the lower bound is always greater than zero, the confidence interval for ρ^2 will **never** encompass $\rho^2 = 0$. This happens because we do not use the asymptotic distribution of $\hat{r}^2$ under the hypothesis $\rho^2 = 0$. The procedure is constructed so that this is the alternative.

Following Phillips and Ouliaris (1988), we recommend using 0.10 as the rejection point for the upper and lower bounds. If the upper bound for ρ^2 is less than 0.10, one could be fairly confident that the true value of the spectrum was sufficiently close to zero so as to be compatible with the alternative hypothesis of $\rho^2 = 0$. If the lower bound for ρ^2 is greater than 0.10, then one could be very confident that the true spectrum at the zero frequency is not zero.

In order to get some indication of how adequate such a decision rule may be, we simulated critical values for $\hat{r}^2$ using randomly-selected processes under the alternative hypothesis of $\rho^2 = 0$ and the null hypothesis of $\rho^2 \neq 0$. The form of the data generation process was assumed to be ARMA(1,1). The series was differenced in order to induce a unit root in its moving average representation for the alternative $\rho^2 = 0$. The parameters of the ARMA(1,1) process were selected randomly from a uniform distribution over the interval [-0.6, 0.6], thereby restricting draws to ensure that the process possessed a unit root in its MA representation. Table I presents the values obtained for $\hat{r}^2$ by averaging the upper and lower percentile values of the empirical distributions of 50 processes. The simulations suggest that an upper bound of 0.10 would provide an extremely conservative decision rule for the upper bound since the 95 percentile point for the average distribution is 0.45.

TABLE I.

Percentiles for ρ^2 under the Null and Alternative

99.00%	97.50%	95.00%	92.50%	90.00%	87.50%	85.00%
			Alternative Hypothesis of Stationarity			
0.2250	0.2026	0.1863	0.1751	0.1670	0.1608	0.1556
			Null Hypothesis of a Unit Root			
0.8989	0.8416	0.7920	0.7618	0.7378	0.7185	0.7014
			Average			
0.5618	0.5221	0.4891	0.4684	0.4524	0.4396	0.4285

Note: These values were obtained by averaging the lower and upper percentiles of the empirical distribution of $\hat{r}^2$ under the null hypothesis of a unit root and the alternative hypothesis of stationarity respectively. The data generation processes were drawn from an ARMA(1,1) process with randomly-selected coefficients. The empirical distributions were simulated using 2500 iterations and 250 observations. Fifty data generation processes were drawn at random.

The above analysis bears directly on recent papers by Cochrane (1986) and Campbell and Mankiw (1986, 1987). These papers analyze the real per capita GNP trend/difference stationarity issue by considering the magnitude of the spectrum of real per capita GNP at the zero frequency. Campbell and Mankiw (1987) find that the long-run variance of real per capita GNP is large, and thus argue that this is strong evidence in favor of the difference stationary model. In contrast, Cochrane (1986) estimates $\hat{r}^2$ for real per capita GNP and argues that since $\hat{r}^2$ was small (0.40) the random walk component of real per capita GNP was negligible. However, neither Cochrane (1986) nor Campbell and Mankiw (1987) compute upper bounds for $\hat{\rho}^2$. If the focus of attention is whether or not $\hat{\rho}^2$ is small (and not necessarily zero), then the appropriate procedure is obviously to compute the upper bound of the confidence limit for ρ^2 using (8).

4. Empirical Applications

The new unit root procedures are particularly useful in applied work which utilizes the theory of cointegration to test steady state models of economic behavior. The steps involved in testing for cointegration may be outlined as follows. First, all the variables in the model should be pre-tested for a unit root, since a regression model involving a mixture of $I(0)$ and $I(1)$ variables is trivially cointegrated. Second, it is necessary to test whether the residuals of the model (or the deviations from the equilibrium condition) possess a unit root. If the residual vector has a unit root, the model is not a cointegrated system. When the cointegrating vector does not need to be estimated, standard unit root tests (such as those developed above) may be applied to the residual vector. If the cointegrating vector needs to be estimated, unit root tests may also be used; however, different critical values apply (see Phillips and Ouliaris, 1987).

We now demonstrate the use of the new tests by applying them to the following standard economic models (all of which have recently been reformulated as cointegrated systems and all of which have known cointegrating vectors under the hypothesis of cointegration): (1) Spot and Forward Exchange Rates (Corbae and Ouliaris, 1986, Corbae, Ouliaris and Zender, 1987); (2) Purchasing Power Parity (Corbae and Ouliaris, 1988) and (3) The Real Monetary Equation (Engle and Granger, 1987). In what follows we are primarily interested in determining whether the existing results for these models are changed by using unit root tests which allow for polynomial trends in the maintained hypothesis. For completeness we briefly review the theory underlying the above models in the context of the cointegration framework.

4.1 SPOT AND FORWARD EXCHANGE RATES

A necessary condition for market efficiency in the forward exchange market is that the difference between the spot and forward exchange rate is equal to the current risk premium plus a white noise error. When the spot and forward exchange rates are integrated processes, and the risk premium is stationary, this condition corresponds to the hypothesis that the spot and forward exchange rate are cointegrated with a known cointegrating vector of $(1, -1)$. Moreover, since the unit root tests allow for innovation sequences which are in the ARMA class, we do not need to identify the risk premium in order to carry out the test. Thus the theory of cointegration provides a robust test for a necessary condition for market efficiency which does not require identification of the risk premium.

We shall consider this hypothesis for six U.S. dollar exchange rates: Canada, Germany, Switzerland, France, Japan, and the United Kingdom. In particular, we are interested in determining whether the spot and forward rates can be modelled individually as integrated processes and whether the difference between the spot and forward exchange rates are stationary. The data are weekly, spanning the flexible exchange rate period January 2, 1976 to January 2, 1986.

4.2 PURCHASING POWER PARITY

According to the absolute version of purchasing power parity, the dollar value of goods produced abroad and the dollar value of goods produced domestically should be equal in equilibrium. In stochastic versions of the standard model, this requirement would correspond to the statement that there should only be stationary fluctuations around the equation $P_t = S_t P_t^*$, which relates the level of domestic prices (P_t) to foreign prices (P_t^*) and the spot exchange rate. Moreover, when P_t, S_t and P_t^* are integrated variables, purchasing power parity is equivalent to the statement that $\log S_t$, $\log P_t^*$ and $\log P_t$ form a cointegrated system with a known cointegrating vector of $(1, -1, -1)$. In other words, if purchasing power parity holds, the logarithm of the real exchange rate should be a stationary variable.

The PPP hypothesis will be tested for five countries: Canada, France, Italy, the United Kingdom, and West Germany. The data are monthly, spanning the 1973(7) - 1986(12) period.

4.3 THE REAL MONETARY EQUATION

If prices, the money supply, and real income are integrated processes then the real monetary equation implies that these variables should form a cointegrated system. In particular, we require that the velocity of circulation displays only stationary fluctuations. Note that the real monetary equation is simply an example of a broader class of models which derive from equilibrium conditions implicit in steady state growth models.

We shall test the hypothesis that velocity is a stationary variable for four alternative definitions of the money supply: M1, M2, M3, and ML (Liquid Assets). The data are quarterly, and span the 1959(1) - 1986(4) period.

Table II presents the results of applying the new statistics to Models (1) - (3). The table contains the computed values of $S_P(\hat{\alpha})$, $G_p(\hat{\alpha}, \hat{\beta}_p)$ and $\hat{r}^2$ for a representative value of p (the order of the time polynomial).

The following conclusions may be drawn from the computed values of $S_p(\hat{\alpha})$, and $G_p(\hat{\alpha}, \hat{\beta}_p)$:

(a.) The spot and forward exchange rates of Germany, Switzerland, France, Japan, and the UK are integrated processes. The null hypothesis of a unit root in the level of these series cannot be rejected at the 5% level of significance using $p = 4$. This finding is not affected by including higher order polynomials in the fitted regression.

In contrast, the spot and forward exchange rates of Canada appear to be stationary. The null hypothesis of a unit root in these series may be rejected at the 5% level of significance using $G_4(\hat{\alpha}, \hat{\beta}_4)$ and at the 10% level of significance using $S_4(\hat{\alpha})$. We may therefore model the spot and forward exchange rates of Canada as a stationary process around a fourth-order polynomial trend. It is interesting to note that this finding depends on the order of the time polynomial which is included in the fitted regression. For example, when $p = 3$, $S_3(\hat{\alpha}) = -2.9240$ and $G_3(\hat{\alpha}, \hat{\beta}_3) = 8.5581$, both of which are smaller than the 5% critical value. This result emphasizes the importance of including the fourth order polynomial term in the fitted regression. It also highlights the importance of adequately modelling the deterministic part of the time series when testing for a unit root. Interestingly, Corbae and Ouliaris (1987) find, using the Phillips-Perron (1988) unit root tests where $p = 1$, that the Canadian exchange rate is an integrated process. The results presented in Table II suggest that this may be due to the omission of higher order polynomial terms.

(b.) The difference between the spot and forward exchange rates, or the implied risk premium, is stationary in the case of Canada, Germany, Switzerland, and France. We may reject the unit root hypothesis at the 5% level of significance using $S_p(\hat{\alpha})$ and $G_p(\hat{\alpha}, \hat{\beta}_p)$ for $p = 2$. It also holds for $p = 0$, and $p = 1$. The Canadian result is to be expected, since the spot and forward exchange rates are themselves stationary processes.

The results for Japan and the United Kingdom are not very favorable to the hypothesis that the implied risk premium is stationary. For these countries one can reject the null hypothesis of no cointegration between the spot and forward exchange rate only at the 15% level of significance using $p = 2$.

(c.) The results for the real exchange rate data do not yield any evidence in favor of purchasing power parity. We cannot reject the null hypothesis of a unit root in the real exchange rate data for any of the countries represented in the data. Moreover, the results are not affected by including higher order polynomials in the fitted regression. These findings are consistent with those reported in Corbae and Ouliaris (1988), which are based on the same tests with p set to zero.

TABLE II. Values of $S_p(\hat{\alpha}), G_p(\hat{\alpha}, \hat{\beta}_p)$ and $\hat{r}^2$ for Models 1-3.

Series	p	$S_p(\hat{\alpha})$	$G_p(\hat{\alpha}, \hat{\beta}_p)$	$\hat{r}^2$	$\hat{r}_L^2$	$\hat{r}_U^2$
1. Spot Exchange Rate						
- Canadian Dollar	4	−4.6406	22.3890	0.5262	0.1364	0.9160 [f]
- Deutsche Mark	4	−2.8141	8.2826	0.6119	0.1586	1.0652
- Swiss Franc	4	−3.0333	9.4625	0.8765	0.2272	1.5259
- French Franc	4	−2.7834	12.2638	0.5859	0.1518	1.0199
- Japanese Yen	4	−3.1699	10.1147	1.3141	0.3406	2.2876
- UK pound	4	−2.7493	11.9862	0.8018	0.2078	1.3958
2. Forward Rate						
- Canadian Dollar	4	−4.7252	22.6782	0.4150	0.1075	0.7224
- Deutsche Mark	4	−3.1526	10.2546	0.6857	0.1777	1.1436
- Swiss Franc	4	−3.3083	11.1881	0.8918	0.2311	1.5525
- French Franc	4	−2.9697	11.6177	0.5772	0.1496	1.0049
- Japanese Yen	4	−3.2066	10.2988	1.3532	0.3507	2.3556
- UK pound	4	−3.1738	13.8568	0.7499	0.1943	1.3055 [f]
3. Risk premium						
- Canadian Dollar	2	−4.3334	19.0590	0.1842	0.0477	0.3207
- Deutsche Mark	2	−3.9186	15.6565	0.3291	0.0853	0.5730
- Swiss Franc	2	−4.1356	17.1039	0.4021	0.1042	0.7000
- French Franc	2	−4.3782	19.2336	0.4016	0.1041	0.6991
- Japanese Yen	2	−3.6850	13.5803	0.4611	0.1219	0.8125
- UK pound	2	−3.5058	12.5471	0.3980	0.1031	0.6929
4. Real Exc. Rate						
- Canadian/USA	2	−2.3318	6.2390	1.1964	0.3101	2.0828
- France/USA	2	−1.0546	2.4047	2.2337	0.5789	3.8885
- Italy/USA	2	−0.9441	2.2236	2.2262	0.5770	3.8755
- UK/USA	2	−1.1451	3.2189	2.4569	0.6368	4.2770
- West Ger/USA	2	−1.5366	3.6827	2.6262	0.6806	4.5717
5. Velocity						
- M1	4	−0.4670	12.7186	0.8014	0.2077	1.3951
- M2	4	−3.0827	10.1963	1.4662	0.3800	2.5524
- M3	4	−2.9562	9.0206	1.2585	0.3262	2.1908
- Liquid Assets	4	−2.9410	8.7984	0.6688	0.1733	1.1643

Notes to Table II

1. Data: (a.) Spot and forward exchange rates, measured in logarithms, January 2, 1976 to January 2, 1985. Number of observations = 458. (b.) Real exchange rate, measured in logarithms, July 1973 to December 1986. Source, CITIBANK databank, December 1987. (c.) Velocity, measured in logarithms, March 1959 to December 1986.

2. See Table III for the critical values of the statistics.

3. Some of the series were passed through an AR(3) filter in order to equalize the periodogram ordinates around frequency zero. These series are tagged by 'f' in the table. The periodogram itself was estimated using the Daniell estimator with $k = 7$.

(d.) The money supply data does not provide any support for the real monetary equation. There is no evidence to suggest that velocity is a stationary variable. Moreover, this finding does not depend on the definition of the money supply, the value of p, and is consistent with the results reported in Phillips and Ouliaris (1988) using principal components methods.

Turning to the computed values of $\hat{r}^2$, the upper bounds for the true value of ρ^2 are all larger than 0.10, irrespective of the value of p used. Thus if we employ the 0.10 decision rule for the upper bound we would conclude that all the series in the data possess a unit root -- a result which is obviously in conflict with that suggested by the $S_p(\hat{\alpha})$ and $G_p(\hat{\alpha}, \hat{\beta}_p)$ statistics. Given that these tests are formal statistical procedures, the results for the bounds test raises doubts about the usefulness of the general approach.

The $\hat{r}^2$ procedure is best interpreted as a diagnostic tool rather than a formal statistical test. It should be evaluated with this qualification in mind. The empirical results suggest that the bounds procedure is quite good at detecting the presence of a unit root. The $\hat{r}^2$ procedure is clearly in agreement with the $S_p(\hat{\alpha})$ and $G_p(\hat{\alpha}, \hat{\beta}_p)$ statistics when these tests imply that a series possesses a unit root, since the corresponding point estimates for the upper bound are all very large. In contrast, the upper bound estimates for the series which $S_p(\hat{\alpha})$ and $G_p(\hat{\alpha}, \hat{\beta}_p)$ imply are stationary around a deterministic trend are uniformly less than 1.0. Thus there is some indication that a stationary series yields consistently smaller values for the upper bounds than a nonstationary series.

The above results suggest that the 0.10 cut-off point in the $\hat{r}^2$ bounds procedure is too conservative for practical applications. A low cut-off point ensures that the probability of a type 1 error will be small for all series except those which are nearly stationary. However, in the absence of a formal statistical procedure which allows for the null hypothesis to be $\rho^2 = 0$, it is obviously difficult to set an upper bound for ρ^2 which is not too conservative. Nevertheless, it is encouraging to find that the point estimates for the upper bound are quite large for those series where there is little evidence in favor of the stationarity hypothesis.

5. Conclusion

This paper has developed a number of procedures for detecting a unit root in a time series model. Unlike existing procedures for testing the unit root hypothesis, which take the null hypothesis to be the difference stationary model with/without drift but with no trend, the tests allow explicitly for polynomial trends and drift in the data generation process.

Our aim was to develop tests which are invariant to the true values of the drift and trend parameters. Two classes of procedures were developed. The first class extended the Wald type tests of Phillips (1987) and Phillips and Perron (1988) to account explicitly for linear trend and drift in the maintained hypothesis. The second class extended the univariate bounds procedure for detecting no cointegration (or a unit root in univariate time series models) to very general (possibly) nonlinear trend/cycle models. These models incorporate the linear trend model as a special case.

The new procedures were illustrated using a number of interesting models in the applied cointegration literature. The results confirmed the importance of carefully modelling the deterministic component of a time series when testing for a unit root. We were able to show that some of the series can be modelled as stationary processes around a polynomial trend, in contrast to previous findings.

Notes

* The first author gratefully acknowledges financial assistance from the College of Behavioral and Social Sciences at the University of Maryland. The paper has benefitted by the probing comments of two anonymous referees of an earlier version. The authors are also grateful to Peter Schmidt for helpful discussions.

1. Notable exceptions are the statistics developed in Perron (1987) which allow for structural breaks in the deterministic component of time series.

2. The univariate bounds test can also allow for structural breaks in the deterministic component of the maintained hypothesis. The interested reader is referred to Perron (1988) for applications of the bounds procedure which allow for structural breaks using $\phi(t, \theta)$.

Appendix 1: Proofs

PROOF OF THEOREM 1. The following results are needed in order to prove Theorem 1. Define $y_t^* = \sum_1^t \xi_j$ and

$$W_n(r) = (\sqrt{n}\,\hat{\omega})^{-1} y_{[nr]}^*$$

where $\hat{\omega}^2$ is a consistent estimate of the long-run variance of $\{y_t\}$. Then we have $W_n \overset{D}{\to} W$ and

$$n^{-2}\sum_1^n (y_t^*)^2 \overset{D}{\to} \omega^2 \int_0^1 W^2 \tag{9}$$

using the results in Phillips (1987).

Now let $f_i(r) = r^i$ and $f_{ni}(r) = \left(\dfrac{[nr]}{n}\right)^i$ for $r \in [0, 1]$. Then $f_{ni} \to f_i$ uniformly. Hence,

$$\frac{1}{n}\sum_1^n \left[n^{-(2i+1)/2} t^i \right] y_t^* = \frac{1}{n}\sum_1^n (\frac{t}{n})^i n^{-1/2} y_t^* = \omega_n \int_0^1 f_{ni} W_n + o_p(1) \overset{D}{\to} \omega \int_0^1 f_i W . \tag{10}$$

Also,

$$\frac{1}{n}\sum_1^n \left[n^{-(2i+1)/2} t^i \right]\left[n^{-(2j+1)/2} t^j \right] = \frac{1}{n}\sum_1^n (\frac{t}{n})^i (\frac{t}{n})^j \to \int_0^1 f_i f_j . \tag{11}$$

Define $g_{ni}(r) = n\left[\left(\dfrac{[nr]+1}{n}\right)^i - \left(\dfrac{[nr]}{n}\right)^i \right]$ for $r \in [0, 1]$. It follows that $g_{ni} \to \dfrac{d}{dr} f_i$ uniformly. We therefore have

$$\sum_1^n n^{-(2i+1)/2} t^i \xi_t = n^{-1/2}\sum_1^n (\frac{t}{n})^i \xi_t$$

$$= n^{-1/2}\sum_1^n \xi_t - n^{-1/2}\sum_1^n \left[(\frac{t}{n})^i - (\frac{t-1}{n})^i \right]\sum_1^{t-1} \xi_j$$

$$= \omega_n \left[W_n(1) - \int_0^1 g_{ni} W_n \right]$$

$$\overset{D}{\to} \omega \left[W(1) - \int_0^1 (\frac{d}{dr} f_i) W \right] = \omega \int_0^1 f_i dW .$$

Finally, we shall make use of the following result which is proved in Phillips (1988b):

$$\frac{1}{n}\sum_1^n y_{t-1}^* \xi_t \overset{D}{\to} \omega^2 \int_0^1 W dW + \lambda , \quad \lambda = \frac{1}{2}(\omega^2 - \sigma^2) . \tag{12}$$

To prove part (a) of the theorem, we write

$$n(\hat{\alpha} - 1) = \left[\sum_1^n y_{t-1}^p y_{t-1}^p \right]^{-1} \left[\sum_1^n y_{t-1}^p \xi_t \right]$$

where

$$y_{t-1}^p = y_{t-1}^* - \left[\sum_1^n y_{t-1}^* \tau_t^{p.} \right] \left[\sum_1^n \tau_t^p \tau_t^{p.} \right]^{-1} \tau_t^p$$

and

$$\tau_t^k = \{ n^{-1/2}, n^{-3/2} t, \ldots, n^{-(2k+1)/2} t^k \} \ .$$

Part (a) is immediate from (9) to (12) and the continuous mapping theorem.

It is easy to prove part (b) since

$$\frac{\hat{\sigma}}{\hat{\omega}} t_p(\hat{\beta}) = \frac{1}{\hat{\omega}} \left[\sum_1^n y_{t-1}^p y_{t-1}^p \right]^{-1/2} \left[\sum_1^n y_{t-1}^p \xi_t \right] .$$

To prove part (c), we use Lemma A1 in Park and Phillips (1988) and write

$$\frac{\hat{\sigma}^2}{\hat{\omega}^2} F_p(\hat{\beta}, \hat{\delta}_p) = \frac{1}{\hat{\omega}^2} \left[\sum_1^n y_{t-1}^p y_{t-1}^p \right]^{-1} \left[\sum_1^n y_{t-1}^p \xi_t \right]^2 + \frac{1}{\hat{\omega}^2} \left[\sum_1^n \eta_t^2 \right]^{-1} \left[\sum_1^n \eta_t \xi_t \right]^2$$

where

$$\eta_t = t^p - \left[\sum_1^n t^p \tau_t^{p-1.} \right] \left[\sum_1^n \tau_t^{p-1} \tau_t^{p-1.} \right]^{-1} \tau_t^{p-1}$$

and τ_t^{p-1} is defined as above. The result follows from (10)-(12), and part (a) of the theorem.

Theorem 2 may be proved in a similar manner. The proof is therefore omitted.

Appendix 2: Critical Values

This appendix contains the critical values for the $K_p(\hat{\alpha})$, $S_p(\hat{\alpha})$, and $G_p(\hat{\alpha}, \hat{\beta}_p)$ statistics for $p = 2, 3, 4, 5$. The critical values are given in Table III. They were estimated using Monte-Carlo techniques. The limiting distributions were tabulated by repeatedly computing the various statistics for a given number of replications. The critical values reported in Table III were computed using 500 observations and 25000 replications. The innovation vector was drawn from a standard normal random number generator.

The critical values reported below may be used for models with a smaller number of observations. In preliminary runs simulations were conducted with 50, 100, and 200 observations without much impact on the critical values.

TABLE III. Critical Values for $K_p(\hat{\alpha})$, $S_p(\hat{\alpha})$, and $G_p(\hat{\alpha}, \hat{\beta}_p)$

Size	$K_2(\hat{\alpha})$	$S_2(\hat{\alpha})$	$G_2(\hat{\alpha}, \hat{\beta}_2)$
20.0	−19.854870	3.239486	11.339620
17.5	−20.657720	3.305651	11.775810
15.0	−21.549160	3.378969	12.284770
12.5	−22.671780	3.466916	12.842630
10.0	−23.890100	3.560110	13.493570
7.5	−25.443810	3.670237	14.362610
5.0	−27.477620	3.827886	15.606460
2.5	−31.167340	4.089778	17.592230
1.0	−36.045680	4.376567	19.954010

Size	$K_3(\hat{\alpha})$	$S_3(\hat{\alpha})$	$G_3(\hat{\alpha}, \hat{\beta}_3)$
20.0	−24.728810	3.590699	13.829130
17.5	−25.621250	3.661849	14.307780
15.0	−26.689450	3.735801	14.884850
12.5	−27.834770	3.821583	15.521640
10.0	−29.281110	3.922786	16.234650
7.5	−30.976720	4.045293	17.224380
5.0	−33.452020	4.206791	18.595130
2.5	−37.316560	4.446673	20.529310
1.0	−41.646470	4.739825	23.409930

Size	$K_4(\hat{\alpha})$	$S_4(\hat{\alpha})$	$G_4(\hat{\alpha}, \hat{\beta}_4)$
20.0	−29.498510	3.918707	16.283230
17.5	−30.491740	3.987659	16.825820
15.0	−31.665810	4.062522	17.439930
12.5	−33.055400	4.152921	18.128020
10.0	−34.532940	4.252258	18.928760
7.5	−36.504790	4.367366	19.940770
5.0	−38.715880	4.512972	21.305270
2.5	−42.764600	4.758404	23.591940
1.0	−48.285360	5.063203	26.649970

Size	$K_5(\hat{\alpha})$	$S_5(\hat{\alpha})$	$G_5(\hat{\alpha}, \hat{\beta}_5)$
20.0	−34.223020	4.215988	18.727650
17.5	−35.334720	4.286277	19.330270
15.0	−36.562040	4.367253	19.975390
12.5	−38.002490	4.453981	20.742790
10.0	−39.596630	4.552657	21.594930
7.5	−41.582940	4.662922	22.642760
5.0	−44.064410	4.824760	24.132100
2.5	−48.524830	5.059557	26.533940
1.0	−54.623880	5.389089	29.997240

Appendix 3: Monte-Carlo Evidence

This appendix presents the results of a simple Monte-Carlo experiment designed to assess the size and power properties of the new statistics. In what follows we assume that the data generation process for $\{\xi_t\}_0^\infty$ is

$$\xi_t = \psi_t + \phi\psi_{t-1}, \quad \psi \equiv N(0, 1).$$

That is, the data generation process for $\{\xi_t\}$ is MA(1) with a moving average parameter ϕ. The fundamental innovations, ψ, are normally distributed with mean zero and unit variance.

In what follows we shall restrict our attention to the case $p = 2$. The size and power of the statistics may be assessed by varying the true parameters of the data generation process. Since the statistics are invariant to the true parameter values under the null hypothesis, size distortion (if any) may be evaluated by setting $\alpha = 1$ in the data generation function and varying the value of ϕ. To assess power we need to set $\alpha < 1$, for arbitrary values of ϕ.

Table IV contains the results of the Monte-Carlo experiment. It tabulates the number of rejections of the null hypothesis, expressed as a percentage of the number of iterations, for various values of α and ϕ. The computations were performed on an IBM/AT using the GAUSS programming language. A copy of the GAUSS code is available from the authors.

Since the rejection rates for $\phi > 0.0$ and $\alpha = 1$ are close to 5%, the nominal size of the test, we can deduce that the tests do not possess any material size distortion for positive values of the moving average parameter. This is not the case for negative values of the MA(1) parameter. The empirical size of the test grows substantially as $\phi \to -1.00$. From a practical standpoint, some size distortion for negative values of ϕ is not surprising in finite samples since the data generation process approaches stationarity as $\phi \to -1.00$. The interested reader is referred to Phillips and Perron (1988) for an analytical assessment of this issue using asymptotic expansions.

The simulations indicate that the statistics have reasonable power for negative values of the MA(1) parameter. However, the power of the statistics falls noticeably as ϕ increases and is quite poor for positive values of ϕ. The results for $\alpha = 1.00$ and $\alpha = 0.95$ indicate that the statistics have trouble discriminating between models with a unit root ($\alpha = 1.00$) and trend stationary models with an autoregressive parameter near unity (e.g., $\alpha = 0.95$). Power, of course, increases as α falls from 0.95 to 0.90.

Additional simulations were performed using smaller values for the maintained trend parameter and a smaller number of observations. The power of the statistics fell slightly (for every value of ϕ) when the maintained trend parameter was reduced to 0.01. Power also fell when the number of observations was reduced to 100. The corresponding tables may be obtained from the authors on request.

TABLE IV. Rejections based on a nominal asymptotic size of 5%

Innovations follow an MA(1) process: $\xi_t = \psi_t + \phi\psi_{t-1}$

True Model: $y_t = 10.0 + 0.1t + \alpha y_{t-1} + \xi_t$

Fitted Model: $y_t = \hat{\beta}_0 + \hat{\beta}_1 t + \hat{\beta}_2 t^2 + \hat{\alpha}y_{t-1}$

MA parameter ϕ	$S_2(\hat{\alpha})$			$G_2(\hat{\alpha}, \hat{\beta}_2)$		
	$\alpha = 1.00$	$\alpha = 0.95$	$\alpha = 0.90$	$\alpha = 1.00$	$\alpha = 0.95$	$\alpha = 0.90$
	Size	Power		Size	Power	
−0.5	82.44	91.84	100.00	80.44	97.08	100.00
−0.4	59.88	80.16	99.96	57.20	89.28	99.92
−0.3	35.36	64.44	99.40	33.20	77.20	99.32
−0.2	19.00	51.48	96.52	17.20	64.60	95.32
−0.1	11.56	40.04	87.84	10.44	51.32	83.44
0.0	6.28	32.44	75.36	6.08	43.00	69.12
0.1	4.16	24.24	62.00	4.20	32.72	54.60
0.2	3.80	19.36	51.36	4.00	25.68	43.80
0.3	2.04	16.20	42.60	2.52	21.92	35.48
0.4	2.20	14.50	40.04	2.68	12.80	31.92
0.5	1.96	12.80	38.64	2.40	16.16	29.40

Notes

a. The fitted regression was completed using 250 observations.

b. Number of iterations = 2500.

c. Fundamental innovations, ψ_t, drawn from $N(0, 1)$ distribution.

d. Computations were carried out using the GAUSS programming language on an IBM/AT.

References

Bhargava, A.: 1986, 'On the Theory of Testing for Unit Roots in Observed Time Series', *Review of Economic Studies*, **53**, 369-384.

Campbell, J. Y., and N. G. Mankiw: 1986, 'Are Output Fluctuations Transitory?', Working Paper No. 1916, National Bureau of Economic Research, May 1986.

Campbell, J. Y., and N. G. Mankiw: 1987, 'Permanent and Transitory Components in Macroeconomic Fluctuations', *American Economic Review*, Papers and Proceedings, 111-117.

Chan, K., J. C. Hung, and J. K. Ord: 1977, 'A Note on Trend Removal Methods: The Case of Polynomial versus Variable Differencing', *Econometrica*, **45**, 737-744.

Cochrane, J. H.: 1986, 'How Big is the Random Walk in GNP?', mimeo, University of Chicago.

Corbae P. D., and S. Ouliaris: 1986, 'Robust Tests for Unit Roots in the Foreign Exchange Market', *Economics Letters*, **22**, 375-80.

Corbae P. D., and S. Ouliaris: 1988, 'Cointegration and Tests of Purchasing Power Parity', *Review of Economics and Statistics*, **70**, 508-511.

Corbae P. D., S. Ouliaris, and J. Zender: 1987, 'Testing a Necessary Condition for Efficiency in the Forward Exchange Market', University of Maryland Working Paper No. 25, College Park, Maryland, U.S.A.

Dickey D. A., and W. A. Fuller: 1979, 'Distribution of the Estimators for Autoregressive Time Series with a Unit Root', *Journal of the American Statistical Association*, **74**, 427-431.

Dickey, D.A.: 1981, 'Likelihood Ratio Statistics for Autoregressive Time Series with a Unit Root', *Econometrica*, **49**, 1057-1072.

Durlauf, S., and P. C. B. Phillips: 1987, 'Trends versus Random Walks in Times Series Analysis', *Econometrica*, forthcoming.

Engle, R. F., and C. W. J. Granger: 1987, 'Co-Integration and Error Correction: Representation, Estimation and Testing', *Econometrica*, **55**, No. 2, 251 - 276.

Hall, P., and C. C. Heyde: 1980, *Martingale Limit Theory and Its Applications*, John Wiley, New York, New York, U.S.A.

Nelson, C. R., and H. Kang: 1982, 'Spurious Periodicity in Inappropriately Detrended Time Series', *Econometrica*, **49**, 741-751.

Nelson, C. R., and C. I. Plosser: 1982, 'Trends and Random Walks in Macroeconomic Times Series', *Journal of Monetary Economics*, **10**, 132-162.

Newey, W. K., and K. D. West: 1987, 'A Simple, Positive Definite, Heteroskedasticity and Autocorrelation Consistent Covariance Matrix', *Econometrica*, **55**, 703-708.

Park, J. Y., and P. C. B. Phillips: 1988, 'Statistical Inference in Regressions with Integrated Processes: Part I', *Econometric Theory*, **4**, 468-497.

Perron, P.: 1986, 'Trend and Random Walks in Macroeconomic Time Series: Further Evidence from a New Approach', Department of Economics, University of Montreal, Montreal, Canada.

Perron, P.: 1987, 'The Great Crash, the Oil Price Shock and the Unit Root Hypothesis', Department of Economics, University of Montreal, Quebec, Canada.

Perron, P.: 1988, 'The Humped-Shaped Behaviour of Macroeconomic Fluctuations', Department of Economics, University of Montreal, Montreal, Canada.

Phillips, P. C. B.: 1987, 'Time Series Regression with Unit Roots', *Econometrica*, **55** (2), 277-302.

Phillips, P. C. B.: 1988a, 'Multiple Regression with Integrated Processes', IMS/SIAM Conference Volume, forthcoming.

Phillips, P. C. B.: 1988b, 'Weak Convergence to the Matrix Stochastic Integral $\int_0^1 BdB$', *Journal of Multivariate Analysis*, **24**, 252-264.

Phillips, P. C. B., and S. N. Durlauf: 1986, 'Multiple Time Series with Integrated Variables', *Review of Economic Studies*, **53**, 473-496.

Phillips, P. C. B., and S. Ouliaris: 1987, 'Asymptotic Properties of Residual Based Tests for Cointegration', Cowles Foundation Discussion Paper No. 847.

Phillips, P. C. B., and S. Ouliaris: 1988 'Testing for Cointegration using Principal Components Methods', *Journal of Economic Dynamics and Control*, **12**, 205-230.

Phillips P. C. B., and P. Perron: 1988, 'Testing for a Unit Root in Time Series Regression', *Biometrika*, **75**, 335-346.

Said, S. E., and D. A. Dickey: 1984, 'Testing for Unit Roots in Autoregressive-Moving Average Models of Unknown Order', *Biometrika*, **71**, 599-607.

CHAPTER 2

RANDOM WALKS VERSUS FRACTIONAL INTEGRATION: POWER COMPARISONS OF SCALAR AND JOINT TESTS OF THE VARIANCE-TIME FUNCTION

FRANCIS X. DIEBOLD *
Board of Governors of the Federal Reserve System
Division of Research and Statistics
20th and Constitution Ave., NW
Washington, DC 20551
U.S.A.

ABSTRACT. A class of tests for the detection of deviations from random-walk behavior in observed time series is examined. The tests are based on the variance-time function, which maps integers k into the variance of k-th differences of a time series. Both simple and joint null hypotheses are considered, and exact finite-sample critical values are tabulated. The power of the tests against fractionally-integrated alternatives, which are argued to have interesting variance-time function interpretations and potential importance in economics, is evaluated.

1. Introduction

Consider an observed time series $\{x_t\}_{t=0}^{T}$. Denote the variances of the k-th differenced series $\{\Delta_1 x\}, \{\Delta_2 x\}, \ldots, \{\Delta_k x\}, \ldots, \{\Delta_K x\}$ by $\sigma_1^2, \sigma_2^2, \ldots, \sigma_k^2, \ldots, \sigma_K^2$, respectively. Then, under the random walk null hypothesis, we have:

$$\sigma_2^2 = 2\sigma_1^2$$
$$\sigma_3^2 = 3\sigma_1^2$$
$$\cdots$$
$$\sigma_K^2 = K\sigma_1^2,$$

or:

$$\frac{2\sigma_1^2}{\sigma_2^2} = \frac{3\sigma_1^2}{\sigma_3^2} = \cdots = \frac{K\sigma_1^2}{\sigma_K^2} = 1.$$

It is well known that if a time series follows a random walk, then the variance of its k-th difference is a linear function of k, i.e., the variance-time function grows linearly. Conversely, if a time series is white noise, then the variance-time function is horizontal at $2\sigma^2$. It may also be shown that the properties of the variance-time functions of random walk and white noise processes also hold for I(1) and I(0) processes, respectively, for large k, as emphasized in Cochrane (1988).[1] In other words, I(1) (e.g., ARIMA) processes have variance-time functions which eventually grow linearly in k, and I(0) (e.g., ARMA) processes have variance-time functions which become flat.

These facts have been exploited at least since Working (1949) in attempts to determine the nature of asset price fluctuations. More recently, authors such as Campbell and Mankiw (1987), Cochrane (1988), Fama and French (1988), Huizinga (1986), Lo and MacKinlay (1988), and Poterba and Summers (1987) have used the variance-time function or closely related constructs to examine long-run mean reversion in both real and financial variables. Explicit hypothesis tests regarding the shape of this function have been proposed and used. The tests are nondirectional, in that they are not directed against a particular alternative, and the null hypotheses are simple, as opposed to composite. It is hoped that the nondirectional nature of the tests will yield power against a variety of (unspecified) alternatives.

The goals of this paper are modest. We focus on the random walk null hypothesis, as opposed to the more general null hypothesis of a unit root in a higher-ordered autoregressive lag-operator polynomial. While the random walk null is obviously too restrictive for some applications (e.g., explorations of the properties of aggregate output fluctuations), it may be quite appropriate for others, particularly those related to asset-price dynamics. We focus on similarly simple alternative hypotheses of fractional integration.

In Section 2 we introduce the class of fractionally-integrated time-series processes and study its properties in terms of the variance-time function, which can grow at increasing or decreasing rates. We motivate this result from a number of perspectives, note that it cannot be achieved with finite ARIMA representations, and argue that the fractionally-integrated process may be useful in macroeconomics and financial economics. In Section 3 we propose a *joint* test for random-walk behavior, which makes use of multiple points of the variance-time function, and we contrast it to the non-joint tests that have appeared in the literature. Exact finite-sample fractiles are tabulated under a normality assumption. It is hoped, of course, that the joint test will have greater power than its non-joint counterparts; this is investigated in Section 4, where the power properties of the various simple and joint tests are evaluated against a range of fractionally-integrated alternatives. The paper therefore extends the work of Lo and MacKinlay (1987), by providing a power evaluation of new as well as existing tests against what may prove to be a useful class of alternatives. In Section 5 we offer our conclusions.

2. Fractionally-Integrated ARIMA Processes

In this section we introduce the class of fractionally-integrated time-series models and provide a brief review of their properties in order to fix ideas and establish notation.[2] In the subsequent Monte Carlo power comparisons of scalar and joint tests of the variance-time function, the alternatives are fractionally integrated. This choice is not accidental; we argue that such processes possess long-memory properties likely to make them useful for modeling both real economic series — like aggregate output, and asset prices — like exchange rates. They provide generalized approximations to low-frequency components in economic time series; in particular, the knife-edged 'unit root' phenomenon arises as a special, and potentially restrictive, case. Consider a simple generalization of a random walk:

$$(1-L)^d x_t = \varepsilon_t , \tag{1}$$

where d takes values in the real, as opposed to integer, numbers. The process is stationary and invertible if $d \in (-1/2, 1/2)$; since d need not take integer value, we refer to the process as *fractionally integrated*. Clearly $d = 1$

We call the process (1) a *pure fractional noise*, in order to distinguish it from its natural generalization - the fractionally integrated ARIMA (ARFIMA) process:

$$\Phi(L)(1-L)^d x_t = \Theta(L)\varepsilon_t \tag{2}$$

where:

$$\Phi(L) = 1 - \phi_1 L - \cdots - \phi_p L^p$$

$$\Theta(L) = 1 - \theta_1 L - \cdots - \theta_q L^q$$

$$\varepsilon_t \sim (0, \sigma_\varepsilon^2),$$

all roots of $\Phi(L)$ and $\Theta(L)$ lie outside the unit circle, and d takes values in the real numbers. In this paper we are concerned only with deviations from random walk behavior that can be represented as pure fractional noise; such alternatives are natural against the random-walk null. The fractional difference operator $(1-L)^d$ may be expanded as:

$$(1-L)^d = 1 - dL + \frac{d(d-1)}{2!} L^2 - \frac{d(d-1)(d-2)}{3!} L^3 + \cdots \tag{3}$$

Econometricians typically have considered only integer values of d; writing the model as in (1), however, makes clear the arbitrary nature of the integer d restriction. The possibility of a graduated range of persistence effects may be entertained in a natural (and general) way by allowing for fractional integration.[4]

The intuition of fractional integration emerges clearly in the frequency domain. A series $\{x_t\}$ displays long memory if its pseudo-spectrum increases without limit as angular frequency tends to zero:

$$\lim_{\lambda \to 0} f_x(\lambda) = \infty.$$

ARFIMA processes have pseudo-spectra that behave like λ^{-2d} as $\lambda \to 0$. I(1) processes emerge as a special case, corresponding to $d = 1$; their pseudo-spectra behave like λ^{-2} near the origin. Note, however, the wider range of spectral behavior near the origin that becomes possible when the 'integer d' restriction is relaxed, which gives the ARFIMA class the potential to provide superior approximations to low-frequency dynamics.

In the time domain, fractional integration imparts 'long memory,' which is associated with significant dependence between observations widely separated in time.[5] The usual ARMA process is a short-memory process, and the autocorrelations decline exponentially:

$$\rho_X(\tau) \sim r^\tau, \quad 0 < r < 1, \quad \tau \to \infty.$$

For the ARFIMA process (2), the autocorrelation function has a slower hyperbolic decline:

$$\rho_X(\tau) \sim \tau^{2d-1}, \quad \tau \to \infty.$$

Additional time-domain motivation is achieved by considering the behavior of expanding sums, which we denote S_T, of T contiguous observations on a pure fractionally integrated process. It is easy to see that the growth of the variance of such sums depends on d, such that

$$var(S_T) = O(T^{1+2d}).$$

Thus, for example, if $d = 0$ so that S_T is a random walk, then the variance grows at the familiar rate $O(T)$.[6] This result has direct implications for the behavior of fractionally-integrated processes in terms of the variance-time function: its growth behavior is $O(k^{2d-1})$. Thus for example if $d < 1/2$, then the variance-time function becomes flat, while if $1/2 < d < 1$ or $1 < d < 3/2$, then the variance-time function eventually grows at decreasing and increasing rates, respectively.

The time-domain behavior of fractionally integrated processes is also nicely illustrated by the calibration of k-step-ahead prediction intervals, for increasing k. The behavior of such intervals for the common trend-stationary and difference-stationary cases is strikingly different and well known.[7] In particular, prediction intervals for trend-stationary processes eventually become constant around trend, while those for difference-stationary processes grow continuously around drift, at the rate $O(k^{1/2})$. The uncertainty associated with forecasts of fractionally integrated processes, on the other hand, grows at rate $O(k^{d-1/2})$, which can be faster or slower than the I(1) case, providing a natural generalization. The point is simply that while many economic series do appear to have long memory, it needn't be associated with a unit autoregressive root.[8] Thus, the uncertainty associated with k-step ahead forecasts might reasonably be expected to be continuously increasing in k, but at a rate different from that associated with a unit root.

3. Joint Diagnostic Tests Based on the Variance-Time Function

The variance-time function can be exploited to obtain tests for random walk behavior. Simple scalar asymptotic tests of the individual points of the variance-time function:

$$\sigma_k^2 = k\sigma_1^2, \quad k = 1, 2, \ldots, K \tag{4}$$

under the null hypothesis of linearity have recently been proposed by Cochrane (1988) and Lo and MacKinlay (1988), and their finite-sample distributions have been tabulated under a normality assumption by Diebold (1988). The test statistics are given by:

$$R(k) = \frac{k\hat{\sigma}_1^2}{\hat{\sigma}_k^2}, \quad k = 2, 3, \ldots, K.$$

If drift is assumed to be zero we use:

$$\hat{\sigma}_k^2 = \frac{1}{(T-k+1)} \sum_{t=k}^{T} (x_t - x_{t-k})^2, \quad k = 1, 2, \ldots, K, \tag{5}$$

and denote the resulting statistic $R1(k)$; if drift is estimated we use:

$$\hat{\sigma}_k^2 = \frac{1}{(T-k+1)} \sum_{t=k}^{T} (x_t - x_{t-k} - k\hat{\mu})^2, \quad k = 1, 2, \ldots, K, \tag{6}$$

where:

$$\hat{\mu} = \frac{1}{T} \sum_{t=1}^{T} (x_t - x_{t-1}),$$

and we denote the resulting statistic $R2(k)$. Fractiles of $R1(k)$ are presented in Table I for various (T, k) combinations, and fractiles of $R2(k)$ for the same (T, k) combinations are given in Diebold (1988) and reproduced for convenience in Table II.[9] The sample size, T, in all tables corresponds to the number of available first-differenced observations. Thus, the 'levels' sample contains $T + 1$ observations. The tabulated critical values correspond to use of differencing intervals of $k = 1, 2, 4, 8, 16$ and 32; sample sizes were accordingly chosen to be divisible by 32. Interpolation may be used to obtain critical values for other sample sizes. Note also that the variance estimators in this paper are not corrected for finite-sample bias; for our purposes, since we are tabulating exact finite-sample distributions, such corrections are unnecessary.

TABLE I. Fractiles of R 1

R1(2)

FRACTILES: T:	0.005	0.025	0.050	0.100	0.250	0.750	0.900	0.950	0.975	0.995
64	0.756	0.799	0.825	0.860	0.921	1.092	1.193	1.260	1.321	1.461
96	0.790	0.831	0.855	0.881	0.935	1.075	1.152	1.201	1.246	1.339
128	0.815	0.854	0.870	0.897	0.943	1.064	1.128	1.172	1.212	1.303
160	0.827	0.865	0.884	0.907	0.949	1.058	1.115	1.149	1.184	1.251
192	0.843	0.876	0.893	0.915	0.952	1.053	1.104	1.137	1.166	1.231
256	0.861	0.889	0.907	0.924	0.959	1.044	1.089	1.115	1.138	1.188
512	0.898	0.919	0.932	0.946	0.970	1.031	1.059	1.078	1.094	1.125
1024	0.927	0.942	0.950	0.961	0.979	1.021	1.042	1.055	1.068	1.093
2048	0.946	0.959	0.965	0.972	0.985	1.015	1.029	1.038	1.045	1.062
4096	0.961	0.970	0.975	0.980	0.990	1.011	1.021	1.027	1.033	1.043

R1(4)

FRACTILES: T:	0.005	0.025	0.050	0.100	0.250	0.750	0.900	0.950	0.975	0.995
64	0.580	0.654	0.699	0.758	0.865	1.197	1.400	1.547	1.709	2.030
96	0.634	0.709	0.748	0.798	0.888	1.157	1.308	1.413	1.512	1.727
128	0.672	0.744	0.777	0.819	0.901	1.133	1.259	1.347	1.440	1.606
160	0.706	0.760	0.792	0.834	0.911	1.119	1.228	1.301	1.370	1.505
192	0.720	0.778	0.810	0.848	0.917	1.108	1.208	1.273	1.338	1.444
256	0.749	0.806	0.833	0.867	0.928	1.088	1.175	1.230	1.281	1.383
512	0.815	0.858	0.878	0.902	0.947	1.059	1.119	1.154	1.186	1.248
1024	0.865	0.894	0.909	0.929	0.963	1.041	1.082	1.106	1.130	1.176
2048	0.901	0.925	0.936	0.949	0.973	1.028	1.056	1.072	1.088	1.114
4096	0.927	0.946	0.953	0.963	0.981	1.021	1.039	1.050	1.062	1.082

R1(8)

FRACTILES: T:	0.005	0.025	0.050	0.100	0.250	0.750	0.900	0.950	0.975	0.995
64	0.426	0.522	0.581	0.655	0.813	1.376	1.775	2.069	2.379	3.075
96	0.497	0.584	0.636	0.710	0.842	1.285	1.566	1.772	1.976	2.465
128	0.546	0.629	0.676	0.734	0.858	1.232	1.460	1.618	1.785	2.128
160	0.584	0.651	0.699	0.758	0.869	1.207	1.399	1.528	1.655	1.956
192	0.607	0.677	0.720	0.775	0.878	1.182	1.359	1.482	1.597	1.825
256	0.644	0.713	0.750	0.800	0.894	1.152	1.300	1.397	1.494	1.673
512	0.730	0.787	0.816	0.853	0.919	1.099	1.198	1.264	1.319	1.418
1024	0.792	0.839	0.863	0.890	0.942	1.066	1.133	1.175	1.214	1.285
2048	0.848	0.881	0.900	0.922	0.958	1.046	1.091	1.117	1.142	1.191
4096	0.888	0.915	0.929	0.943	0.970	1.033	1.061	1.080	1.097	1.129

R1(16)

FRACTILES: T:	0.005	0.025	0.050	0.100	0.250	0.750	0.900	0.950	0.975	0.995
64	0.296	0.385	0.450	0.543	0.765	1.748	2.567	3.254	3.992	5.871
96	0.366	0.461	0.525	0.607	0.795	1.518	2.074	2.473	2.943	3.985
128	0.414	0.504	0.560	0.641	0.812	1.410	1.840	2.132	2.471	3.218
160	0.451	0.535	0.592	0.667	0.827	1.352	1.703	1.959	2.210	2.828
192	0.481	0.566	0.621	0.694	0.835	1.314	1.618	1.833	2.056	2.541
256	0.528	0.612	0.659	0.724	0.853	1.257	1.507	1.676	1.834	2.204
512	0.631	0.703	0.742	0.792	0.890	1.162	1.318	1.424	1.514	1.736
1024	0.714	0.770	0.804	0.844	0.915	1.106	1.204	1.277	1.338	1.460
2048	0.783	0.830	0.853	0.886	0.940	1.072	1.140	1.181	1.221	1.303
4096	0.842	0.877	0.896	0.919	0.956	1.049	1.094	1.123	1.148	1.200

R1(32)

FRACTILES: T:	0.005	0.025	0.050	0.100	0.250	0.750	0.900	0.950	0.975	0.995
64	0.179	0.263	0.333	0.449	0.742	2.751	4.802	6.534	8.500	13.567
96	0.255	0.337	0.405	0.506	0.756	2.045	3.258	4.218	5.340	7.991
128	0.288	0.385	0.449	0.548	0.769	1.781	2.646	3.356	4.072	5.592
160	0.330	0.421	0.484	0.579	0.778	1.635	2.340	2.860	3.441	4.871
192	0.354	0.453	0.509	0.601	0.785	1.549	2.135	2.581	3.080	4.218
256	0.404	0.500	0.556	0.632	0.807	1.433	1.890	2.235	2.586	3.442
512	0.522	0.606	0.655	0.718	0.850	1.256	1.523	1.698	1.893	2.268
1024	0.626	0.691	0.734	0.786	0.887	1.167	1.327	1.433	1.520	1.724
2048	0.704	0.768	0.801	0.843	0.915	1.110	1.214	1.280	1.339	1.468
4096	0.781	0.826	0.855	0.885	0.938	1.073	1.140	1.184	1.228	1.303

TABLE II. Fractiles of $R2$

R2(2)

FRACTILES: T:	0.005	0.025	0.050	0.100	0.250	0.750	0.900	0.950	0.975	0.995
64	0.767	0.810	0.837	0.871	0.934	1.112	1.217	1.286	1.353	1.486
96	0.799	0.839	0.862	0.890	0.944	1.087	1.164	1.217	1.264	1.356
128	0.821	0.858	0.877	0.903	0.950	1.073	1.138	1.183	1.227	1.313
160	0.830	0.869	0.889	0.912	0.954	1.064	1.122	1.157	1.193	1.256
192	0.847	0.879	0.897	0.919	0.957	1.058	1.112	1.144	1.173	1.238
256	0.864	0.892	0.910	0.928	0.962	1.049	1.093	1.119	1.144	1.194
512	0.901	0.921	0.934	0.948	0.972	1.033	1.062	1.080	1.096	1.128
1024	0.928	0.943	0.951	0.961	0.980	1.023	1.043	1.056	1.069	1.093
2048	0.947	0.959	0.965	0.973	0.985	1.016	1.029	1.038	1.046	1.063
4096	0.962	0.970	0.975	0.980	0.990	1.011	1.021	1.028	1.033	1.043

R2(4)

FRACTILES: T:	0.005	0.025	0.050	0.100	0.250	0.750	0.900	0.950	0.975	0.995
64	0.605	0.680	0.732	0.794	0.906	1.264	1.487	1.635	1.806	2.202
96	0.651	0.730	0.770	0.820	0.916	1.193	1.353	1.467	1.573	1.785
128	0.684	0.759	0.794	0.837	0.923	1.162	1.294	1.387	1.481	1.653
160	0.716	0.773	0.807	0.847	0.928	1.141	1.254	1.328	1.400	1.542
192	0.728	0.788	0.823	0.861	0.931	1.127	1.229	1.294	1.361	1.474
256	0.757	0.815	0.842	0.877	0.939	1.101	1.187	1.244	1.296	1.407
512	0.821	0.863	0.882	0.907	0.953	1.065	1.126	1.162	1.194	1.258
1024	0.867	0.895	0.912	0.932	0.965	1.044	1.085	1.110	1.133	1.180
2048	0.901	0.926	0.937	0.951	0.974	1.030	1.058	1.074	1.090	1.117
4096	0.928	0.946	0.954	0.964	0.982	1.022	1.040	1.051	1.062	1.083

R2(8)

FRACTILES T	0.005	0.025	0.050	0.100	0.250	0.750	0.900	0.950	0.975	0.995
64	0.477	0.580	0.646	0.730	0.914	1.569	2.035	2.347	2.692	3.581
96	0.525	0.631	0.685	0.759	0.906	1.399	1.706	1.937	2.150	2.639
128	0.574	0.663	0.710	0.773	0.906	1.306	1.558	1.742	1.915	2.307
160	0.601	0.679	0.726	0.788	0.908	1.264	1.465	1.609	1.741	2.056
192	0.623	0.701	0.745	0.803	0.912	1.228	1.417	1.542	1.657	1.902
256	0.653	0.732	0.771	0.821	0.918	1.186	1.337	1.437	1.534	1.727
512	0.738	0.796	0.826	0.862	0.932	1.117	1.215	1.284	1.338	1.445
1024	0.796	0.844	0.869	0.897	0.948	1.075	1.141	1.184	1.222	1.295
2048	0.849	0.884	0.903	0.925	0.961	1.050	1.095	1.122	1.148	1.197
4096	0.890	0.916	0.930	0.945	0.972	1.035	1.063	1.082	1.099	1.132

R2(16)

FRACTILES:	0.005	0.025	0.050	0.100	0.250	0.750	0.900	0.950	0.975	0.995
T:										
64	0.381	0.507	0.588	0.712	1.007	2.313	3.374	4.219	5.082	6.832
96	0.419	0.540	0.612	0.720	0.939	1.829	2.463	2.988	3.549	4.839
128	0.454	0.556	0.629	0.723	0.919	1.620	2.101	2.454	2.833	3.646
160	0.479	0.585	0.644	0.732	0.908	1.501	1.891	2.170	2.448	3.116
192	0.509	0.614	0.670	0.750	0.906	1.431	1.758	2.007	2.244	2.777
256	0.552	0.643	0.696	0.767	0.906	1.338	1.602	1.783	1.950	2.343
512	0.651	0.720	0.762	0.816	0.915	1.195	1.365	1.470	1.564	1.810
1024	0.723	0.781	0.815	0.856	0.930	1.125	1.227	1.300	1.360	1.478
2048	0.789	0.835	0.858	0.893	0.947	1.081	1.149	1.190	1.231	1.315
4096	0.843	0.881	0.899	0.922	0.960	1.052	1.098	1.126	1.151	1.204

R2(32)

FRACTILES:	0.005	0.025	0.050	0.100	0.250	0.750	0.900	0.950	0.975	0.995
T:										
64	0.455	0.632	0.745	0.939	1.460	4.412	7.281	9.603	11.926	17.481
96	0.362	0.508	0.604	0.755	1.133	3.008	4.500	5.669	6.947	9.988
128	0.366	0.488	0.584	0.714	1.015	2.386	3.492	4.286	5.217	7.138
160	0.384	0.509	0.585	0.707	0.959	2.048	2.909	3.578	4.239	5.838
192	0.411	0.531	0.609	0.712	0.940	1.864	2.561	3.120	3.657	4.987
256	0.452	0.560	0.626	0.716	0.914	1.648	2.155	2.571	2.945	3.886
512	0.554	0.640	0.694	0.759	0.903	1.346	1.629	1.824	2.025	2.440
1024	0.639	0.710	0.757	0.809	0.912	1.207	1.376	1.480	1.570	1.801
2048	0.712	0.781	0.814	0.855	0.929	1.128	1.232	1.299	1.363	1.482
4096	0.786	0.830	0.860	0.892	0.945	1.082	1.150	1.193	1.234	1.315

Due to the potential power advantages of a joint test of:

$$\frac{2\sigma_1^2}{\sigma_2^2} = \frac{3\sigma_1^2}{\sigma_3^2} = \cdots = \frac{K\sigma_1^2}{\sigma_K^2} = 1, \tag{7}$$

as opposed to the sequence of component 'scalar' tests (4), availability of a joint test may be useful. It is well known (e.g., Snedecor and Cochrane, 1980) that the negative of twice the log likelihood ratio for testing equality of variances from independent samples is given by:

$$J \equiv S \ln \hat{\sigma}^2 - \sum_{k=1}^{K} \left[\Psi_k \ln \left(\frac{\hat{\sigma}_k^2}{k} \right) \right],$$

where:

$$\Psi_k = F\left(\frac{T}{k} \right)$$

$$S = \sum_{k=1}^{K} \Psi_k$$

$$\hat{\sigma}^2 = \frac{1}{S} \sum_{k=1}^{K} \left[\Psi_k \left(\frac{\hat{\sigma}_k^2}{k} \right) \right],$$

$\hat{\sigma}_k^2$ is as defined earlier in (5) or (6), depending on whether drift is estimated, and $F(\cdot)$ rounds down to the nearest integer. Under the null (7) and independence of the samples from which the $\hat{\sigma}_k^2$ are calculated, $J \xrightarrow{d} \chi_{K-1}^2$. In the present context, this limiting result is invalid due to sample dependence. The null distribution is easily characterized (in small as well as large samples) by

Monte Carlo, however; tabulations corresponding to the cases of zero drift and estimated drift appear in Tables III and IV. In accordance with earlier notation, they are denoted $J1$ and $J2$. The tabulated critical values for the J statistics are for joint tests of five points on the variance-time function corresponding to use of differencing intervals of $k = 1, 2, 4, 8, 16$ and 32.[10]

TABLE III. Fractiles of $J1$

FRACTILES: T:	0.005	0.025	0.050	0.100	0.250	0.750	0.900	0.950	0.975	0.995
64	0.079	0.172	0.248	0.369	0.727	2.809	4.794	6.272	7.776	11.103
96	0.067	0.146	0.222	0.340	0.650	2.678	4.621	6.070	7.621	11.121
128	0.072	0.150	0.213	0.323	0.639	2.606	4.559	6.008	7.542	10.990
160	0.067	0.137	0.203	0.317	0.635	2.633	4.505	6.005	7.673	11.206
192	0.066	0.136	0.205	0.314	0.634	2.592	4.531	6.090	7.578	11.574
256	0.065	0.136	0.201	0.308	0.598	2.600	4.492	5.930	7.533	11.134
512	0.061	0.128	0.184	0.293	0.582	2.494	4.375	5.873	7.491	11.292
1024	0.051	0.126	0.183	0.286	0.580	2.460	4.440	6.027	7.587	11.179
2048	0.056	0.130	0.184	0.279	0.557	2.453	4.352	5.941	7.577	11.970
4096	0.053	0.116	0.177	0.286	0.564	2.371	4.292	5.897	7.438	11.152

TABLE IV. Fractiles of $J2$

FRACTILES: T:	0.005	0.025	0.050	0.100	0.250	0.750	0.900	0.950	0.975	0.995
64	0.086	0.187	0.281	0.429	0.874	3.513	5.579	7.064	8.548	12.382
96	0.071	0.161	0.242	0.382	0.776	3.244	5.259	6.920	8.647	12.006
128	0.076	0.151	0.222	0.354	0.734	3.094	5.262	6.815	8.599	12.051
160	0.073	0.153	0.232	0.352	0.714	3.046	5.116	6.768	8.291	11.954
192	0.066	0.149	0.220	0.335	0.683	2.897	4.977	6.686	8.301	12.277
256	0.069	0.147	0.209	0.326	0.658	2.786	4.917	6.487	8.120	11.711
512	0.064	0.130	0.196	0.311	0.610	2.603	4.628	6.137	7.842	11.986
1024	0.052	0.121	0.183	0.284	0.587	2.571	4.542	6.181	7.830	11.275
2048	0.057	0.126	0.185	0.278	0.562	2.496	4.425	5.993	7.630	11.985
4096	0.055	0.114	0.177	0.288	0.563	2.387	4.280	5.901	7.496	11.267

4. Monte Carlo Power Evaluation

We consider fractionally-integrated data-generating processes, as discussed above. We use d values of $0.3, 0.45, 0.6, 0.7, 0.8, 0.9, 1.0, 1.1, 1.2$, and 1.3. In all cases the innovation variance σ_ε^2 is held fixed at 1.0. Sample sizes of $T = 64, 128$ and 256 are examined, with $N = 1000$ replications performed for each sample size.

Samples of size T from the ARFIMA process (1) with $d = 0.3$ and $d = 0.45$ (stationary parameter configurations) are formed as follows. First, a vector, v, consisting of $TN(0, 1)$ deviates is generated using IMSL subroutine GGNML. Then the desired $T \times T$ data covariance matrix (Σ) is constructed. This is simply the Toeplitz matrix formed from the autocovariances, which are given by:

$$\gamma_x(\tau) = \frac{\Gamma(1-2d)\Gamma(d+\tau)}{\Gamma(d)\Gamma(1-d)\Gamma(1-d+\tau)} \sigma_\varepsilon^2,$$

where $\Gamma(\cdot)$ is the gamma function. We next obtain the Choleski factorization of Σ, $\Sigma = PP'$, where P is lower triangular, using IMSL subroutine LUDECP. Finally the sample, x, is generated as

$x = Pv$.[11] Construction of x in this way eliminates dependence on presample startup values, which can be particularly problematic with long-memory models. For the nonstationary parameter configurations $d = 0.6, 0.7, 0.8, 0.9, 1.0, 1.1, 1.2,$ and 1.3, we generate fractional noise with parameter $d^* = d - 1$, which yields observations on $(1-L)x_t$. Then, taking $x_0 = 0$, we construct the sample $\{x_1, \ldots, x_T\}$ by cumulating.

TABLE V. Sample Powers of Variance-Time Function Tests, Two-Tailed, No Estimated Drift

	0.3	0.45	0.6	0.7	0.8	d 0.9	1.0	1.1	1.2	1.3
T=64										
R1(2)	95,98	85,91	64,76	45,58	26,36	10,18	05,10	15,23	47,57	81,87
R1(4)	01,01	97,99	81,90	59,73	30,47	11,20	05,11	18,27	52,63	83,88
R1(8)	01,01	99,01	84,93	59,74	30,45	11,19	05,11	19,27	50,60	79,85
R1(16)	01,01	98,99	76,88	48,64	23,36	09,16	05,10	16,24	42,51	70,76
R1(32)	01,01	91,97	57,74	34,48	17,27	08,14	05,11	13,20	32,40	55,63
J1	01,01	99,01	83,92	54,68	24,36	09,16	05,10	12,18	34,42	65,72
T=128										
R1(2)	01,01	99,01	92,96	74,86	45,58	17,27	05,10	26,32	74,79	98,98
R1(4)	01,01	01,01	99,01	92,97	61,75	22,33	05,10	29,39	77,84	98,98
R1(8)	01,01	01,01	01,01	94,98	65,77	24,35	05,11	29,37	75,82	95,97
R1(16)	01,01	01,01	99,01	90,96	56,70	17,28	06,11	26,36	66,73	91,94
R1(32)	01,01	01,01	97,99	78,87	41,54	14,22	06,11	22,29	56,64	81,85
J1	01,01	01,01	01,01	93,97	58,72	18,28	06,11	21,29	61,68	91,93
T=256										
R1(2)	01,01	01,01	01,01	01,01	77,86	33,43	05,10	41,53	95,98	01,01
R1(4)	01,01	01,01	01,01	01,01	90,95	39,50	05,09	53,62	97,98	01,01
R1(8)	01,01	01,01	01,01	01,01	92,96	35,50	04,09	51,62	95,97	01,01
R1(16)	01,01	01,01	01,01	01,01	89,95	31,43	05,10	46,55	91,94	99,01
R1(32)	01,01	01,01	01,01	01,01	78,89	23,35	04,09	36,44	81,86	97,98
J1	01,01	01,01	01,01	01,01	91,96	31,43	05,09	38,46	91,93	99,01

Note: Each cell of the table has two entries, separated by a comma. The first is estimated power for a 5% level test, while the second is estimated power for a 10% level test. The data-generating process is:
$$\Delta x_t = (1-L)^{d-1}\varepsilon_t \qquad \varepsilon_t \overset{iid}{\sim} N(0,1).$$

At each Monte Carlo replication $i = 1, \ldots, N$, the processes corresponding to each of the various d values are constructed using the same vector v of random numbers, to aid in variance-reduction. Each test at each replication is assigned a 1 if rejection occurs, and 0 otherwise. After completion of the N replications the power estimates are computed as the relative rejection frequencies. The power estimates are asymptotically normally distributed around the true power p, with variance $p(1-p)/N$; thus, $\pm 1.96 \, [\hat{p}(1-\hat{p})/N]^{1/2}$ provides an estimate of the approximate 95 percent confidence interval.[12]

Estimated powers for two-tailed $R1$ and $J1$ tests are presented in Table V, for which the true data-generating process (DGP) is:[13]

$$\Delta x_t = (1-L)^{d-1}\varepsilon_t \qquad (8)$$
$$\varepsilon_t \overset{iid}{\sim} N(0,1).$$

Note first that power equals nominal size under the null of $d = 1$ for all tests and sample sizes, which must be the case since we are using exact finite-sample critical values. The power curves of all tests are asymmetric around $d = 1$; power grows more quickly for $d > 1$ than for $d < 1$. Power of all tests grows rapidly with sample size as well.

For each sample size, a consistent power pattern emerges for the five two-sided $R\,1(\cdot)$ tests. Power is generally highest for $R\,1(4)$ or $R1(8)$, with $R\,1(2)$, $R\,1(16)$ and $R\,1(32)$ displaying somewhat less power. The power of the two-sided joint test $J\,1$ is generally less than that of the best $R\,1$ statistic, but greater than that of the worst $R\,1$ statistic.

TABLE VI. Sample Powers of Variance-Time Function Tests, Lower-Tailed, No Estimated Drift

	0.3	0.45	0.6	0.7	0.8	d 0.9	1.0	1.1	1.2	1.3
T=64										
R1(2)	00,00	00,00	00,00	00,00	00,00	01,02	05,10	22,35	57,69	87,92
R1(4)	00,00	00,00	00,00	00,00	00,00	00,01	05,11	26,38	62,73	88,93
R1(8)	00,00	00,00	00,00	00,00	00,00	00,01	05,10	26,37	60,69	85,90
R1(16)	00,00	00,00	00,00	00,00	00,00	00,01	04,10	23,32	50,61	76,83
R1(32)	00,00	00,00	00,00	00,00	00,00	00,02	05,10	18,27	40,50	62,71
J1	00,00	00,00	00,00	00,00	00,00	03,06	05,10	04,07	01,02	00,01
T=128										
R1(2)	00,00	00,00	00,00	00,00	00,00	00,01	04,09	32,48	79,86	98,99
R1(4)	00,00	00,00	00,00	00,00	00,00	00,01	05,09	39,51	84,90	98,99
R1(8)	00,00	00,00	00,00	00,00	00,00	00,00	05,10	36,49	81,88	97,98
R1(16)	00,00	00,00	00,00	00,00	00,00	00,01	05,10	34,43	73,81	94,96
R1(32)	00,00	00,00	00,00	00,00	00,00	00,00	05,10	28,40	64,72	85,89
J1	00,00	00,00	00,00	00,00	00,00	02,05	05,08	02,05	00,01	00,00
T=256										
R1(2)	00,00	00,00	00,00	00,00	00,00	00,00	06,10	53,63	98,99	01,01
R1(4)	00,00	00,00	00,00	00,00	00,00	00,00	05,10	62,73	98,99	01,01
R1(8)	00,00	00,00	00,00	00,00	00,00	00,00	04,09	61,74	97,99	01,01
R1(16)	00,00	00,00	00,00	00,00	00,00	00,00	04,09	54,66	94,97	01,01
R1(32)	00,00	00,00	00,00	00,00	00,00	00,00	04,08	44,56	86,91	98,99
J1	00,00	00,00	00,00	00,00	01,02	00,00	05,09	01,02	00,00	00,00

Note: Each cell of the table has two entries, separated by a comma. The first is estimated power for a 5% level test, while the second is estimated power for a 10% level test. The data-generating process is:

$$\Delta x_t = (1-L)^{d-1}\varepsilon_t \qquad \varepsilon_t \overset{iid}{\sim} N(0,1).$$

The above results may appear to bode poorly for the $J\,1$ test, but such is not the case. In the absence of prior information on the nature of allowable deviations of d from 1.0, the $R\,1(\cdot)$ tests should be used in two-tailed mode, but $J\,1$ should always be used as a one-tailed test (specifically, upper-tailed), which yields considerable power gains. The intuition is straightforward. By virtue of the definitions of the $R\,1(\cdot)$ and $J\,1$ statistics, one-sided lower-tailed $R\,1(\cdot)$ tests will have power *only* against alternatives for which $d > 1$, and one-sided upper-tailed $R\,1(\cdot)$ tests will have power *only* against alternatives for which $d < 1$. Conversely, one-sided upper-tailed $J\,1$ tests will have power against *all* alternatives.[14] These assertions are clearly illustrated in Tables VI and VII. The lower-tailed $R\,1(\cdot)$ tests in Table VI have no power against alternatives for which $d < 1$, and the lower-tailed $J(\cdot)$ tests have no power against *any* alternatives. The upper-tailed $R\,1(\cdot)$ tests of Table VII have no power against alternatives for which $d > 1$, while the upper-tailed $J\,1$ tests have power against *all* alternatives. Comparison of the power of upper-tailed $J\,1$ tests and two-tailed $R\,1$ tests reveals the superiority of the joint test, for all d and T values.[15] To solidify these ideas consider a representative case: $d = 0.7$ and $T = 64$. To test the null that d equals one against the alternative of d not equal to one, use of the the two-sided $R\,1(\cdot)$ tests and the one-sided upper-tailed

J 1 test is appropriate. From Table V, we see that the power of the R 1($\cdot$) tests (at the 5% level) ranges from 0.34 (R 1(32)) to 0.59 (R 1(8)), while Table VII reports the power of J 1 as 0.68.

TABLE VII. Sample Powers of Variance-Time Function Tests, Upper-Tailed, No Estimated Drift

	0.3	0.45	0.6	0.7	0.8	d 0.9	1.0	1.1	1.2	1.3
T=64										
R1(2)	98,99	91,96	76,87	58,73	36,52	17,28	05,10	01,03	00,00	00,00
R1(4)	01,01	99,01	90,96	73,85	47,63	20,32	06,11	01,03	00,00	00,00
R1(8)	01,01	01,01	93,98	74,87	45,61	19,31	06,11	01,03	00,01	00,00
R1(16)	01,01	99,01	88,96	64,81	36,53	16,27	06,11	02,04	00,01	00,00
R1(32)	01,01	97,99	74,88	48,66	27,42	14,23	06,11	02,05	01,02	00,01
J1	01,01	01,01	92,97	68,81	35,51	13,23	05,10	14,21	41,50	71,78
T=128										
R1(2)	01,01	01,01	96,99	86,93	58,72	27,39	05,11	00,01	00,00	00,00
R1(4)	01,01	01,01	01,01	97,99	75,87	33,49	05,11	00,01	00,00	00,00
R1(8)	01,01	01,01	01,01	98,99	77,89	35,48	06,10	00,02	00,00	00,00
R1(16)	01,01	01,01	01,01	96,98	70,83	28,44	06,11	02,03	00,00	00,00
R1(32)	01,01	01,01	01,01	87,96	54,72	22,36	06,11	01,03	00,01	00,00
J1	01,01	01,01	01,01	97,99	72,83	26,38	06,11	26,34	68,76	93,95
T=256										
R1(2)	01,01	01,01	01,01	98,01	86,92	43,56	05,10	00,00	00,00	00,00
R1(4)	01,01	01,01	01,01	01,01	95,98	50,66	04,09	00,00	00,00	00,00
R1(8)	01,01	01,01	01,01	01,01	96,99	50,65	05,09	00,00	00,00	00,00
R1(16)	01,01	01,01	01,01	01,01	95,99	43,60	05,10	00,00	00,00	00,00
R1(32)	01,01	01,01	01,01	01,01	89,95	35,52	05,10	00,00	00,00	00,00
J1	01,01	01,01	01,01	01,01	96,99	42,55	05,09	46,56	93,96	01,01

Note: Each cell of the table has two entries, separated by a comma. The first is estimated power for a 5% level test, while the second is estimated power for a 10% level test. The data-generating process is:

$$\Delta x_t = (1-L)^{d-1}\varepsilon_t \qquad \varepsilon_t \overset{iid}{\sim} N(0, 1).$$

Variations on the above themes are explored in Tables VIII-XI.[16] The R 2($\cdot$) and J 2 are evaluated in Table VIII, while the DGP is still the no-drift model (8). As expected, there is a consistent (but very slight) power loss for all tests in Table VIII, since a drift has been needlessly estimated. The result is of practical importance: since only a *slight* power loss occurs, it is clear that little penalty is incurred when drift is needlessly estimated.

In Table IX, the true DGP displays drift:

$$\Delta x_t = 1.0 + (1-L)^{d-1}\varepsilon_t \tag{9}$$

$$\varepsilon_t \overset{iid}{\sim} N(0, 1),$$

but the no-drift R 1($\cdot$) and J 1 test statistics are used. It is at once apparent that severe penalties, in terms of departures of empirical from nominal test sizes, are incurred when drift is incorrectly assumed to be zero.

In Table X the power properties of the estimated-drift statistics R 2($\cdot$) and J 2 are evaluated for DGP (9); thus, the scenario corresponds to the correct inclusion of drift. As expected, power is qualitatively the same as in Table V, which corresponds to the correct exclusion of drift.[17]

Finally, in Table XI, the effects of violation of the normality assumption on empirical test size are investigated. The DGP is:

$$\Delta x_t = (1-L)^{d-1} \ [sign(\varepsilon_t)*(\varepsilon_t^2)]$$

$$\varepsilon_t \overset{iid}{\sim} N(0,1),$$

which has leptokurtic (but symmetric) innovations. All tests appear quite robust; empirical size stays very close to nominal size.

TABLE VIII. Sample Powers of Variance-Time Function Tests, Two-Tailed, Estimated Drift

					d					
	0.3	0.45	0.6	0.7	0.8	0.9	1.0	1.1	1.2	1.3
T=128										
R2(2)	01,01	99,01	88,95	70,82	42,56	13,24	05,09	21,30	66,73	95,97
R2(4)	01,01	01,01	98,99	88,93	54,70	17,29	05,10	25,35	73,81	96,97
R2(8)	01,01	01,01	99,01	88,94	54,69	16,27	05,09	24,33	68,76	92,95
R2(16)	01,01	01,01	98,99	83,91	43,60	14,22	04,09	19,28	54,64	82,87
R2(32)	01,01	01,01	90,96	64,78	31,45	09,17	04,10	15,23	41,51	65,73
J2	01,01	01,01	01,01	91,95	55,69	15,24	05,10	08,14	32,41	72,80

Note: Each cell of the table has two entries, separated by a comma. The first is estimated power for a 5% level test, while the second is estimated power for a 10% level test. The data-generating process is:
$$\Delta x_t = (1-L)^{d-1}\varepsilon_t \qquad \varepsilon_t \overset{iid}{\sim} N(0,1).$$

TABLE IX. Empirical Sizes of Variance-Time Function Tests, No Estimated Drift

	Upper-tailed	Lower-tailed	Two-sided
T=128			
R1(2)	00,00	01,01	01,01
R1(4)	00,00	01,01	01,01
R1(8)	00,00	01,01	01,01
R1(16)	00,00	01,01	01,01
R1(32)	00,00	01,01	01,01
J1	01,01	00,00	01,01

Note: Each cell of the table has two entries, separated by a comma. The first is estimated power for a 5% level test, while the second is estimated power for a 10% level test. The data-generating process is:
$$\Delta x_t = 1.0 + (1-L)^{d-1}\varepsilon_t \qquad \varepsilon_t \overset{iid}{\sim} N(0,1).$$

TABLE X. Sample Powers of Variance-Time Function Tests, Two-Tailed Tests, Estimated Drift

					d					
	0.3	0.45	0.6	0.7	0.8	0.9	1.0	1.1	1.2	1.3
T=128										
R2(2)	01,01	99,99	91,96	72,83	44,57	16,25	05,10	21,29	66,74	94,96
R2(4)	01,01	01,01	99,99	89,95	56,70	17,28	04,09	26,36	73,81	96,97
R2(8)	01,01	01,01	99,01	89,95	56,70	16,26	06,10	26,34	68,75	92,95
R2(16)	01,01	01,01	98,99	81,91	42,58	15,23	08,11	20,30	53,65	83,88
R2(32)	01,01	01,01	91,96	63,79	30,46	10,18	04,10	14,22	39,50	66,74
J2	01,01	01,01	01,01	91,95	55,69	15,26	05,10	07,13	30,41	72,80

Note: Each cell of the table has two entries, separated by a comma. The first is estimated power for a 5% level test, while the second is estimated power for a 10% level test. The data-generating process is:
$$\Delta x_t = 1.0 + (1-L)^{d-1}\varepsilon_t \qquad \varepsilon_t \overset{iid}{\sim} N(0,1).$$

TABLE XI. Empirical Sizes of Variance-Time Function Tests, No Estimated Drift

T=256	Upper-tailed	Lower-tailed	Two-tailed
R1(2)	06,10	05,10	06,11
R1(4)	05,11	05,10	06,10
R1(8)	06,11	04,10	05,10
R1(16)	05,11	04,08	05,10
R1(32)	05,10	05,10	04,09
J1	04,09	05,09	04,09

Note: Each cell of the table has two entries, separated by a comma. The first is estimated power for a 5% level test, while the second is estimated power for a 10% level test. The data-generating process is:
$$\Delta x_t = (1-L)^{d-1} [\, sign(\varepsilon_t) * (\varepsilon_t^2) \,] \qquad \varepsilon_t \overset{iid}{\sim} N(0, 1).$$

5. Concluding Remarks

It is argued that the class of fractionally-integrated processes may prove useful in empirical economics, due to its ability to approximate a wide range of low-frequency dynamics, and the power properties of tests based on the variance-time function against fractionally-integrated alternatives are examined. All test comparisons are performed using exact finite-sample fractiles, which are presented in tabular form. A new joint test is proposed and found to be more powerful than currently popular tests based on scalar variance ratios. Finally, some preliminary evidence indicates that the variance-time tests may display robustness to fat-tailed innovations.

If a particular time series *does* in fact possess long memory, but not a unit root, it is natural to ask whether a researcher would be able to detect such deviation from unit-root behavior using conventional tests.[18] Formally, the problem amounts to determining the power properties of various unit-root tests against fractionally-integrated alternatives. One such test has been examined in the present paper, for the simplest null (random walk) against a very simple alternative (pure fractional integration). Others, such as the Dickey-Fuller tests and their relatives, are examined in Diebold and Rudebusch (1988b).

Finally, we note that the spectral procedure of Geweke and Porter-Hudak (1983) for estimating (posssibly) fractionally-integrated models holds promise as a unit root test against fractional as well as nonfractional alternatives. The semiparametric nature of the first-stage d estimate makes such an approach particularly attractive — consistent and asymptotically normal estimates of d are obtained *independent* of the potentially infinite-dimensional nuisance parameter in $\Phi^{-1}(L)\Theta(L)$.[19]

Notes

* The author expresses appreciation to two referees for constructive and useful comments. He would also like to thank Anil Bera, Rob Engle, Tarhan Feyzioglu, Roger Koenker, Jim Nason, Marc Nerlove, Fallaw Sowell, Pravin Trivedi, Jim Stock, Sam Yoo, and especially Glenn Rudebusch, all of whom provided useful input, but who are not to be held responsible for the outcome. The views expressed are solely those of the author; they do not necessarily reflect those of the Federal Reserve System or its staff.

1. I(1) and I(0) denote, respectively, integrated processes of order one and zero. I(1) processes are commonly referred to as 'difference stationary', or 'homogeneous nonstationary of order one,' and are made stationary by taking a first difference. The leading example of an I(1) process is the finite-ordered ARIMA, while the stationary finite-ordered ARMA is a commonly-encountered I(0) process.

For purposes of this paper, we use I(1) to denote a finite-ordered ARIMA $(p, 1, q)$ process with a positive, real, unit autoregressive root.

2. For in-depth treatments of various aspects of these processes, see Granger and Joyeux (1980), Hosking (1981), Geweke and Porter-Hudak (1983), Li and McLeod (1986), Brockwell and Davis (1987), Sowell (1987), and Diebold and Nerlove (1989), *inter alia*.

3. The range $1/2 < d < 3/2$ may be of special interest in economics, due to the local generalization of unit-root behavior that it permits. Such processes are stationary in first differences, since the first-differentiated series will be fractionally integrated of order d^*, where $-1/2 < d^* < 1/2$.

4. Note, however, that the spectrum of the first difference of a fractionally-integrated series is 0 if $d < 1$ and ∞ if $d > 1$. In the time domain, this corresponds to the fact that the sum of (infinitely many) coefficients of the moving-average representation of the first difference of a fractionally-integrated series is 0 if $d < 1$ and ∞ if $d > 1$. Thus, fractional integration allows for richer cumulative impulse-response effects only at finite horizons — but these are, of course, the horizons of greatest economic interest.

5. In particular, fractionally-integrated processes are *not* strong mixing. Thus, the assumptions underlying much of the asymptotic theory recently popularized in econometrics (e.g., White (1984), *inter alia*) do not hold. Under suitable regularity conditions, however, they are stationary, ergodic, regular, and weak mixing, so that (weaker) asymptotic results are available. See Graf, et al. (1984), Samarov and Taqqu (1988), and Gourieroux et al. (1987).

6. Stock (1988) develops a class of unit-root tests based upon these ideas.

7. See Dickey, Bell and Miller (1986) and Stock and Watson (1988) for nice expositions.

8. Furthermore, standard unit root tests (e.g., the Dickey-Fuller tests and their relatives) may have low power against fractionally-integrated alternatives, as argued by Diebold and Rudebusch (1988b).

9. The fractiles given in Diebold (1988) are based on 25000 replications and are therefore somewhat more accurate than those given here, which are based on 10000 replications. A detailed description of the procedures used to tabulate the various test statistics is given in the appendix.

10. Different sets of points on the variance-time function may be jointly tested by first temporally aggregating the data to the desired degree.

11. Quick calculation verifies that $cov(x) = PP' = \Sigma$.

12. For $N = 1000$, the maximum width of the estimated confidence interval (occurring when $p = 1/2$) is ±0.03.

13. Use of the $R\,1$ and $J\,1$ tests exploits the knowledge that drift is not present; in practice such information may be uncommon. Alternative scenarios are subsequently explored, such as allowance for a nonexisting drift, or failure to allow for an existing drift.

14. This is analogous to the standard χ^2 test, which could be used if the samples were independent.

15. If, however, prior information is available indicating that a one-sided alternative (either $d < 1$ or $d > 1$) is appropriate, then maximal power may be attained by using the appropriate one-sided $R\,1(\cdot)$ test. Such prior information is rarely available.

16. Tables VIII-XI report results for two-sided tests only, for comparison with Table V. It should be kept in mind that, in practice, the $J\,1$ and $J\,2$ tests would never be used in two-sided mode. Our intent is comparison *of relative powers*, however, so that, for example, comparison of the power of $J\,2$ in Table VIII and $J\,1$ in Table V *does* convey useful information.

17. Power is slightly reduced in Table X, however, due to the loss of one degree of freedom in estimating the drift.

18. Note, for example, that the Dickey-Fuller tests allow for fractional integration neither under the null nor under the alternative.

19. For an application to aggregate output dynamics, see Diebold and Rudebusch (1988a).

Appendix: Details of Numerical Procedure

The simulation for each of the test statistics is executed as follows. Consider first $R1(k)$, the scalar test statistic for the no-drift case. A sample of $T N(0, 1)$ deviates is generated by IMSL subroutine GGNML; these are the values of $\Delta_1 x_t$. A distributional assumption is of course necessary for finite-sample tabulation. In some economic contexts the normality assumption may be inappropriate, but judicious choice of sampling frequency will usually enable its approximate satisfaction. For example, while daily stock returns are known to be leptokurtic, monthly returns are approximately normal. Furthermore, as argued in the text, the test sizes appear robust to innovation non-normality.

The level series is obtained by cumulating the $\Delta_1 x_t$ series from an initial value of 0. Then $\hat{\sigma}_1^2$ is calculated, imposing the zero-drift restriction. Next, the data are k-th differenced and $\hat{\sigma}_k^2$ is calculated, again imposing the zero-drift restriction, and the test statistic is formed. This is repeated 10000 times, whereupon the resulting sequence of 10000 values of the test statistic is ordered and the fractiles extracted. This is repeated for all of the various (T, k) pairs that are tabulated. An identical procedure is followed when drift is allowed, except that the sample k-variances are for data centered around an estimated mean, as discussed in the text. The true (but unknown) mean, μ, is maintained at 0. The joint test statistics $J1$ and $j2$ are tabulated in similar fashion, using k values of 2, 4, 8, 16 and 32.

Precision of the fractile estimates may be evaluated using the well-known result (e.g., Rao, 1973) that the sample fractiles are asymptotically normal. Specifically, the p-th fractile of a distribution function F is any value δ_p such that:

$$P(x \leq \delta_p) \geq p$$

$$P(x \geq \delta_p) \geq q,$$

where $q = 1 - p$. If $F(x)$ has a density function f continuous in x, δ_p is unique, and $f(\delta_p) > 0$, then:

$$n^{1/2}(\hat{\delta}_p - \delta_p) \xrightarrow{d} X \sim N\left(0, \frac{p(1-p)}{[f(\delta_p)]^2}\right),$$

where n is the number of replications upon which the fractile estimates are based. The fact that the asymptotic standard error depends on the height of the unknown density function f and δ_p is inconvenient, but f may be estimated by nonparametric methods in order to obtain estimated standard errors. Alternatively, nonasymptotic distribution-free fractile confidence intervals may be obtained as in David (1981) or Rohatgi (1984). Let $X_{(1)}, \ldots, X_{(n)}$ be the order statistic for the sample of replications, and let $x = \upsilon_p$ be the population fractile which we are attempting to estimate (i.e., $F(x) = p$, $0 < p < 1$, is uniquely solved by $x = \upsilon_p$). It may then be shown that:

$$P[\upsilon_p \varepsilon(X_{(r)}, X_{(s)})] \geq \pi(r, s, n, p) = \sum_{i=r}^{s-1} \binom{n}{i} p^i (1-p)^{n-1}.$$

References

Brockwell, P. J., and R. A. Davis: 1987, *Time Series: Theory and Models*, Springer-Verlag, New York, New York, U.S.A.

Campbell, J. Y., and N. G. Mankiw: 1987, 'Permanent and Transitory Components in Macroeconomic Fluctuations', *American Economic Review*, **77**, 111-117.

Cochrane, J. H.: 1988, 'How Big is the Random Walk in GNP?', *Journal of Political Economy*, **96**, 893-920.

Cochrane, J. H.: 1987, 'Spectral Density Estimates of Unit Roots', manuscript, Department of Economics, University of Chicago, Chicago, Illinois, U.S.A.

David, H. A.: 1970, *Order Statistics*, John Wiley, New York, New York, U.S.A.

Dickey, D. A.: 1976, 'Estimation and Testing of Nonstationary Time Series', Ph.D. Dissertation, Department of Statistics, Iowa State University, Ames, Iowa, U.S.A.

Dickey, D. A., W. R. Bell, and R. B. Miller: 1986, 'Unit Roots in Time Series Models: Tests and Implications', *The American Statistician*, **40**, 12-26.

Diebold, F. X.: 1988, 'Testing for Bubbles, Reflecting Barriers and Other Anomalies', *Journal of Economic Dynamics and Control*, **12**, 63-70.

Diebold, F. X., and M. Nerlove: 1989, 'Unit Roots in Economic Time Series: A Selective Survey', forthcoming in T. B. Fomby and G. F. Rhodes, (eds.), *Advances in Econometrics: Co-Integration, Spurious Regressions, and Unit Roots*, JAI Press, Greenwich, Connecticut, U.S.A.

Diebold, F. X., and G. D. Rudebusch: 1988a, 'Long Memory and Persistence in Aggregate Output', Finance and Economics Discussion Series #7, Federal Reserve Board, Washington, D.C., U.S.A.

Diebold, F. X., and G. D. Rudebusch: 1988b, 'Why Unit Root Tests on Macroeconomic Variables May be Misleading', manuscript in progress, Federal Reserve Board, Washington, D.C., U.S.A.

Fama, E. F., and K. R. French: 1988, 'Permanent and Temporary Components of Stock Prices', *Journal of Political Economy*, **96**, 246-273.

Geweke, J., and S. Porter-Hudak: 1983, 'The Estimation and Application of Long Memory Time Series Models', *Journal of Time Series Analysis*, **4**, 221-238.

Gourieroux, C., F. Maurel, and A. Monfort: 1987, 'Regression and Nonstationarity', Working Paper #8708, INSEE, Paris, France.

Graf, H., F. R. Hampel, and J. D. Tacier: 1984, 'The Problem of Unsuspected Serial Correlations', in J. Franke, W. Hardle and D. Martin (eds.), *Robust and Nonlinear Time Series Analysis (Lecture Notes in Statistics, Volume 26)*, Springer-Verlag, New York, New York, U.S.A.

Granger, C. W. J.: 1981, 'Some Properties of Time Series Data and their Use in Econometric Model Specification', *Journal of Econometrics*, **16**, 121-130.

Granger, C. W .J., and R. Joyeux: 1980, 'An Introduction to Long-Memory Time Series Models and Fractional Differencing', *Journal of Time Series Analysis*, **1**, 15-39.

Hosking, J. R. M.: 1981, 'Fractional Differencing', *Biometrika*, **68**, 165-176.

Huizinga, J.: 1986, 'An Empirical Investigation of the Long-Run Behavior of Real Exchange Rates', manuscript, Department of Economics, University of Chicago, Chicago, Illinois, U.S.A.

Li, W. K., and A. E. McLeod: 1986, 'Fractional Time Series Modelling', *Biometrika*, **73**, 217-21.

Lo, A. W., and A. C. MacKinlay: 1987, 'The Size and Power of the Variance Ratio Test in Finite Samples: A Monte Carlo Investigation', Working Paper 28-87, Rodney L. White Center for Financial Research, Department of Finance, Wharton School, University of Pennsylvania, Philadelphia, Pennsylvania, U.S.A. Forthcoming, *Journal of Econometrics*.

Lo, A. W., and A. C. MacKinlay: 1988, 'Stock Market Prices do not Follow Random Walks: Evidence From a Simple Specification Test', *Journal of Financial Research*, **1**, 41-66.

Mandelbrot, B. B.: 1972, 'Statistical Methodology for Nonperiodic Cycles: From the Covariance to R/S Analysis', *Annals of Economic and Social Measurement*, **1**, 259-290.

Poterba, J. M., and L. H. Summers: 1987, 'Mean Reversion in Stock Prices: Evidence and Implications', manuscript, Sloan School, M.I.T., and Department of Economics, Harvard University, Cambridge, Massachusetts, U.S.A.

Rao, C. R.: 1973, *Linear Statistical Inference and Its Applications*, John Wiley, New York, New York, U.S.A.

Rohatgi, V. K.: 1984, *Statistical Inference*, John Wiley, New York, New York, U.S.A.

Samarov, A,. and M. S. Taqqu: 1988, 'On the Efficiency of the Sample Mean in Long-Memory Noise', *Journal of Time Series Analysis*, **9**, 191-200.

Shea, G. S.: 1987, 'Long-Memory Models of Interest Rates: Estimation, Forecasting and Inference for Variance Bounds on the Interest Rate Term Structure', manuscript, Department of Finance, Pennsylvania State University, University Park, Pennsylvania, U.S.A.

Sowell, F. B.: 1987, 'Maximum-Likelihood Estimation of Fractionally Integrated Time-Series Models', Research Paper 87-07, Institute of Statistics and Decision Sciences, Duke University, Durham, North Carolina, U.S.A.

Stock, J. H.: 1988, 'A Class of Tests for Integration and Cointegration', manuscript, Kennedy School, Harvard University, Cambridge, Massachusetts, U.S.A.

Stock, J. H., and M. W. Watson: 1988, 'Variable Trends in Economic Time Series', *Economic Perspectives*, **2**, 147-174.

White, H.: 1984, *Asymptotic Theory for Econometricians*, Academic Press, New York, New York, U.S.A.

Working, H.: 1949, 'The Investigation of Economic Expectations', *American Economic Review*, **39**, 164-165.

CHAPTER 3

TESTING FOR A RANDOM WALK: A SIMULATION EXPERIMENT OF POWER WHEN THE SAMPLING INTERVAL IS VARIED

PIERRE PERRON*
Princeton University
Department of Economics
Princeton, New Jersey
U.S.A.
and C.R.D.E.

ABSTRACT. This paper analyzes the power of various tests for the random walk hypothesis against AR(1) alternatives when the sampling interval is allowed to vary. The null and alternative hypotheses are set in terms of the parameters of a continuous time model. The discrete time representations are derived and it is shown how they depend on the sampling interval. The power is simulated for a grid of values of the number of observations and the span of the data available (hence for various sampling intervals). Various test statistics are considered among the following classes: (a) test for a unit root on the original series and (b) tests for randomness in the differenced series. Among class (b), we consider both parametric and nonparametric tests, the latter including tests based on the rank of the first-differenced series. The paper therefore not only provides information as to the relative power of these tests but also about their properties when the sampling interval varies. This work is an extension of Perron (1987) and Shiller and Perron (1985).

1. Introduction

An interesting feature in time series analysis is that a given stochastic process can be parameterized in different ways corresponding to different specifications of the sampling frequency. Indeed, an infinity of combinations is theoretically possible by fixing different values of the number of observations T, the span of the data available S, and the sampling frequency h. By definition, these parameters are related as $T = S/h$.

Consider, for example, the following simple continuous time Ornstein-Uhlenbeck process:

$$dy_t = -\gamma y_t dt + \sigma dw_t$$

where w_t is the unit Wiener process. The discrete time representation of the stochastic variable y_t is given by (see Section 2):

$$y_{ht} = \beta_h y_{ht-1} + v_{ht}$$

where $\beta_h = \exp(-\gamma h)$ and h is the sampling interval. Suppose we wish to test the null hypothesis of a random walk, i.e., $\gamma = 0$ and hence $\beta_h = 1$ for all h. Under the null hypothesis, the discrete time autoregressive parameter β_h is independent of h. However, under the alternative hypothesis that the process is stationary ($\gamma > 0$), the autoregressive parameter β_h depends on the specified sampling interval h for any fixed value of the continuous time parameter γ.

The usual analysis concerning the power properties of various tests of the random walk hypothesis does not explicitly take into account the dependence of the power on the sampling interval. The autoregressive parameter is usually treated as fixed and the power analyzed for various sample sizes. Indeed, the usual consistency criterion considers a test consistent if its power function converges to one as the sample size converges to infinity for any given fixed alternative β_h.

Yet, this framework does not permit the raising of some interesting issues. For instance, does an increase in the sample size lead to the same increase in power if it is achieved by keeping a fixed span (i.e., reducing the sampling interval) or by increasing the span one for one with the number of observations (i.e., keeping the sampling interval fixed)? Is it possible to have higher power with fewer observations if these observations are spread out over a longer period? Is it possible that the power of some test statistics can actually be increased by simply deleting some observations (i.e., keeping the same span but with a larger sampling interval)?

These questions and others can be answered by an analysis of the power function of the test which explicitly takes into account the dependence of the autoregressive parameter β_h on the sampling interval h and evaluates the power directly in terms of the fixed alternative value of the continuous time parameter γ.

Similarly, asymptotic analysis can be used to shed some light on the above issues. Indeed, one can consider the consistency property of a test statistic for a given fixed alternative $\gamma(\gamma > 0)$ as the sample size increases to infinity allowing any path for the sampling interval. For example, one could consider the consistency of a test statistic as the sample size converges to infinity with a given fixed span S; i.e., when the sampling interval converges to zero at rate T. If a test is inconsistent under this path for h, the sampling interval, one could expect low power, in finite samples, with a data set sampled frequently. On the other hand, if a test is consistent allowing h to increase as the sample size increases (i.e., allow the span S to increase faster than T), then one could expect large power in a data set that extends over a long horizon even with a relatively small number of observations.

The aim of the paper is to analyze the power properties of various tests of the random walk hypothesis against stationary alternatives in a context which allows for different sampling intervals. Section 2 introduces the continuous time model and considers its properties in more detail. The test statistics are presented in Section 3. We include statistics that test for a unit root in the original data and statistics that test for randomness in the first-differenced series. In the latter class, we include parametric as well as nonparametric statistics (including some nonparametric rank statistics). Hence, a by-product of our study is also a comparison of power among a wide number of statistics from different classes (13 statistics are considered in all). The simulation experiment to assess the power in finite samples is presented in Section 4 and the results are discussed in Section 5.

Section 6 presents some theoretical results concerning the consistency properties of the tests analyzed when we allow an arbitrary path for the sampling interval as the sample size increases. These results draw heavily from the study of Perron (1987) which used methods first introduced by Phillips (1987a, 1987b and 1988) in the context of continuous asymptotic records for integrated series and asymptotic analyses of near-integrated series. Section 7 presents some concluding comments, and a mathematical appendix contains the proofs of the theorems in Section 6.

2. The Null and Alternative Hypotheses

The simplest and most sensible way to approach the problem of differential sampling interval and its effect on the properties of test statistics is to consider the general case of correlation in continuous time records. Our null hypothesis is that the changes in the random variable of interest are independently and identically distributed and the alternative is that the process is mean reverting. These null and alternative hypotheses are succinctly represented by the stochastic differential equations:

$$H_0: \quad dy(t) = \sigma dw(t) \quad t > 0, \ y(0) = 0 \tag{1}$$

$$H_1: \quad dy(t) = -\gamma y(t)dt + \sigma dw(t), \quad -\infty < t < \infty, \gamma > 0 \tag{2}$$

where $w(t)$ is a unit Wiener process and γ and σ are constant. Under the null hypothesis $y(0)$ is fixed at 0 while, since the alternative hypothesis specify a stationary process, we can equivalently specify H_1 as holding for $t \geq 0$ with $y(0)$ having the stationary distribution (see below). The null hypothesis is, in fact, that $\gamma = 0$.

These systems of stochastic differential equations can be solved in order to derive discrete time representations of the processes. Let h be the sampling interval. Consider first the alternative hypothesis where $y(t)$ is simply an Ornstein-Uhlenbeck process having a unique solution of the form (see, e.g., Arnold, 1974, pp. 134-135):

$$y(th) = e^{-\gamma ht} y(0) + \sigma \int_0^{ht} e^{-\gamma(ht-s)} dw(s), \quad t \geq 0.$$

Simple manipulations (see, e.g., Arnold, p. 134) yield the following discrete time representation of the alternative hypothesis (imposing stationarity):

$$H_1: \quad y(ht) = e^{-\gamma h} y\Big(h(t-1)\Big) + v(ht) \quad t = 1, 2, \ldots \tag{3}$$

where $y(0) \sim N(0, \sigma^2/2\gamma)$ and $v(ht) \sim N\Big(0, \sigma^2(1 - \exp(-2\gamma h))/2\gamma\Big)$. Under the null hypothesis H_0, the unique solution to the stochastic differential equation (1) is:

$$y(ht) = \sigma \int_0^{ht} dw(s) = \sigma \int_0^{h(t-1)} dw(s) + \sigma \int_{h(t-1)}^{ht} dw(s).$$

Let $u(th) = \sigma \int_{h(t-1)}^{ht} dw(s)$. From the properties of the Brownian motion $w(t)$, it is easy to deduce that $Var\Big(u(th)\Big) = h\sigma^2$ (see Arnold, 1974 and Bergström, 1984). Therefore, in discrete time, we have the following null hypothesis:

$$H_0: \quad y(ht) = y\Big(h(t-1)\Big) + u(ht) \quad t = 1, 2, \cdots \tag{4}$$

where $y(0) = 0$ and $u(ht) \sim N(0, h\sigma^2)$. If we let $\beta_h = \exp(-\gamma h)$, the alternative hypothesis has the form

$$H_1: \quad y(ht) = \beta_h y\Big(h(t-1)\Big) + v(ht),$$

and a test of the null hypothesis that $\gamma = 0$ is equivalent in discrete time to a test that $\beta_h = 1$, i.e., the random walk hypothesis; the test being carried out against an alternative that the process is a stationary first-order autoregressive process.

Of course, in practice only a finite amount of data is available, say T. In the following, we will denote by S the span of the data available, where $S = hT$. Therefore, in discrete time, the index t is in the range $t = 0, 1, ..., T = S/h$.

Four of the tests we study deal directly with the sample series $\{y(ht)\}_{t=0}^{T}$ but the rest of them treat the series $\Delta y(ht) \equiv y(ht) - y[h(t-1)] \ (t = 1,...,T)$. Indeed under the null hypothesis that $\beta_h = 1$ (for all *h*) we have that $\Delta y(ht)$ is a sequence of independent and identically distributed random variables so that we can simply apply various tests of randomness readily available in the literature. It is therefore of interest to derive the null and alternative hypotheses in terms of the sample of first-differences $\{\Delta y(ht)\}_{t=1}^{T}$. In what follows, we will omit the suffix *h* and simply write Δy_t and y_t.

Of course, under the null hypothesis $\Delta y_t = u_t$ ($t = 1,...,T$) where u_t is a sequence of iid normal random variables with mean 0 and variance $h\sigma^2$. Under the alternative hypothesis, the sequence of first differences $\{\Delta y_t\}$ is an ARMA (1,1) process with a moving average parameter on the unit circle, i.e.,

$$\Delta y_t = \beta_h \Delta y_{t-1} + v_t - v_{t-1}.$$

Some algebra yields the following representation for the *k*th order autocorrelation of the sequence $\{\Delta y_t\}$, ρ_k:

$$\rho_k = \tfrac{1}{2}(\beta_h - 1)\beta_h^{k-1} = \tfrac{1}{2}(\exp(-\gamma h) - 1)\exp(-\gamma h(k-1)).$$

The autocorrelations are negative at all lags and have a maximum in absolute value when $k = 1$. Note the fact that $\rho_k \to 0$ for all k as $h \to 0$. As $h \to \infty$, we have $\rho_1 \to -\tfrac{1}{2}$ and $\rho_k \to 0$ for all $k \geq 2$. These observations will be useful when interpreting the behavior of the power of the tests. [1]

3. Description of the Statistics

In this section we describe various test statistics which can be used to test the random walk hypothesis. Thirteen test statistics are described. Four of these tests are based upon the original series of $T + 1$ observations $y_0, \ldots, y_T$. The other tests are based upon the series of first differences $\Delta y_t = y_t - y_{t-1}$ ($t = 1, \ldots, T$). [2] In this section we pay special attention to the asymptotic distribution of these tests and to the determination of the appropriate critical values to be used in the simulation study. For simplicity of notation we suppress the dependence of the coefficients and variables on the parameter *h*, the sampling interval.

3.1 TEST STATISTICS BASED UPON THE SERIES $\{y_t\}_0^T$

(i) Normalized OLS Coefficient: An obvious test statistic to consider is the ordinary least squares estimate of the autoregressive parameter β, $\hat{\beta}$, in a regression of y_t against y_{t-1} (this is also the maximum likelihood estimator of β conditional upon y_0):

$$\hat{\beta} = \sum_{t=1}^{T} y_t y_{t-1} \Big/ \sum_{t=1}^{T} y_{t-1}^2 .$$

It is easy to verify that $\hat{\beta}$ is invariant with respect to σ^2, the variance of the errors term. Therefore it can be used directly as a basis for testing $\beta = 1$. The distribution of $T(\hat{\beta} - 1)$ has been tabulated using Monte Carlo methods by Dickey (1976) and a table of values can be found in Fuller (1976), Table 8.5.1, for certain values of T which, however, do not fit our experiment. We obtained the required critical values by simulation using 10000 replications (see the methodology section) for all values of T considered in this study.

(ii) t-statistic on $\hat{\beta}$: Another natural statistic to consider is the *t*-statistic associated with the previous regression

$$t_{\hat{\beta}} = (\hat{\beta}-1)\left(\sum_{t=1}^{T} y_{t-1}^2\right)^{1/2}/\hat{\sigma} \text{ where } \hat{\sigma}^2 = (T-1)^{-1} \sum_{t=1}^{T}(y_t - \hat{\beta}y_{t-1})^2.$$

Percentage points of the distribution of $t_{\hat{\beta}}$ have been evaluated by Monte Carlo method by Dickey (1976) and the values are tabulated in Table 8.5.2 in Fuller (1976). Since this table does not include exact values for the values of T which are of interest to us, these were estimated by Monte Carlo method using 10000 replications (see the methodology section).

(iii) Locally Best Invariant: King (1981) derived the locally best invariant test for the hypothesis that $\beta = 1$ against $\beta < 1$, i.e., a one-sided test (see also Dufour and King, 1986.) This test consists in rejecting the null hypothesis for low values of d, where d is defined as:

$$d = y_T^2 / \sum_{t=1}^{T}(y_t - y_{t-1})^2.$$

Under the null hypothesis, we can write d in terms of the innovation sequence $\{u_t\}$ as $d = u'ss'u / u'u$ where $s = (1,\ldots,1)'_{(T \times 1)}$, $y_T = s'u$ and $u' = \{u_1,\ldots,u_T\}$. The $T \times T$ matrix ss' is of rank 1 and therefore has $T-1$ zero eigenvalues and one non-zero eigenvalue taking the value T. Therefore, we can also write d as $d = T\xi_1^2 / \xi'\xi$ where $\xi = (\xi_1,\ldots,\xi_T)'$ and $\xi_i \sim IN(0,1)$. Finally, we note that d/T is of the form $X_1/(X_1+X_2)$ where X_1 and X_2 are independent X^2 variates and thus d/T has a beta type I distribution with parameters $1/2, (T-1)/2$.

(iv) Uniformly Most Powerful Invariant: Bhargava (1986) extended the work of Sargan and Bhargava (1983) to provide uniformly most powerful invariant tests of the random walk hypothesis. As with the previous test of King the resulting test statistics are different for stationary and explosive alternatives. We shall be concerned here with the former only. In the case studied here, the statistic reduces to

$$R = \sum_{t=1}^{T}(y_t - y_{t-1})^2 / \sum_{t=0}^{T}(y_t - \bar{Y})^2, \quad \bar{Y} = (T+1)^{-1}\sum_{0}^{T} y_t.$$

It is a ratio of quadratic forms in normal random variables and therefore the critical values can be evaluated with the Imhof routine. Since the critical values tabulated by Bhargava are not for sample sizes used in this study, we derived them independently using the Imhof routine as programmed by Koerts and Abrahamse (1969). Note that Bhargava provides the appropriate eigenvalues to be used as weights in this routine.

3.2 PARAMETRIC TESTS BASED ON THE SERIES $\Delta y_t = y_t - y_{t-1}$ $(t = 1,\ldots,T)$

(v) The von Neumann Ratio: von Neumann (1942) suggested as a statistic the ratio of successive mean squared differences to the variance:

$$V = (T/T-1)\sum_{t=2}^{T}(\Delta y_t - \Delta y_{t-1})^2 / \sum_{t=1}^{T}(\Delta y_t - \overline{\Delta y})^2 \text{ where } \overline{\Delta y} = T^{-1}\sum_{t=1}^{T}\Delta y_t.$$

Under the null hypothesis, von Neumann (1942) showed that with normal errors, $E(V) = 2T/(T-1)$ and $VAR(V) = 4/T$. It is also shown that $[V - E(V)]/\sqrt{Var(V)}$ is asymptotically $N(0,1)$. Since V is a ratio of quadratic forms, its exact distribution can be computed using the Imhof routine. This was done by Dufour and Perron (1985) for a wide range of values of T and percentage points. For T up to 64, we take the critical values from this study which also showed that the normal approximation is indeed very good for T greater than 60. Therefore, for values of T greater than 64 we determine the critical values from the asymptotic normal distribution.

(vi) First-Order Correlation Coefficient: Consider the first-order serial correlation coefficient defined by:

$$r = (T/T-1)\sum_{t=2}^{T}\Delta y_t \Delta y_{t-1} / \sum_{t=1}^{T}\Delta y_t^2.$$

Under our null hypothesis, Moran (1948) shows that $E(r) = 0$ and $Var(r) = T(T-1)^{-1}(T+2)^{-1}$. Anderson (1942) shows that, under normality of the errors, $[r - E(r)] / \sqrt{Var(r)}$ is asymptotically $N(0,1)$. In this study we used the critical values derived from the asymptotic distribution.

3.3 NONPARAMETRIC TESTS BASED ON THE LEVEL OF THE SERIES $\{\Delta y_t\}$ [3]

(vii) Turning Points Test: We define the series $\Delta y_1, \ldots, \Delta y_T$ as having a turning point at t if $\Delta y_{t-1} > \Delta y_t$ and $\Delta y_t < \Delta y_{t+1}$ or if $\Delta y_{t-1} < \Delta y_t$ and $\Delta y_t > \Delta y_{t+1}$. The statistic of interest, say D, is simply the number of such turning points present in the series. That is,

$$D = \sum_{t=2}^{T-1} Y_i \text{ where } Y_i = 1 \text{ if there is a turning point at } i \text{ and } Y_i = 0 \text{ otherwise.}$$

If $T > 4$, we have $E(D) = 2(T-2)/3$ and $VAR(D) = (16T - 29)/90$ (see Kendall and Stuart, 1976). It can also be shown that this test is equivalent to a test based upon the number of runs (see Mood, 1940) a version of which was studied in Shiller and Perron (1985).

(viii) Wald-Wolfowitz Statistic: Wald and Wolfowitz (1943) proposed the following transformation of the serial correlation coefficient

$$R = \sum_{t=2}^{T} \Delta y_t \Delta y_{t-1} + \Delta y_1 \Delta y_T$$

which is designed especially to test against serial behavior. They show that

$$E(R) = (S_1^2 - S_2)/(T-1)$$
$$Var(R) = (T-1)^{-1}[S_2^2 - S_4] + [(T-1)(T-2)]^{-1}[S_1^4 - 4S_1^2 S_2 + 4S_1 S_3 + S_2^2 - 2S_4] - (T-1)^{-2}[(S_1^2 - S_2)^2]$$

where $S_k = \sum_{t=1}^{T} \Delta y_t^k$.

3.4 NONPARAMETRIC TESTS BASED ON THE RANKS OF $\{\Delta y_t\}_1^T$

(ix) Rank Correlation Coefficient: If we apply the ordinary correlation coefficient to the ranks of the series Δy_t, we can define the following rank correlation coefficient, where $\{R_t\}$ is the series of ranks associated with the series $\{\Delta y_t\}$.

$$r_k = (T/T-1) \sum_{t=2}^{T}(R_t - \bar{R})(R_{t-1} - \bar{R}) / \sum_{t=1}^{T}(R_t - \bar{R})^2.$$

Since $\sum_{t=1}^{T} R_t = \sum_{t=1}^{T} t = T(T+1)/2$ and $\sum_{t=1}^{T} R_t^2 = \sum_{t=1}^{T} t^2 = T(T+1)(2T+1)/6$, using r_k is equivalent to using the statistic

$$K = \sum_{t=2}^{T} (R_t - \bar{R})(R_{t-1} - \bar{R}) \text{ where } \bar{R} = (T+1)/2.$$

Knoke (1977) studied the statistic K and its power against autocorrelated alternatives. It can be shown that $E(K) = -(T^2-1)/12$ and $Var(K) = (T+1)T^2(T-3)(5T+6)/720$.

(x) Rank Version of von Neumann Ratio: Bartels (1982) studied the rank version of the von Neumann ratio given by

$$G' = \sum_{t=2}^{T} (R_t - R_{t-1})^2 / \sum_{t=1}^{T} (R_t - \bar{R})^2$$

where $\bar{R} = T^{-1} \sum_{t=1}^{T} R_t = (T+1)/2$. Since the denominator is equal to $T(T^2-1)/12$, using G' is equivalent to using:

$$G = \sum_{t=2}^{T} (R_t - R_{t-1})^2.$$

Under H_0, Bartels obtained $E(G) = T(T^2-1)/6$ and $Var(G) = T(T+1)(T-2)(5T^2-2T-9)/180$.

3.5 NONPARAMETRIC TESTS BASED ON THE RANKS OF $\{\Delta y_t \Delta y_{t+1}\}$

Dufour (1981) introduced a family of linear rank test statistics to test the independence of a sequence of random variables under the assumption that the marginal probability density function of the series is symmetric with zero median but without requiring the assumption that the series is identically distributed. These tests are aimed against alternatives of serial dependence.

Dufour motivates the statistics by noting that under the symmetry and independence assumptions, we have $med(\Delta y_t \Delta y_{t+k}) = 0$ $(t = 1, \ldots, T-k)$ where $med(\cdot)$ refers to the median. If there is positive serial dependence (at lag k) $med(\Delta y_t \Delta y_{t+k}) > 0$ and with negative serial dependence $med(\Delta y_t \Delta y_{t+k}) < 0$. The following tests are therefore aimed at testing the null hypothesis that $med(\Delta y_t \Delta y_{t+k}) = 0$ against the alternative hypothesis that $med(\Delta y_t \Delta y_{t+k}) \neq 0$, with $t = 1, \ldots, T-k$ and k an integer $(1 < k < T)$. The family of rank statistics is described as follows:

$$S_k = \sum_{t=1}^{T-k} \mu(Z_t) a_{T-k}(R_t^+)$$

where $Z_t = \Delta y_t \Delta y_{t+k}$, $R_t^+ = $ rank of $|Z_t|$ and $\mu(Z_t) = 1$ if $Z_t \geq 0$ and 0 otherwise. It is shown that the mean and variance of S_k under H_0 are given by $E(S_k) = 1/2 \sum_{t=1}^{T-k} a_T(t)$ and $Var(S_k) = 1/4 \sum_{t=1}^{T-k} a_T^2(t)$. Furthermore, the distribution of S_k is symmetric about $E(S_k)$ and approximately normal under some regularity conditions. The choice of the function $a_T(t)$ defines the particular statistics.

(xi) Sign Test: If we let $a_T(t) = 1$ for all t $(t = 1, \ldots, T)$, we have:

$$S_k^{(1)} = \sum_{t=1}^{T-k} \mu(Z_t).$$

In this case, $S_k^{(1)}$ is the number of non-negative values in the sequence $Z_1, \ldots, Z_{T-k}$, i.e., the statistic of the sign test applied to $Z_1, \ldots, Z_{T-k}$. Under H_0, the exact distribution of $S_k^{(1)}$ is $Bin(T-k, \ 1/2)$ where $Bin(\cdot)$ is the binomial distribution.

If we let $k = 1$, $S_1^{(1)}$ is the number of times consecutive Δy_t's have the same sign. Thus $T - S_1^{(1)}$, is the total number of runs in the sequence $\mu(\Delta y_1), \ldots, \mu(\Delta y_T)$. We approximate the distribution using the asymptotic normality property with $E(S_1^{(1)}) = (T-1)/2$ and $Var(S_1^{(1)}) = (T-1)/4$.

(xii) Wilcoxon Signed-Rank Test: If we let $a_T(t) = t$, we get $S_k^{(2)} = \sum_{t=1}^{T} \mu(Z_t) R_t^+$ which is the sum of the ranks of the non-negative Z_t's. This test statistic is associated with the Wilcoxon signed-rank test for symmetry about zero when applied to $Z_1, \ldots, Z_T$. The exact distribution of $S_k^{(2)}$ under H_0 is the same as the null distribution of the Wilcoxon test statistic. In this study, we let $k = 1$ and it can be verified that in this case $E(S_1^{(2)}) = T(T-1)/4$ and $Var(S_1^{(2)}) = T(T-1)(2T-1)/24$.

(xiii) van Der Waerden Test Statistic: If we let $a_T(t) = \phi^{-1}((1 + t(T+1)^{-1})/2)$ where ϕ^{-1} is the inverse of the cumulative distribution function of a $N(0,1)$ random variable, with $k = 1$ we get the analog of the van der Waerden (1952) test statistic:

$$S_1^{(3)} = \sum_{t=1}^{T-1} \phi^{-1}((1 + R_t^+(T+1)^{-1})/2) \ \mu(Z_t).$$

Under H_0 : $E(S_1^{(3)}) = \sum_{t=1}^{T-1} \phi^{-1}((1 + R_t^+(T+1)^{-1})/2)/2$ and $Var(S_1^{(3)}) = \sum_{t=1}^{T-1} \phi^{-1}((1 + R_t^+(T+1)^{-1})/2)^2/4$.

4. Methodology for the Simulations

All simulations were carried out on a CDC Cyber 915 at the Université de Montréal. The $N(0,1)$ random deviates were obtained from the subroutine GGNML of the International Mathematical and Statistical Library (IMSL). The critical values for $\hat{\beta}$ and $t_{\hat{\beta}}$ were obtained using 10000 replications. The starting value $y(0)$ was set at 0. All tests considered here are one-tailed 5% size tests against stationary alternatives. The power estimates were obtained using 2000 replications. Hence the standard error of any entry in the tables is $\sqrt{P(1-P)/2000}$ if P is the true power, which gives a maximum standard error of 0.0112 (when $P = \frac{1}{2}$).

Since the tests statistics are invariant to the value of σ^2, we let $\sigma^2 = 1/h$ under the null hypothesis and $\sigma^2 = 2\gamma/(1 - \exp(-2\gamma h))$ under the alternative hypothesis. This implies that u_{ht} and v_{ht} are $N(0,1)$ in (3) and (4) and $y(0)$ is $N(0, (1 - \exp(-2\gamma h))^{-1})$ in (3). The experiment was performed for an alternative hypothesis specified as $\gamma = 0.2$ and the following grid of values for both the span S and the number of observations T: 8, 16, 32, 64, 128, 256, 512. The power against alternatives other than $\gamma = 0.2$ can be obtained from the tables. Since $\beta_h = \exp(-\gamma h)$, one can read the power of a test against the alternative that $\gamma = 0.2 * 2^j$ by reading j rows down.

The row 'inf' gives the power of a test in the limiting case where the span tends to infinity. Since $\beta_h = \exp(-\gamma S/T)$, we have $\beta \to 0$ as $S \to \infty$ and the values reported in 'row inf' are simply the powers of a test that $\beta = 1$ against an alternative that $\beta = 0$. Finally, the row labelled 'size' gives the estimated exact size of the test obtained again using 2000 replications by simulating the model under the null hypothesis of a random walk. The standard error of each entry is, in this case, 0.005.

5. Analysis of the Results

Table I presents the results concerning the normalized least-squares coefficient in a first-order autoregression using the level of the series $\{y_t\}$. The results are similar to those obtained in Shiller and Perron (1985) which considers the coefficient in a regression that includes a constant term. Here the power is slightly higher since some variability is excluded due to the fact that the mean of the series is not estimated. To summarize, with a small span the power is low and does not significantly increase as T increases. As the span increases the power increases significantly. For any given span the power appears to converge to a limit between 0 and 1, this limit increasing with the span. The results for the t-statistic (Table II) are similar except for the fact that the power is somewhat higher.

TABLE I. Normalized OLS Coefficient

S \ T	8	16	32	64	128	256	512
8	0.078	0.077	0.080	0.069	0.069	0.071	0.075
16	0.148	0.158	0.166	0.155	0.166	0.155	0.155
32	0.303	0.359	0.407	0.413	0.430	0.431	0.421
64	0.519	0.740	0.839	0.868	0.903	0.903	0.908
128	0.670	0.947	0.996	1.000	1.000	1.000	1.000
256	0.704	0.988	1.000	1.000	1.000	1.000	1.000
512	0.705	0.992	1.000	1.000	1.000	1.000	1.000
INF	0.705	0.992	1.000	1.000	1.000	1.000	1.000
Size	0.057	0.053	0.050	0.051	0.057	0.053	0.053

TABLE II. t-Statistic on $\hat{\beta}$

S \ T	8	16	32	64	128	256	512
8	0.150	0.142	0.141	0.132	0.116	0.122	0.132
16	0.232	0.225	0.229	0.224	0.216	0.212	0.222
32	0.396	0.436	0.488	0.480	0.463	0.473	0.477
64	0.609	0.778	0.863	0.892	0.903	0.912	0.913
128	0.737	0.948	0.995	0.999	0.999	1.000	1.000
256	0.769	0.987	1.000	1.000	1.000	1.000	1.000
512	0.770	0.990	1.000	1.000	1.000	1.000	1.000
INF	0.770	0.990	1.000	1.000	1.000	1.000	1.000
Size	0.067	0.060	0.054	0.050	0.056	0.047	0.056

TABLE III. Locally Best Invariant

S \ T	8	16	32	64	128	256	512
8	0.085	0.095	0.085	0.098	0.093	0.099	0.091
16	0.120	0.131	0.127	0.120	0.117	0.124	0.138
32	0.158	0.168	0.166	0.168	0.161	0.179	0.174
64	0.186	0.207	0.211	0.234	0.236	0.248	0.244
128	0.199	0.268	0.280	0.325	0.345	0.335	0.330
256	0.207	0.263	0.350	0.410	0.430	0.473	0.460
512	0.214	0.286	0.382	0.469	0.537	0.593	0.605
INF	0.214	0.286	0.385	0.515	0.681	0.857	0.948
Size	0.047	0.046	0.045	0.050	0.053	0.049	0.050

Table III presents the results concerning the locally best invariant test statistic proposed by King (1981). As expected from a locally best invariant test the power for small spans (which correspond to higher frequencies for a given T and therefore alternatives closer to the null) is higher than for most other tests. This is verified for span of 8 and 16 units. Nevertheless, the power remains rather low. For spans greater than 16 the power of King's test gets comparatively worse than the power of the previous two tests. As is the case for the statistics analyzed previously, the power increases in both directions, i.e., as T increases and as S increases. The power seems to level to some limit as T increases for a given span. This limit is lower than for the previous two tests for spans greater than 16.

Table IV presents the results concerning the uniformly most powerful invariant test proposed by Bhargava (1986). The results are very similar to the ones with the OLS coefficient and its t-statistic with the power marginally greater for low spans and marginally smaller for large spans. Bhargava's test appears to provide an interesting alternative to the serial correlation coefficient.

TABLE IV. Uniformly Most Powerful Invariant

S \ T	8	16	32	64	128	256	512
8	0.059	0.065	0.067	0.075	0.074	0.074	0.053
16	0.097	0.094	0.106	0.099	0.088	0.110	0.101
32	0.163	0.183	0.215	0.234	0.234	0.238	0.225
64	0.290	0.455	0.547	0.599	0.621	0.641	0.626
128	0.400	0.770	0.932	0.987	0.991	0.991	0.992
256	0.444	0.901	1.000	1.000	1.000	1.000	1.000
512	0.427	0.921	1.000	1.000	1.000	1.000	1.000
INF	0.427	0.923	1.000	1.000	1.000	1.000	1.000
Size	0.058	0.057	0.062	0.054	0.049	0.055	0.051

The tests analyzed so far are the only ones for which the power does not eventually decrease as T increases with a given fixed span. It is noteworthy that all the following tests interestingly share this feature.

Table V presents the results for the von Neumann test. Compared to the other tests the power is much lower, e.g., 0.11 for a span as large as 64 and any value of T. For a given span the power increases until $T = 64$ and then decreases significantly. Note that the test is significantly biased for low values of T and S. The results for the first-order correlation coefficient of the first-differences are presented in Table VI. The same comments apply as for the von Neumann statistic. The power here is maximized when $T = 32$ for all values of S except when $S = 512$ for which it is maximized at $T = 64$.

TABLE V. The von Neumann Ratio

S \ T	8	16	32	64	128	256	512
8	0.053	0.050	0.054	0.051	0.051	0.053	0.048
16	0.054	0.075	0.064	0.073	0.056	0.064	0.059
32	0.096	0.090	0.086	0.084	0.078	0.062	0.063
64	0.149	0.175	0.160	0.150	0.110	0.090	0.077
128	0.194	0.327	0.360	0.306	0.233	0.157	0.127
256	0.220	0.498	0.682	0.691	0.555	0.396	0.255
512	0.211	0.513	0.854	0.950	0.949	0.851	0.667
INF	0.218	0.497	0.888	0.997	1.000	1.000	1.000
Size	0.047	0.059	0.051	0.058	0.054	0.058	0.058

TABLE VI. First-Order Correlation Coefficient

S\T	8	16	32	64	128	256	512
8	0.039	0.046	0.067	0.055	0.058	0.064	0.055
16	0.050	0.060	0.086	0.064	0.066	0.068	0.058
32	0.082	0.111	0.116	0.089	0.081	0.074	0.067
64	0.158	0.224	0.200	0.161	0.132	0.107	0.089
128	0.225	0.416	0.430	0.343	0.257	0.199	0.139
256	0.250	0.582	0.766	0.718	0.581	0.412	0.280
512	0.251	0.620	0.900	0.965	0.953	0.854	0.650
INF	0.251	0.622	0.928	0.997	1.000	1.000	1.000
Size	0.027	0.039	0.056	0.047	0.051	0.061	0.053

The turning points test (Table VII) has very low power, a maximum of 0.224 is obtained for $S = 512$ and $T = 64$ but does not appear to be biased for any pairs of values of T and S. It is clear in this case that the power tends to the size of the test as T increases for any given fixed span. Here the power is maximized at a value of T between 8 and 32 depending on the magnitude of the span. The Wald-Wolfowitz test statistic (Table VIII) and the rank correlation coefficient (Table IX) are appreciably more powerful and do not appear biased. Again the power eventually decreases as T increases for a given fixed span and is maximized at $T = 32$ or 64. The same comments apply to the rank version of the von Neumann ratio proposed by Bartels (Table X).

TABLE VII. Turning Points Test

S\T	8	16	32	64	128	256	512
8	0.073	0.073	0.061	0.050	0.048	0.048	0.045
16	0.077	0.078	0.061	0.050	0.047	0.048	0.044
32	0.090	0.085	0.071	0.053	0.048	0.045	0.044
64	0.112	0.102	0.080	0.054	0.049	0.043	0.045
128	0.134	0.139	0.098	0.065	0.058	0.049	0.046
256	0.141	0.184	0.160	0.110	0.083	0.058	0.046
512	0.141	0.194	0.224	0.216	0.151	0.088	0.062
INF	0.141	0.194	0.240	0.363	0.568	0.812	0.978
Size	0.069	0.069	0.057	0.048	0.047	0.046	0.045

TABLE VIII. Wald-Wolfowitz Statistic

S\T	8	16	32	64	128	256	512
8	0.047	0.051	0.063	0.054	0.052	0.061	0.055
16	0.054	0.054	0.070	0.060	0.058	0.064	0.056
32	0.073	0.089	0.095	0.076	0.074	0.072	0.065
64	0.119	0.166	0.173	0.142	0.111	0.099	0.085
128	0.167	0.326	0.363	0.308	0.231	0.183	0.132
256	0.184	0.482	0.691	0.672	0.541	0.385	0.270
512	0.184	0.524	0.861	0.947	0.945	0.843	0.633
INF	0.184	0.526	0.889	0.996	1.000	1.000	1.000
Size	0.045	0.048	0.060	0.050	0.050	0.060	0.054

TABLE IX. Rank Correlation Coefficient

S\T	8	16	32	64	128	256	512
8	0.029	0.037	0.048	0.047	0.056	0.062	0.051
16	0.031	0.044	0.053	0.053	0.061	0.067	0.053
32	0.044	0.061	0.082	0.076	0.071	0.074	0.061
64	0.067	0.132	0.146	0.128	0.108	0.101	0.077
128	0.093	0.253	0.321	0.265	0.212	0.164	0.119
256	0.104	0.384	0.619	0.616	0.491	0.354	0.249
512	0.104	0.429	0.809	0.928	0.923	0.811	0.611
INF	0.104	0.430	0.849	0.992	1.000	1.000	1.000
Size	0.024	0.034	0.048	0.046	0.056	0.062	0.051

TABLE X. Rank Version of the von Neumann Ratio

S\T	8	16	32	64	128	256	512
8	0.054	0.045	0.055	0.049	0.059	0.062	0.052
16	0.069	0.054	0.064	0.054	0.062	0.067	0.053
32	0.090	0.080	0.092	0.079	0.074	0.074	0.061
64	0.141	0.161	0.158	0.132	0.118	0.101	0.076
128	0.188	0.296	0.335	0.274	0.213	0.165	0.120
256	0.199	0.429	0.644	0.620	0.496	0.356	0.249
512	0.201	0.472	0.811	0.928	0.922	0.808	0.610
INF	0.201	0.473	0.853	0.993	1.000	1.000	1.000
Size	0.049	0.041	0.053	0.046	0.059	0.062	0.050

The test statistics based on the ranks of the series $\{\Delta y_t \Delta y_{t-1}\}$ are presented in Table XI (sign test), Table XII (Wilcoxon signed-rank test), and Table XIII (van der Waerden test statistic). These tests have very low power up to a span of 64 units for all values of T. The power is noticeably higher for larger spans. It is maximized at $T = 32$ for any given fixed span except for a span of 512 where it is maximized at $T = 64$. Again the power seems to converge towards the size of the test as T increases for any fixed value of S.

TABLE XI. Sign Test

S\T	8	16	32	64	128	256	512
8	0.069	0.060	0.038	0.043	0.059	0.060	0.046
16	0.086	0.075	0.044	0.048	0.062	0.062	0.043
32	0.118	0.101	0.063	0.054	0.071	0.070	0.053
64	0.169	0.157	0.092	0.080	0.094	0.089	0.062
128	0.208	0.247	0.175	0.151	0.152	0.120	0.090
256	0.219	0.336	0.334	0.340	0.309	0.224	0.154
512	0.219	0.359	0.476	0.621	0.669	0.515	0.345
INF	0.219	0.360	0.517	0.844	0.995	1.000	1.000
Size	0.056	0.054	0.038	0.040	0.059	0.053	0.040

Several interesting features emerge from this simulation experiment. First, one can compare the various tests in terms of their power properties. Among the class of non-parametric tests analyzed, the Wald-Wolfowitz statistic performs best, closely followed by the Wilcoxon signed-rank test and the van der Waerden statistic. The Wald-Wolfowitz statistic seems almost as good as the parametric test based on the first-order correlation coefficient of the first-differences and better than the von Neumann ratio. However, the best tests are those based on the original series $\{y_t\}$: the normalized least squares coefficient in a first-order autoregression and its t-statistic and Bhargava's test.

TABLE XII. Wilcoxon Signed-Rank Test

S\T	8	16	32	64	128	256	512
8	0.070	0.060	0.057	0.055	0.064	0.062	0.054
16	0.083	0.078	0.069	0.064	0.068	0.066	0.057
32	0.123	0.109	0.099	0.085	0.081	0.074	0.062
64	0.191	0.208	0.171	0.134	0.117	0.100	0.076
128	0.266	0.355	0.344	0.276	0.209	0.160	0.120
256	0.282	0.506	0.634	0.595	0.461	0.327	0.237
512	0.282	0.538	0.806	0.892	0.883	0.751	0.540
INF	0.282	0.539	0.842	0.987	1.000	1.000	1.000
Size	0.050	0.048	0.058	0.045	0.057	0.055	0.053

TABLE XIII. van der Waerden Test Statistic

S\T	8	16	32	64	128	256	512
8	0.070	0.054	0.058	0.058	0.065	0.064	0.055
16	0.083	0.073	0.071	0.068	0.072	0.068	0.057
32	0.123	0.107	0.110	0.089	0.085	0.080	0.063
64	0.191	0.212	o.183	0.147	0.124	0.106	0.080
128	0.266	0.366	0.370	0.304	0.225	0.183	0.127
256	0.282	0.521	0.672	0.651	0.512	0.372	0.265
512	0.282	0.557	0.841	0.924	0.927	0.817	0.615
INF	0.282	0.562	0.871	0.995	1.000	1.000	1.000
Size	0.050	0.045	0.055	0.048	0.056	0.059	0.052

However, the most interesting feature emerging from the simulation experiment is the behavior of the power function of the tests as the sampling interval is varied. The common pattern is that all tests of the random walk based on a test of randomness in the first-differenced series have a power that eventually declines as the sampling interval decreases. Furthermore, the evidence for low spans suggests that the limit of the power as the sampling interval converges to zero is the size of the test. On the other hand, tests based on the original series $\{y_t\}$ have power that increases as more observations are added keeping a fixed span, though the power tends to level off as the sampling interval converges to zero.

This power property has interesting implications. First, when the power function converges to the size of the test as the sampling interval converges to zero, more observations are not necessarily better and too many may yield useless tests if they are concentrated in a data set with a small span. Indeed, it may be the case that higher power can be achieved by throwing away observations if the span is kept fixed, for example, by going from monthly to quarterly observations. Secondly, for test statistics having this property, there appears to be an optimal sampling interval (for any given fixed span) that maximizes the power of the test. This number of observations appears, from the simulation results, to be relatively small. This is not the case when considering tests based on the original series $\{y_t\}$. Here more observations are always better, though the contribution of each addition is marginal if the span is fixed.

The feature that is common to both classes of tests is that the power is much more influenced by the span of the data than by the number of observations per se. While each increases in T, the sample size, has at most a marginally declining effect, the power appears to converge rapidly to one if both the span and the number of observations are increased.

In the notation of Perron (1987), the results suggested by the experiments are that tests based on the original series $\{y_t\}$ are consistent as long as the span increases with the sample size and this at any positive rate. Equivalently, they are consistent as long as the sampling interval does not converge to zero at a rate greater or equal to T (recall that $T = S/h$). On the other hand, tests of the random walk based on a test of randomness on the first-differences of the data are consistent only if the span increases with T at a higher rate. From the arguments presented in the next section, this rate is $T^{1/2}$, i.e., the span must increase at least at rate $T^{1/2}$ for the tests to be consistent. These empirical results are justified theoretically in the next section.

It must be stressed that the conclusions reached apply to the particular setting considered, i.e., testing the random walk hypothesis against an alternative that the process is stationary. The properties described above may not hold against other alternatives such as a random walk with correlated residuals. However, the results appear to be robust to other specifications concerning the distribution of the errors (see Perron, 1986, chap. 1).

6. A Theoretical Analysis of the Consistency Property

The results described in Perron (1987) can be used to analyse the consistency properties of the tests described here. The presentation is informal and more details on the method can be found in that paper. For ease of presentation, we analyze the special case where the initial observation is set at 0, i.e., $y(0) = 0$. The same conclusions follow letting y(0) have an arbitrary pre-specified distribution including the one described in Section 2.

To analyze the limiting distribution of the statistics, we consider the process (3) embedded in a triangular array which allows the sampling interval h and the sample size T to be related as T increases. Each variable is then indexed by, say, n such that $T_n = S_n / h_n$. We require $T_n \to \infty$ as $n \to \infty$. We can then define a triangular array of random variables $\{\{y_{nt}\}_{t=1}^{T_n}\}_{n=1}^{\infty}$. For a given n, the sequence $\{y_{nt}\}_{t=1}^{T_n}$ is generated by

$$y_{nt} = \exp(-\gamma h_n)y_{nt-1} + u_{nt} \qquad t = 1, \ldots, T_n \tag{5}$$

where the innovation sequence $\{u_{nt}\}_{t=1}^{T_n}$ is i.i.d. normal with mean 0 and variance $\sigma^2(1 - \exp(-2\gamma h_n))/2\gamma$, and $y(0) = 0$.

The following Lemma, proved in Perron (1987), describes the limiting distribution of the sample moment of $\{y_{nt}\}$ as $T_n \to \infty$ with the span S fixed for all n. The proof uses methods originally introduced in a series of papers by Phillips (1987a, 1987b, 1988) concerning continuous records asymptotic and near-integrated systems.

LEMMA 1

If $\{\{y_{nt}\}_1^{T_n}\}_1^{\infty}$ is a triangular array of random variables defined by (5) and $y(0) = 0$, then as $n \to \infty$ and $h_n \to 0$ with $S_n = S$ for all n:

(a) $\quad y_{T_n} \to S^{1/2} \sigma J_c(1)$

(b) $\quad h_n \sum_1^{T_n} y_{nt} \to S^{3/2} \sigma \int_0^1 J_c(r)dr$

$$(c) \quad h_n \sum_{t=1}^{T_n} y_{nt}^2 \to S^2 \sigma^2 \int_0^1 J_c(r)^2 dr$$

$$(d) \quad \sum_{t=1}^{T_n} y_{nt-1} u_{nt} \to S\sigma^2 \int_0^1 J_c(r) dw(r)$$

$$(e) \quad \sum_{t=1}^{T_n} u_{nt}^2 \to S\sigma^2$$

where $J_c(r) = \int_0^r e^{(r-s)c} dw(s)$ and $c = -\gamma S$.

The statistics described in Section 3.1 can be written in terms of the triangular array of random variables defined by (5). These depend only on the sample moments defined in Lemma 1. The results in Lemma 1 can be used directly to derive the limiting distribution of these statistics both under the null $(\gamma = 0)$ and the alternative $(\gamma > 0)$ hypotheses. The statistics are now indexed by the subscript n to emphasize that they are analysed under the triangular array of random variables defined by (5).

THEOREM 1

If $\{\{y_{nt}\}_1^{T_n}\}_1^\infty$ is a triangular array of random variables defined by (5) and $y(0) = 0$, then as $n \to \infty$ and $h_n \to 0$, with S fixed:

$$(a) \quad T_n(\hat{\beta}_n - 1) \to c + \{ \int_0^1 J_c(r)^2 dr \}^{-1} \{ \int_0^1 J_c(r) dw(r) \}$$

$$(b) \quad t_{\hat{\beta}_n} \to [c + \{\int_0^1 J_c(r)^2 dr\}^{-1} \{\int_0^1 J_c(r) dw(r)\}] \, [\int_0^1 J_c(r)^2 dr]^{1/2}$$

$$(c) \quad d_n \to J_c(1)^2$$

$$(d) \quad T_n R_n \to [\int_0^1 J_c(r)^2 dr - (\int_0^1 J_c(r) dr)^2]^{-1} .$$

As a corollary to Theorem 1, we can obtain the limiting distribution of the various statistics under the null hypothesis of a random walk. To do this we simply let $\gamma = 0$ and hence $c = 0$ and $J_c(r) = w(r)$.

COROLLARY 1

If $\{\{y_{nt}\}_1^{T_n}\}_1^\infty$ is a triangular array of random variables defined by (5) with $\gamma = 0$ and $y(0) = 0$, then as $n \to \infty$ and $h_n \to o$ with S fixed:

$$(a) \quad T_n(\hat{\beta}_n - 1) \to [\int_0^1 w(r)^2 dr]^{-1} \int_0^1 w(r) dw(r) = [\int_0^1 w(r)^2 dr]^{-1} (\tfrac{1}{2})(w(1)^2 - 1)$$

$$(b) \quad t_{\hat{\beta}_n} \to [\int_0^1 w(r)^2 dr]^{-1/2} (\tfrac{1}{2})(w(1)^2 - 1)$$

$$(c) \quad d_n \to w(1)^2$$

$$(d) \quad T_n R_n \to [\int_0^1 w(r)^2 dr - (\int_0^1 w(r) dr)^2]^{-1}$$

It can be shown that the results of Corollary 1 apply under any path for the sampling interval (see Perron, 1987). The same is not true for the limiting distribution under the alternative as given in Theorem 1. A few interesting results emerge from Theorem 1 and Corollary 1. First, the limiting distributions of the statistics are non-degenerate and finite as $h \to 0$ keeping a fixed span. This proves the conjecture from the Monte Carlo experiment to the effect that the power function of tests based on the original series $\{y_t\}$ have a non-degenerate limiting power function as $h \to 0$. That is, the power does not converge to 1 but to some value which depends on the span. Some exact values were obtained for the statistic $T(\hat{\beta} - 1)$ in Perron (1987).

One can also easily obtain the limiting power function as both the sampling interval and the span converge to zero. Since $c = -\gamma S$, the limiting distribution of the statistics as $S \to 0$ are obtained by taking the limit as $c \to 0$. This implies that the limiting distributions under the alternative are the same as the limiting distributions under the null (see Corollary 1); hence, the power function converges to the size of the tests as $S \to 0$ with $T \to \infty$, i.e., when the sampling interval converges to zero at a rate faster than T.

Arguments similar to those given in Perron (1987) can be used to show that the statistics considered in Theorem 1 all converge to $-\infty$ (a, b) and $+\infty$ (c, d), under the alternative, if $S \to \infty$ as $T \to \infty$. Hence, if the span is increasing (at whatever rate) with the sample size, the test statistics are consistent. This confirms the conjecture from the Monte Carlo study.

When considering tests of the random walk hypothesis based on a test of randomness on the first-differenced data, a different approach must be taken. We shall, however, not be as precise as above. Our argument is based on the results of Theorem 2 below which shows that for a well-defined class of test statistics, we obtain consistency if and only if the span is increasing at a rate greater than $T^{1/2}$. This class of statistics has a root T convergence rate and satisfies the so-called Pitman's conditions for a non-degenerate local asymptotic power function with contiguous alternatives that approach the null at a rate $T^{1/2}$. Our claim is that the tests presented here that use the first-differenced data satisfy those conditions. To be more precise we would have to verify on a case-by-case basis whether or not they apply. For the moment this is a conjecture except for the statistics based on the first-order correlation coefficient where it was formally shown in Perron (1987) that the conditions were satisfied.

THEOREM 2

Let J_n be a test statistic based on the first T_n observations sampled at intervals of length h_n, and let the critical region be $J_n \geq \lambda_n$. Suppose that

(a) $\lim_{n \to \infty} P(J_n \geq \lambda_n) = \alpha > 0$.

(b)   there exist functions $\mu(\theta)$ and $\sigma(\theta)$ such that

$$\lim_{n \to \infty} P\left\{ T_n^{1/2} \frac{J_n - \mu(\theta_0 + \delta T_n^{-1/2})}{\sigma(\theta_0 + \delta T_n^{-1/2})} < y \mid \theta_0 + \delta T_n^{-1/2} \right\} = \Phi(y)$$

for every real y, where $\Phi(y)$ is the distribution function of $N(0,1)$.

(c) $\mu(\theta)$ has a derivative $\mu'(\theta_0)$ at $\theta = \theta_0$, which is positive and $\sigma(\theta)$ is continuous at θ_0.

Then J_n is a consistent test of the random walk hypothesis against stationary alternatives if and only if $h_n = O(T_n^a)$ for any $a > -\frac{1}{2}$.

The conditions of Theorem 2 are usually referred to as Pitman's conditions. They are related to the concept of the Pitman efficiency which considers the local asymptotic power of test statistics under contiguous alternatives of the form $\theta_0 + \delta T_n^{-1/2}$ (for details see Rao, 1973, Section 7.a.7).

The proof of the theorem is presented in the appendix. To get some intuition about the result, note first that we can write $\theta_n = \beta_n = \exp(-\gamma h_n)$ and therefore $\theta_n = \theta_0 + T_n^{-1/2}\delta_n$ where $\delta_n = T_n^{1/2}(\exp(-\gamma h_n) - 1)$ and $\theta_0 = 1$. Given condition (b) of the theorem, the statistic J_n has a non-degenerate limiting distribution against local alternatives that approach the null value at a rate of $T_n^{1/2}$. If the alternative value approaches the null at a rate lower than $T_n^{1/2}$, the power function converges to 1. However, if it approaches the null at a rate faster than $T_n^{1/2}$, the power converges to the size of the test. When the sampling interval is varied, the value of the autoregressive parameter changes. When the sampling interval decreases, β_n converges to 1 at a rate which depends on the rate at which h the sampling interval converges to 0 relative to the sample size. For instance, if the span of the data is fixed, the sampling interval converges to 0 at the same rate as the sample size converges to infinity. Hence, in this case we expect the test to be inconsistent. This is proved formally in Theorem 2. In general, test statistics which satisfy the conditions of Theorem 2 will be consistent tests of the random walk hypothesis against stationary alternatives only if the sampling interval does not decrease at a rate greater or equal to $T^{1/2}$.

7. Conclusions

This paper has presented an extended analysis of the behavior of the power function for a wide class of tests of the random walk hypothesis against stationary first-order autoregressive alternatives.

Several features that emerged are worth mentioning. First, the power depends more importantly on the span of the data rather than the number of observations *per se* for all statistics considered. It is preferable to have a large span of data even, in most cases, if this entails a smaller number of observations available. Second, there is a notable difference between tests using the original level of the series and tests based on testing for randomness in first-differenced data. In the latter case too many observations, for a given fixed span, may destroy the power. It was shown, in particular, that as the number of observations increases keeping a fixed span, the power converges to the size of the test. It may be the case that higher power can be obtained by deleting observations while keeping the span fixed. This feature is not present for the class of tests based on the original undifferenced series. In that case, more observations always lead to higher power though the marginal contribution of each additional observation is quickly declining. Finally, when comparing the power of the various tests, our results suggest that the Dickey-Fuller type procedure and Barghava's test stand out as the preferred tests.

These results relate interestingly to the concept of consistency of a testing procedure. The usual consistency criterion states that a test is consistent if the power function converges to one as the number of observations increases to infinity for any given fixed alternative. The requirement of a fixed alternative has led, in a time series context, to analyze the asymptotic behavior with a fixed sampling interval as T increases. However, one can view the fixed alternative in terms of the parameters of the continuous time model and, in this case, there is no need to consider the sampling interval fixed as the sample size increases. As shown here (and detailed in Perron, 1987), a richer set of properties concerning the behavior of the power function can be obtained by considering a continuum of consistency criteria indexed by the possible paths of the sampling interval as T increases. What has been shown here is that tests of the random walk hypothesis

($\gamma = 0$) based on the original series are consistent against a fixed mean-reverting alternative ($\gamma > 0$) if and only if the sampling interval does not decrease at a rate faster or equal to T; or, equivalently, if and only if the span is increasing as the sample size increases. On the other hand, tests based on the differenced series are consistent if and only if the span increases at least at rate $T^{1/2}$. Therefore in a well-defined sense, the former class of tests can be said to dominate the latter since they are consistent over a wider range of possible paths for the sampling interval.

The Monte Carlo experiment showed how these consistency properties are valuable in providing information on the behavior of the power of the tests in finite samples. Of course, the results presented here need not carry over to different models. Nevertheless they show that in a time series context the notion that more observations is desirable clearly depends not only on the statistics and the null and alternative hypotheses considered but also on the time interval between each observation.

Notes

* The author is assistant Professor, Department of Economics, Princeton University and research associate, Centre de recherche et développement en économique, Université de Montréal. The material in this paper is drawn from chapter 1 of the author's Ph.D. dissertation, Perron (1986). I wish to thank Peter C. B. Phillips and Robert J. Shiller for their useful comments. Funding is acknowledged from SSHRC (Canada) and FCAR (Quebec).:

1. The framework considered here may seem overly restrictive with the normality and independence assumptions for the error sequence and the fact that no constant nor deterministic time trend are included. The latter could be relaxed by using different statistics than the ones presented in the next sections. Much the same conclusions regarding the behavior of the power functions as the sampling frequency is changed would remain. The present study is simply illustrative of some phenomena that occur in a more general context. The normality assumption has been relaxed in Perron (1986) and the conclusions are basically the same. Our study, however, cannot generalize to the case where additional correlation is present in the errors since the test statistics based on the sequence $\{\Delta y_t\}$ are indeed constructed for testing the null hypothesis that Δy_t is uncorrelated.

2. See also Lepage and Zeidan (1981) and Girard (1983) who analyzed some of the statistics described here in a different context.

3. A comment about the determination of the critical values is in order. In this section all the tests considered have the property that $[J - E(J)] / \sqrt{Var(J)}$ tends asymptotically to a $N(0,1)$ variable as $T \to \infty$, under the null hypothesis. For most statistics, the asymptotic approximation is very good even for quite small values of T. Nevertheless, there may be a significant discrepancy for values of T as small as 8, and even 16, studied in this paper. The exact distributions have been tabulated in most cases for such small sample sizes. However, due to the discreteness of the exact distributions we cannot get critical values for which tests of size 0,05 can be constructed. A possible resolution of this problem would be to use randomized test procedures which would create a test of exact size 0,05. Since the main concern of this paper is the behavior of the power function as h tends to 0 with T increasing, it is not worthwhile to carry such a procedure. We therefore use the asymptotic critical values for all sample sizes. The effect on the size of the tests can be evaluated and the estimated sizes are presented with the power results.

Appendix

PROOF OF THEOREM 1

Part (a) is proved in Perron (1987). To prove part (b), the t-statistic should be written as:

$$t_{\hat{\beta}_n} = T_n(\hat{\beta}_n - 1)(h_n S^{-1} \sum_1^{T_n} y_{nt-1}^2)^{1/2} / T_n^{1/2} \, \hat{\sigma}_n.$$

Now

$$T_n \hat{\sigma}_n^2 = \sum_1^{T_n} (y_{nt} - \hat{\beta}_n y_{nt-1})^2$$

$$= \sum_1^{T_n} u_{nt}^2 - 2(\hat{\beta}_n - \beta_n) \sum_1^{T_n} u_{nt} y_{nt-1} + (\hat{\beta}_n - \beta_n)^2 \sum_1^{T_n} y_{nt-1}^2.$$

Noting that $h_n^{-1}(\hat{\beta}_n - \beta_n) = O(1)$ (see Perron, 1987) and using Lemma 1, we have $T_n \hat{\sigma}_n^2 \to S\sigma^2$ as $n \to \infty$ and $h_n \to 0$ with S fixed. Hence

$$t_{\hat{\beta}_n} \to [c + \int_0^1 J_c(r)dw(r) \{ \int_0^1 J_c(r)^2 dr \}^{-1}] \cdot [S\sigma^2 \int_0^1 J_c(r)^2 dr]^{1/2} (S\sigma^2)^{1/2}$$

which proves part (b) upon simplification. To prove part (c), we first note that

$$d_n = y_{T_n}^2 / \sum_1^{T_n} (y_{nt} - y_{nt-1})^2.$$

The denominator can be written as:

$$\sum_1^{T_n} (y_{nt} - y_{nt-1})^2 = (\beta_n - 1)^2 \sum_1^{T_n} y_{nt-1}^2 + 2(\beta_n - 1)\sum_1^{T_n} y_{nt-1}u_{nt} + \sum_1^{T_n} u_{nt}^2.$$

Since $h_n^{-1}(\beta_n - 1) = h_n^{-1}(\exp(-\gamma h_n) - 1) \to -\gamma$ as $h_n \to 0$, the first two terms vanish asymptotically and

$$\sum_1^{T_n} (y_{nt} - y_{nt-1})^2 \to S\sigma^2. \tag{6}$$

Finally

$$d_n \to S\sigma^2 J_c(1)^2 / S\sigma^2 = J_c(1)^2$$

using Lemma 1. To prove part (d), $T_n R_n$ should be written as:

$$T_n R_n = \sum_{t=1}^{T_n} (y_{nt} - y_{nt-1})^2 / T_n^{-1} \sum_{t=0}^{T_n} (y_{nt} - \bar{Y}_n)^2$$

$$= S\sum_1^{T_n} (y_{nt} - y_{nt-1})^2 / [h_n \sum_1^{T_n} y_{nt}^2 - h_n^2 S^{-1} (\sum_1^{T_n} y_{nt})^2] + o(1)$$

$$\to S^2\sigma^2 / [S^2\sigma^2 \int_0^1 J_c(r)^2 dr - S^2\sigma^2 (\int_0^1 J_c(r)dr)^2]$$

$$= [\int_0^1 J_c(r)^2 dr - (\int_0^1 J_c(r)dr)^2]^{-1} \text{ using (6) and Lemma 1.}$$

PROOF OF THEOREM 2

The proof is closely related to the development in Rao (1973), section 7.a.7. Here $\theta = \beta_n = \exp(-\gamma h_n)$ and $\theta_0 = 1$ since under the null hypothesis $\gamma = 0$. Hence, under the alternative hypothesis we can write $\theta = \theta_0 + (\exp(-\gamma h_n) - 1) = \theta_0 + \delta_n T_n^{-1/2}$ where $\delta_n = T_n^{1/2}(\exp(-\gamma h_n) - 1)$. Now denote the power function of J_n by $P_n(\theta_0 + \delta_n T_n^{-1/2})$ under the alternative hypothesis that $\theta = \theta_0 + \delta_n T_n^{-1/2}$. By definition, we have:

$$P_n(\theta_0 + \delta_n T_n^{-1/2}) = P[J_n \geq \lambda_n \mid \theta_0 + \delta_n T_n^{-1/2}]$$

$$= P\left\{ T_n^{1/2} \frac{J_n - \mu(\theta_0 + \delta_n T_n^{-1/2})}{\sigma(\theta_0 + \delta_n T_n^{-1/2})} \geq T_n^{1/2} \frac{\lambda_n - \mu(\theta_0 + \delta_n T_n^{-1/2})}{\sigma(\theta_0 + \delta_n T_n^{-1/2})} \mid \theta_0 + \delta_n T_n^{-1/2} \right\}$$

$$= \Phi\left(-T_n^{1/2} \frac{\lambda_n - \mu(\theta_0 + \delta_n T_n^{-1/2})}{\sigma(\theta_0 + \delta_n T_n^{-1/2})} \right) + \varepsilon_n(\delta_n) \tag{7}$$

using condition (b), where the convergence is uniform in y, although not in δ_n. Here $\varepsilon_n(\delta_n) \to 0$ as $n \to \infty$. Substituting $\delta_n = 0$ we have

$$P_n(\theta_0) = \Phi\left(-T_n^{1/2} \frac{\lambda_n - \mu(\theta_0)}{\sigma(\theta_0)} \right) + \varepsilon_n(0). \tag{8}$$

Taking the limit of both sides of (8) and noting that $\lim_{n \to \infty} P_n(\theta_0) = \alpha$ using condition (a), we have $\alpha = \lim_{n \to \infty} \Phi(-T_n^{1/2}(\lambda_n - \mu(\theta_0)) / \sigma(\theta_0))$ which shows that $-T_n^{1/2}(\lambda_n - \mu(\theta_0)) / \sigma(\theta_0) = a + \eta_n$ with $\eta_n \to 0$ as $n \to \infty$ and $\alpha = \Phi(a)$. Therefore $\lambda_n = -T_n^{-1/2}(a + \eta_n) \sigma(\theta_0) + \mu(\theta_0)$. Hence, the argument of Φ in (7) has the following limit:

$$-T_n^{1/2}(\lambda_n - \mu(\theta_0) + \delta_n T_n^{-1/2})) / \sigma(\theta_0 + \delta_n T_n^{-1/2})$$

$$= [-\delta_n [\mu(\theta_0 + \delta_n T_n^{-1/2}) - \mu(\theta_0)] / \delta_n T_n^{-1/2} + (a + \eta_n) \sigma(\theta_0)] / \sigma(\theta_0 + \delta_n T_n^{-1/2})$$

$$= [-\delta_n \mu'(\theta_0) + a\sigma(\theta_0)] / \sigma(\theta_0) + \varepsilon_n'$$

$$= a - \delta_n \mu'(\theta_0) / \sigma(\theta_0) + \varepsilon_n'$$

where $\varepsilon_n' \to 0$ as $n \to \infty$. Hence

$$\lim_{n \to \infty} P_n(\theta_0 + \delta_n T_n^{-1/2}) = \Phi[\lim_{n \to \infty} (a - \delta_n \mu'(\theta_0) / \sigma(\theta_0))].$$

Now, $\delta_n = T_n^{1/2}(\exp(-\gamma h_n) - 1)$ and we have: i) $\delta_n \to 0$ if $h_n = O(T_n^a)$ for any $a < -1/2$; ii) $\delta_n \to -\infty$ if $h_n = O(T_n^a)$ for any $a > -1/2$ and iii) $\delta_n \to -\gamma$ if $h_n = O(T_n^{-1/2})$.

Finally, this shows that

$$\lim_{n \to \infty} P_n(\theta_0 + \delta_n T_n^{-1/2}) = \Phi(a) = \alpha \quad \text{if} \quad h_n = O(T_n^a) \text{ for any } a < -1/2$$

$$\Phi(\infty) = 1 \quad \text{if} \quad h_n = O(T_n^a) \text{ for any } a > -1/2$$

$$\Phi[a + \gamma \mu'(\theta_0) / \sigma(\theta_0)] \quad \text{if} \quad h_n = O(T_n^{-1/2}).$$

References

Anderson, R. L.: 1942, 'Distribution of the Serial Correlation Coefficient', *Annals of Mathematical Statistics*, **13**, 1-13.

Arnold, L.: 1974, *Stochastic Differential Equations: Theory and Applications*, John Wiley and Sons, New York, New York, U.S.A.

Bartels, R.: 1982, 'The Rank Version of Neumann's Ratio Test for Randomness', *Journal of the American Statistical Association*, **77**, 40-46.

Bergström, A. R.: 1984, 'Continuous Time Stochastic Models and Issues of Aggregation Over Time', in M. D. Intriligator and Z. Griliches (eds.), *Handbook of Econometrics*, **2**, North-Holland, Amsterdam, Holland, pp. 1145-1212.

Bhargava, A.: 1986, 'On the Theory of Testing for Unit Roots in Observed Time Series', *Review of Economic Studies*, **53**, 369-384.

Dickey, D. A.: 1976, 'Estimation and Hypothesis Testing for Nonstationary Time Series', Ph.D. Thesis, Iowa State University, Ames, Iowa, U.S.A.

Dufour, J. M.: 1981, 'Rank Tests for Serial Dependence', *Journal of Time Series Analysis*, **2**, 117-126.

Dufour, J. M., and M. L. King: 1986, 'Optimal Invariant Test for the Autocorrelation Coefficient in a Linear Regression Model', mimeo, Université de Montréal, Montreal, Quebec, Canada.

Dufour, J. M., and P. Perron: 1984, 'Extended Tables for the von Neumann Test of Independence', mimeo, Université de Montréal, Montreal, Quebec, Canada.

Fuller, W. A.: 1976, *Introduction to Statistical Time Series*, John Wiley and Sons, New York, New York, U.S.A.

Girard, M.: 1983, 'Comportement experimental de divers tests d'indépendance pour des contre-hypothèses issues des modèles de séries chronologiques', unpublished M.Sc. Thesis, Département de mathématiques et de statistique, Université de Montréal, Montreal, Quebec, Canada.

Kendall, M. G., and A. Stuart: 1976, *The Advanced Theory of Statistics*, 3rd edition, Haffner Press, London.

King, M. L.: 1981, 'Notes on Testing for Unit Roots', mimeo.

Knoke, J.: 1977, 'Testing for Randomness Against Autocorrelation: Alternative Tests', *Biometrika*, **64**, 523-529.

Koerts, J., and A. P. J. Abrahamse: 1969, *On the Theory and Applications of the General Linear Model*, Rotterdam University Press, Rotterdam, Holland.

Lepage, Y., and H. Zeidan: 1981, 'L'indépendance d'une série d'observations', *Annales des sciences mathématiques du Québec*, **5**, 169-184.

Mood, A. M.: 1940, 'The Distribution Theory of Runs', *Annals of Mathematical Statistics*, **11**, 367-392.

Moran, P. A. P.: 1948, 'Some Theorems on Time Series II. The Significance of the Serial Correlation Coefficient', *Biometrika*, **35**, 255-260.

Neumann, J. von: 1942, 'Distribution of the Ratio of the Mean Square Successive Difference to the Variance', *Annals of Mathematical Statistics*, **13**, 367-395.

Perron, P.: 1986, 'Hypothesis Testing in Time Series Regressions with a Unit Root', Ph.D. Dissertation, Yale University, New Haven, Connecticut, U.S.A.

Perron, P.: 1987, 'Test Consistency with Varying Sampling Interval', Cahier de recherche no 4187, C.R.D.E., Université de Montréal, Montréal, Québec, Canada.

Phillips, P. C. B.: 1987a, 'Time Series Regression with Unit Roots', *Econometrica*, **55**, 277-302.

Phillips, P. C. B.: 1987b, 'Towards a Unified Asymptotic Theory for Autoregression', *Biometrika*, **74**, 535-47.

Phillips, P. C. B.: 1988, 'Regression Theory for Near-Integrated Time Series', *Econometrica*, **56**, 1021-1044.

Rao, C. R.: 1973, *Linear Statistical Inference and Its Applications*, 2nd edition, John Wiley and Sons, New York, New York, U.S.A.

Rao, M. M.: 1978, 'Asymptotic Distribution of an Estimator of the Boundary Parameter of an Unstable Process', *Annals of Statistics*, **6**, 185-190.

Sargan, J. D., and A. Bhargava: 1983, 'Testing Residuals from Least Squares Regression for Being Generated by a Gaussian Random Walk', *Econometrica*, **51**, 153-174.

Shiller, R. J., and P. Perron: 1985, 'Testing the Random Walk Hypothesis: Power Versus Frequency of Observation', *Economics Letters*, **18**, 381-386.

Waerden, B. W. van der: 1952, 'Order Tests for the Two-sample Problem and Their Power', *Indagationes Mathematicae*, series A, **14**, 453-458.

Wald, A., and J. Wolfowitz: 1943, 'An Exact Test for Randomness in the Non-parametric Case Based on Serial Correlation', *Annals of Mathematical Statistics*, **14**, 378-388.

PART TWO

NONPARAMETRIC ECONOMETRICS

CHAPTER 4

ESTIMATION OF A PROBABILITY DENSITY FUNCTION WITH APPLICATIONS TO NONPARAMETRIC INFERENCE IN ECONOMETRICS

AMAN ULLAH*
University of Western Ontario
Department of Economics
London, Ontario

RADHEY S. SINGH
University of Guelph
Department of Mathematics and Statistics
Guelph, Ontario

ABSTRACT. In this paper we present a class of nonparametric estimates of densities which are asymptotically unbiased and consistent. We point out various applications of these density estimates in econometrics. Some illustrative examples, using economic data, are also given.

1. Introduction

It is now well known that parametric inference in econometrics is carried on under various assumptions. For example, consider y and x as two economic variables, say consumption and income, respectively. First, it is usually assumed that y is stochastic but x is controlled (nonstochastic) when in fact both are stochastic. Second, even if both y and x are stochastic the conditional model ($E(y \mid x)$) is used under the assumption that the parameters of the conditional and marginal distributions are variation free so that x is weakly exogenous (Engle, et al., 1983). Third, the functional form of the conditional model is taken as linear when in fact it may be nonlinear. Fourth, the joint density (data generating process) of y and x is usually assumed to be normal. These are some basic assumptions, among others, which are considered in the empirical research in econometrics (although see, for example, the recent work by Engle, et al., 1986, Gallant and Tauchen, 1987, and Powell, 1986).

Here we explore an alternative procedure which is free of the assumptions indicated above. This alternative is based on the estimation of a probability density function and this has drawn considerable attention in the statistical literature (see, e.g., Rosenblatt, 1956 and the recent books by Prakasa Rao, 1983, Devroye and Gyorfi, 1985, and Silverman, 1986). However, very few attempts have been made to explore the application of density estimates to any area of applied research although Singh (1977) has pointed out some applications to statistical problems. The modest aim of this paper is to explore the applications of density function estimation in various areas of econometrics.

In Section 2 we present a class of nonparametric estimates of densities which are asymptotically unbiased and consistent. In Section 3 we point out the applications of density estimates to several problems that arise in econometrics. Some illustrative examples are presented in Section 4.

2. Estimators of a Probability Density Function

Consider the density function of a random variable X at a point x as $f = f(x)$. Further, let $x_1, \ldots, x_n$ be independent identically distributed i.i.d. observations on X. Then Rosenblatt's 1956 class of 'kernel' estimates of $f(x)$ is

$$\hat{f}(x) = h^{-1} n^{-1} \sum_{t=1}^{n} K\left(\frac{x_t - x}{h}\right), \tag{1}$$

where $h = h_n$, a positive function of n approaching to zero as $n \to \infty$, is called the window-width function and $K(w)$ is the nonnegative kernel satisfying $\int K(w)dw = 1$. The estimator in (1) is well known to be asymptotically unbiased and consistent.

Among the various methods of univariate density estimation are: the polynomial series, the maximum likelihood, the histogram, and the nearest neighborhood methods. The most widely used one is the kernel method of estimation, and this has been considered throughout this paper. For details about other methods, see Silverman (1986) and Prakasa Rao (1983).

Parzen (1962) extended Rosenblatt's estimator to cases where the weight function need not be non-negative. For any Borel measurable function $K(w)$ satisfying

$$\int K(w)dw = 1, \quad \underset{-\infty < w < \infty}{Sup} |K(w)| < \infty, \quad \int |K(w)| \, dw < \infty \text{ and } \lim_{|w| \to \infty} |wK(w)| = 0,$$

he showed that $\hat{f}(x)$ in (1) is asymptotically unbiased and mean square consistent at every continuity point of f. The asymptotic distribution of $(\hat{f}(x) - E\hat{f}(x)) / V(\hat{f}(x))$ is shown to be standard normal.

In the case of dependent observations the density estimation has been considered by Ahmad (1979) and Robinson (1983) among others.

The kernel estimator of a univariate density function in (1) was first generalized to the multivariate density function by Cacoullos (1966). Let $x_t, t = 1, \ldots, n$ be n independent $m \times 1$ random vectors generated from an unknown m-variate density function. Consider κ to be a class of all Borel-measurable real valued bounded functions K on the m-dimensional Euclidean space R^m such that

$$\int K(w)dw = 1, \quad \int |K(w)| \, dw < \infty, \quad \|w\|^m |K(w)| \to 0 \text{ as } \|w\| \to \infty, \tag{2}$$

where $\|w\|$ is the usual Euclidean norm of w in R^m. Then Cacoullos estimated f at a point x in R^m by

$$\hat{f}(x) = n^{-1} h^{-m} \sum_{t=1}^{n} K\left(\frac{x_t - x}{h}\right) \tag{3}$$

where, as before, $h = h_n \to o$ as $n \to \infty$. He showed that the estimator $\hat{f}(x)$ is asymptotically unbiased and mean square consistent. Further for $x_1, \ldots, x_j$, distinct continuity points of f in R^m, the vector $(\hat{f}(x_1), \ldots, \hat{f}(x_j))$ is asymptotically j-variate normal. For details on the asymptotic properties, in the independent observations case, see Prakasa Rao (1983) and Devroye and Gyorfi (1986) and the references therein. For the independent observations case, see Robinson (1983), Castellana and Leadbetter (1986), and Collomb and Hardle (1986).

For the estimators of marginal and conditional densities let us write the m components of the $m \times 1$ vector x_t of Section 2 as

$$x_t = [y'_t, z'_t]', \quad t = 1, \ldots, n \tag{4}$$

where y_t is a $p \times 1$ vector and z_t is a $q \times 1$ vector such that $p + q = m$. Similarly, as in Section 2, let K_1 and K_2 be p and q variate functions obtained after integrating $K(w_1, \ldots, w_m)$ with respect to $(w_{p+1}, \ldots, w_m)$ and with regard to $(w_1, \ldots, w_p)$ respectively. Further, consider $x = [y', z']'$ be a point in R^m at which the density is to be estimated. Now the estimator of the joint density f at x from (3) is

$$\hat{f}(x) = n^{-1} \sum_{t=1}^{n} h^{-m} K\left(\frac{x_t - x}{h}\right) = \hat{f}(y, z). \tag{5}$$

Using this we can write the marginal density of z_t at z as

$$\hat{f}(z) = \int \hat{f}(y, z) dy = n^{-1} \sum_{t=1}^{n} h^{-m} \int K\left(\frac{x_t - x}{h}\right) dy = n^{-1} \sum_{t=1}^{n} h^{-q} K_2\left(\frac{z_t - z}{h}\right). \tag{6}$$

The marginal density of y can be similarly written.

Next, the estimator of the conditional density of y_t given $z_t = z$ can be obtained as

$$\hat{f}(y \mid z) = \frac{\hat{f}(y, z)}{\hat{f}(z)} = \frac{\sum_{t=1}^{n} h^{-m} K\left(\frac{y_t - y}{h}, \frac{z_t - z}{h}\right)}{\sum_{t=1}^{n} h^{-q} K_2\left(\frac{z_t - z}{h}\right)} \tag{7}$$

where $\hat{f}(y, z)$ and $\hat{f}(z)$ are as given in (5) and (6) respectively.

These estimators of conditional and marginal densities are asymptotically unbiased and mean squared consistent. These and other distributional properties have been discussed in Rosenblatt (1969) for independent observations and in Robinson (1983) for dependent observations. For the independent case, see details in Prakasa Rao (1983).

3. Applications

In this section we investigate the application of density estimates, given in Section 2, for the various problems in econometrics.

3.1 ESTIMATION OF CONDITIONAL MEAN-REGRESSION FUNCTION

Let y and $z_1, \ldots, z_q$ be a set of $q+1$ random variables. The conditional expectation of y given the values of $z_1, \ldots, z_q$ is then given by

$$E(y \mid z_1, \ldots, z_q) = M(z_1, \ldots, z_q) = M(z) \tag{8}$$

The function M shows how the average values of y change with values of $z_1, \ldots, z_q$. This function plays a significant role in econometrics for the purposes of prediction and testing economic theories. However, we note that g is known only if either the data generating process (joint density $f(y, z_1, \ldots, z_q)$) is known or the true $f(y \mid z_1, \ldots, z_q)$ is known. Since these are rarely, if ever, known, the econometricians have invariably specified, *a priori*,

$$E(y \mid z_1, \ldots, z_q) = M(z_1, \ldots, z_q) = z_1\beta_1 + \cdots z_q\beta_q \tag{9}$$

and labelled it 'the linear regression function' or 'the linear conditional model'. The least square theory is then used for estimation and prediction purposes.

A useful alternative proposed here is to estimate directly the multivariate density $f(y, z_1, \ldots, z_q)$ and the marginal density $f(z_1, \ldots, z_q)$ by the methods discussed in (2) and (3) and then estimate (9). For example, using (7) we can get

$$\hat{f}(y \mid z) = \frac{\hat{f}(y,z)}{\hat{f}(z)} = \frac{h^{-1}\sum_{t=1}^{n} K\left(\frac{y_t - y}{h}, \frac{z_t - z}{h}\right)}{\sum_{t=1}^{n} K_2\left(\frac{z_t - z}{h}\right)} \tag{10}$$

and

$$\hat{E}(y \mid z_1, \ldots, z_q) = \int y\hat{f}(y \mid z_1, \ldots, z_q)dy \tag{11}$$

$$= \frac{\sum_{t=1}^{n} y_t K_2\left(\frac{z_t - z}{h}\right)}{\sum_{t=1}^{n} K_2\left(\frac{z_t - z}{h}\right)} = \sum_{t=1}^{n} y_t r_t(z) = \hat{M}(z)$$

where

$$r_t(z) = K_2\left(\frac{z_t - z}{h}\right) \Big/ \sum_{t=1}^{n} K_2\left(\frac{z_t - z}{h}\right). \tag{12}$$

Thus $\hat{M}(z)$ is simply the weighted average of y_t with weights $r_t(z)$ once z is given. The $\hat{M}(z)$ in (11) is the Nadaraya (1964) and Watson (1964) estimator, which can be used for econometric analysis. For example, the forecast of y for a given value of z can be obtained from (11). Also the change of y due to a unit change in, say z_1, can be determined by calculating partial derivatives of (11). See the illustrative examples in Section 4 for the estimates of (11).

We note that the nonparametric conditional model in (11), unlike (9) is obtained without making assumptions about the functional form, the joint density of y and z's, and non-stochastic behavior of z's. Further, since (11) has been obtained by estimating joint density we do not require to check up the weak exogeneity of z. Thus the four assumptions of parametric inference indicated in the beginning of Section 1 are not needed in the nonparametric estimator (11).

The asymptotic properties (consistency, normality, etc.) can be found in Rosenblatt (1969), Prakasa Rao (1983), Bierens (1987), and Hardle (1987).

3.1.1 Estimation of Linear Probability Model. The estimator (11) can also be used in the context of a regression model in which the dependent variable y is a binary variable taking the value $y_t = 1$ with probability p_t if the event occurs and $y_t = 0$ with probability $1 - p_t$ otherwise, $t = 1, \ldots, n$. Examples of this are participation in the labor force, decision to marry, bankruptcy, etc. Note that for the binary variable y_t

$$Ey_t = p_t \quad \text{and} \quad V(y_t) = p_t(1 - p_t). \tag{13}$$

In empirical econometrics work various assumptions regarding p_t have been made. Some of these are as given below

(i) Probit: $p_t = (2\pi)^{-1/2} \int\limits_{-\infty}^{z_t'\beta} e^{-w^2/2}\, dw$ and

(ii) Logit: $p_t = (1 + e^{-z_t'\beta})^{-1}$

so that p_t in these cases becomes cumulative probability distribution function $F(z_t'\beta) = E(y_t \mid z_t)$, where z_t is a $q \times 1$ given vector and β is a $q \times 1$ vector of parameters. The likelihood function $L = \prod\limits^{n} p^{y_t}(1 - p_t)^{1-y_t}$ is then written and the parameters are estimated.

It is clear from (13) that the specification of the linear probability model amounts to specifying the probability $p_t = E(y_t \mid z_t)$ by a suitable cumulative probability density. An alternative is to consider the nonparametric approach discussed in Section 2. That is, if our interest is to estimate the conditional expectation with respect to vector z_t $(p_t = E(y_t \mid z_t))$ then we can see that it would be as given in (11). Note, however, that in our present model y_t is either 1 or 0. Thus, $\hat{p}_t$ from (11) will be between 0 and 1.

The qualitative response models discussed in McFadden (1984) can also be similarly analyzed.

3.1.2 Censored and Truncated Models.

The statistical literature on the estimation of censored normal and truncated normal distribution is very long (see Cohen, 1950). In econometrics, censored normal models have been used extensively by Tobin (1958), Amemiya (1973) and Heckman (1976), and truncated normal models have been used by Hausman and Wise (1976, 1978) among others.

Suppose $f(y^*, z)$ is the joint density function of y^* and z. Let $y_1^*, \ldots, y_n^*$ and $z_1, \ldots, z_n$ be the samples of size n. For y^* we record only those values which are greater than a constant c. For those values of $y^* \leq c$, we record the value c. Thus, for $t = 1, \ldots, n$,

$$y_t = y_t^* \quad \text{if } y_t^* > c \tag{14}$$
$$= c \quad \text{otherwise}.$$

The resulting sample $y_1, \ldots, y_n$ is said to be a censored sample.

For the above case

$$E(y \mid z) = cP[y = c \mid z] + \int\limits_{c}^{\infty} y f(y \mid z)\, dy \tag{15}$$

or

$$E(y \mid z) = c\,\frac{f[y = c, z]}{f(z)} + \int\limits_{c}^{\infty} y\,\frac{f(y, z)}{f(z)}\, dy . \tag{16}$$

The model in (16) can then be analyzed by using the nonparametric estimates of the marginal and joint densities given in Section 2.

Now consider the truncated model. Suppose $y_1, \ldots, y_n$ is a sample drawn from the truncated population of $y < c_0$. Then the truncated model is

$$f(y_t) = f(y_t \mid y_t < c_0) = \frac{f(y_t)}{F(c_0)} \tag{17}$$

where $F(c_0)$ is the cumulative distribution of $f(y)$. And in the case of two variables y_t and z_t

$$f(y_t \mid z_t) = \frac{f(y_t, z_t \mid y_t \leqq c_0)}{f(z_t)} = \frac{f(y_t, z_t)}{F(c_0)f(z_t)} . \tag{18}$$

Again for prediction $E(y \mid z)$ and other econometric analyses the estimates of the marginal and conditional densities given in Section 2 can be used. This would overcome the specification of $E(y \mid z) = z\beta$ as well as the normality assumption used by Hausman and Wise (1976, 1978) or the assumption of Edgeworth density by Lee (1982).

3.2 ESTIMATION OF CONDITIONAL VARIANCE (CONDITIONAL HETEROSKEDASTICITY)

Let us write the conditional variance of y given $z_1, \ldots, z_q$ as

$$V(y \mid z_1, \ldots, z_q) = V(z) = E(y^2 \mid z) - [E(y \mid z)]^2 . \tag{19}$$

Then a consistent nonparametric estimator (see for example, Carroll, 1982) is given by

$$\hat{V}(z) = \sum y_t^2 r_t(z) - \hat{M}^2(z) \tag{20}$$

where $r_t(z)$ and $\hat{M}(z) = \sum y_t r_t(z)$ are as given in (12) and (11), respectively. The higher order conditional moments of y can similarly be estimated (see Singh and Tracy, 1977).

The estimation of variability is of interest due to various reasons. First, there are many economic models in which the risk term appears as a regressor and, second, variability in economic variables such as inflation and interest rates is in itself of interest to the policymakers. For details see Friedman (1977). In addition there are many economic models in which the conditional variance of the dependent variable is heteroskedastic. Thus a nonparametric estimator (20), which does not use any functional form of heteroskedasticity, is useful for the efficient generalized least squares estimation of the model.

3.3 MODEL ADEQUACY AND OTHER TESTS

It was noted in Section 3.1 that the nonparametric estimator $\hat{E}(y \mid z)$ in (11) is obtained without making assumptions about the weak exogeneity of z, functional form, and the joint density of y and z. Thus the nonparametric residuals

$$y_t - \hat{E}(y_t \mid z_t) = \hat{u}_t, \quad t = 1, \ldots, n$$

are robust and they can be used to perform meaningful diagnostic tests for the adequacy of the model

$$y_t = E(y_t \mid z_t) + u_t .$$

This can be done by using nonparametric residuals $\hat{u}_t$ and the fitted values $\hat{E}(y_t \mid z_t)$, instead of non-robust least squares residuals and fitted values, in various diagnostic tests (for normality, heteroskedasticity, serial correlation, exogeneity, misspecification, and encompassing) given in Pagan et al. (1983) and Ullah (1985). A point to be noted here is that the nonparametric residual $\hat{u}_t$ is such that for large n, $\hat{u}_t \approx u_t$.

Since most of the diagnostic tests may be nonrobust under misspecifications a better alternative will be to use the results of Section 2 directly. For example, the normality can be checked up by estimating $f(\hat{u})$ and calculating its confidence interval. Similarly, the misspecification, heteroskedasticity, and serial correlation can be analyzed by using nonparametric estimates of $E(\hat{u} \mid z)$, $V(\hat{u} \mid z)$ and $cov(\hat{u}_t, \hat{u}_{t-1} \mid z)$, respectively. Some other tests can also be performed and these are given below.

3.3.1 Test of Independence. For the test of independence (see Hausman, 1978) we can estimate the conditional and marginal densities, $f(z \mid \hat{u})$ and $f(z)$, respectively by using the methods of Section 2 and calculate

$$d^2 = \sum_{\hat{u}}^{l} \sum_{z}^{m} d^2(z \mid \hat{u}), \text{ where } d = (\hat{f}(z \mid \hat{u}))^{1/2} - (\hat{f}(z))^{1/2}. \tag{21}$$

The statistic d^2 is then the statistic for checking the independence of x and $\hat{u}$. Notice that d^2 is Bhattacharya's (1967) distance measure which satisfies all the properties of a metric. An alternative to Bhattacharya's distance would be to use Kulback-Leibler information divergence measure in which $d(z \mid \hat{u}) = -(\log \dfrac{\hat{f}(z)}{\hat{f}(z \mid \hat{u})})\hat{f}(z \mid \hat{u})$. For details on divergence see Burbea and Rao (1982).

It is our conjecture that d^2 may follow chi-square asymptotically. The work on this will follow in a future paper.

3.3.2 Testing Causality. In most economic models not only is a cause and effect relationship assumed to hold but, furthermore, the direction of causality is also taken to be known. The truth is, however, that in nonexperimental subjects like economics it is difficult to find convincing evidences in favor of such assumptions. In view of this, following the work of Weiner, Granger (1969) first formalized the idea of causality. The essence of Granger's causality is that z does not cause y if

$$f(y_t \mid \Omega_{t-1}) = f(y_t \mid \Omega_{t-1}^y) \tag{22}$$

where $\{\Omega_{t-1} = \Omega_{t-1}^y, \Omega_{t-1}^z\}$ is the information set consisting of past values of y as well as z. Note that (22) is the 'causality with respect to the particular Ω_{t-1} used.' Since the conditional distribution functions in (22) are unknown, a testable definition has been used in terms of a summary statistic, viz., linear predictions. More precisely z causes y if

$$MSE(y \mid \Omega_{t-1}) < MSE(y \mid \Omega_{t-1}^y). \tag{23}$$

An alternative but equivalent test proposed in the literature is to regress the current value of y on the lagged values of z as well as y and test for the significance of lagged values of z by the F-test. If the hypothesis is accepted z is said to be not causing y in Granger's sense.

Note that the Granger's causality test would be useful, that is the F-test proposed would have power, if there are no misspecifications in the specified variables z and y and there is no misspecification in the error term of the regression indicated above. Further, although the definition in (23) is simple, it is a long way from the rather general definition started with in (22). The true causality may be missed, or spurious causality observed, because of these simplifications. Thus, again an alternative is to use nonparametric methods to estimate the conditional density $f(y_t \mid z_1, \ldots, z_{t-1}, y_1, \ldots, y_{t-1})$ and the marginal density $f(y_t \mid y_1, \ldots, y_{t-1})$ and compare them. The variable z does not cause y if these two estimated densities are the same, that is

$$\hat{f}(y_t \mid z_1, \ldots, z_{t-1}, y_1, \ldots, y_{t-1}) = \hat{f}(y_t \mid y_1, \ldots, y_{t-1}). \tag{24}$$

We can also check whether or not there is a significant difference between the conditional and marginal densities by using the statistic

$$d^2 = \sum_z^l \sum_y^m d^2 \ (y_t \mid z_{t-1}, y_{t-1});$$ (25)

where $d(y_t \mid z_{t-1}, y_{t-1}) = \hat{f}(y_t \mid z_1, \ldots, z_{t-1}, y_1, \ldots, y_{t-1}) - \hat{f}(y_t \mid y_1, \ldots, y_{t-1})$. We can also check for the instantaneous independence of z and y by using

$$d^2 = \sum_z^l \sum_y^m d^2 \ (y_t \mid z_t); \text{ where } d(y_t \mid z_t) = \hat{f}(y_t \mid z_t - \hat{f}(y_t).$$ (26)

3.3.3 Non-Nested Model Selection. Let x, y and z be three economic variables such that there are two data generating processes for y, that is $f(y \mid x)$ and $f(y \mid z)$. If the maintained hypothesis is $f(y \mid z)$ then the non-nested model selection problem is to see if $f(y \mid z)$ is significantly different from $f(y \mid x)$. Usually the parametric specification in terms of regression models is used in order to test such an hypothesis (see e.g., Davidson and Mackinnon, 1981). We propose the estimation of $f(y \mid x)$ and $f(y \mid z)$ first and then the use of

$$d^2 = \sum_y^m \{g_1^{1/2}(y) - g_2^{1/2}(y)\}^2; \ g_1(y) = \sum_x^l \hat{f}(y \mid x), g_2(y) = \sum_z^l \hat{f}(y \mid z)$$

where l is l-number of points of x and z. Again, as in the case a, one can use Kulback-Leibler divergence measure

$$d^2 = \sum_y^m \log \frac{\hat{g}_2(y)}{\hat{g}_1^{(y)}} \hat{g}_1(y).$$

3.3.4 Finite Sample Econometrics. There is a large literature in econometrics on deriving the exact and approximate densities and moments of various econometric estimators (see, e.g., Phillips, 1983, among others). These works are of great importance for proper inference in finite sample situations, particularly since the concept of a 'large' sample is fuzzy for practical situations. However, despite its great importance, work in this area has so far not been very useful because of the complicated expressions of exact results and their nonlinear dependence on unknown parameters.

We propose a nonparametric Monte-Carlo integrated approach here. Suppose, based on the 5000 random samples of size 10 we generate 5000 observations on the estimator of a parameter ($\hat{\beta}$) in a parametric specification. Using these observations on $\hat{\beta}$ we can then easily estimate the unknown exact density of $\hat{\beta}$, $f(\hat{\beta})$, by the nonparametric method discussed in Section 2, say $\hat{f}(\hat{\beta})$. Moments of the estimators, based on $\hat{f}(\hat{\beta})$ can then be analyzed easily. The results can be compared with the Monte-Carlo results as well as the exact results, available in the literature. Notice that the procedure can be extended to the estimation of multivariate or marginal density of a parameter vector β appearing in an econometric model. Similarly, kernel density estimation can be integrated with the bootstrapping approach of Efron (1979).

4. Illustrative Examples

Here we present some examples, based on Monte-Carlo as well as real world data sets, to illustrate the technique of Section 2 in the context of econometric problems discussed in Sections 3.1 and

3.2. The illustrations for the issues in Sections 3.3 and 3.4 are beyond the scope of this paper, and they will be subjects of a future study.

4.1 ESTIMATION OF CONDITIONAL MEAN AND VARIANCE (MONTE-CARLO)

The objective of the experiment here is to verify how the nonparametric estimates of conditional mean (regression function) and variance (heteroskedasticity) perform when the true forms of the conditional mean and variance are known, and the data are generated from a known population.

Consider the true model as a quadratic regression function given by

$$y_t = \beta_0 + \beta_1 z_t + \beta_2 z_t^2 + u_t, \quad t = 1, \ldots, n \tag{27}$$

where y is a dependent variable, z is an exogenous variable, β's are regression parameters, and u is the disturbance term such that

$$u_t \sim N(0, \sigma^2) . \tag{28}$$

From (27) and (28), the parametric forms of the conditional mean and variance are

$$E(y_t \mid z_t) = \beta_0 + \beta_1 z_t + \beta_2 z_t^2 \text{ because } E(u_t \mid z_t) = E u_t = 0 \tag{29}$$

$$V(y_t \mid z_t) = V(u_t \mid z_t) = V(u_t) = \sigma^2 .$$

To generate the observations on y we (i) specify $\beta_0 = 5$, $\beta_1 = 1$, $\beta_2 = 3$, (ii) choose $n = 50$ values of z of an economic variable, and (iii) generate random samples of sizes $n = 50, 100, 400$ from $u \sim N(0, 1)$. This gives samples of sizes $n = 50, 100, 400$ for the y from (27). Note that the values of z for $n = 100$ and 400 are generated by repeating its 50 values.

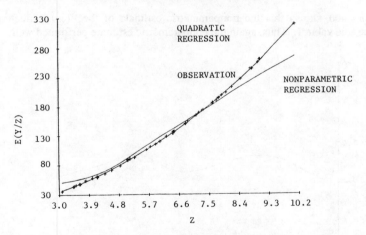

Figure 1. Nonparametric regression ($N = 50$)

The nonparametric estimates of $E(y \mid z)$ given in (11), are plotted in Figures 1 and 2, respectively for $n = 100$ and 400. The kernel chosen for this purpose was

$$K\left(\frac{z_t - z}{h}\right) = \frac{1}{\sqrt{2\pi}} e^{-\frac{1}{2}(\frac{z_t - z}{h})^2} \tag{30}$$

where $h = s_z n^{-1/5}$, $s_z^2 = \sum_1^n (z_t - \bar{z})^2 / n$. For these choices of h and k, see Silverman (1986), Prakasa Rao (1983), Ullah (1985) and Singh, Ullah and Carter (1987). It is evident from the figures that the nonparametric estimates of the conditional mean approximate the true model in (27) extremely well for both $n = 50$ and 400 but specially for $n = 400$. The plot for $n = 100$ was similar to that for $n = 400$. Though not plotted here, the 95 percent confidence interval, based on (15), contained the true model except in the tail ends. Similar results were obtained with various other choices of K.

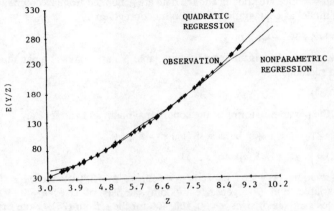

Figure 2. Nonparametric regression ($N = 400$)

Figure 3, for $n = 400$, shows that the nonparametric estimate of the $V(u \mid z)$ fluctuates very closely around the true value 1. Thus, again the nonparametric estimate performed well.

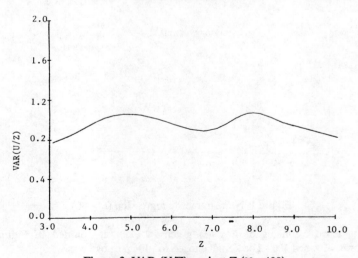

Figure 3. VAR (U/Z) against Z ($N = 400$)

   The implication of the above results is that the nonparametric estimates can be taken as a reasonably good approximation of the conditional mean (econometric model) and variance whose functional forms are usually unknown.

4.1.1 Forecast and Variability of Inflation. The questions of accurate forecasting and the variability of inflation rates are of significant interest for the macroeconomists and the policymakers in the government and industries. In fact, Friedman's Nobel Prize Lecture (1977) ascribes real effects in an economy to a higher rate of inflation if that higher rate is accompanied by increased variability.

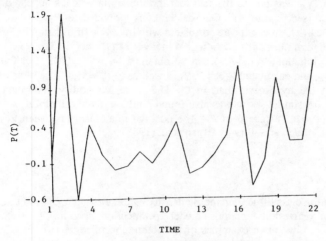

Figure 4. US inflation

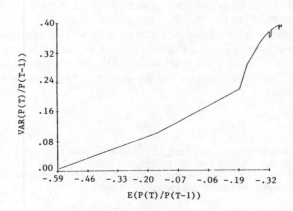

Figure 5. The relationship of variability of inflation and inflation forecast.

Both the issues of forecasting and variability can be analyzed by the nonparametric estimates of the conditional mean and variance, that is,

$$\hat{E}(P_t \mid I_{t-1}) \quad \text{and} \quad \hat{V}(P_t \mid I_{t-1})$$

where P_t is the inflation rate and I_{t-1} is the information available up to the period $t-1$. For this purpose we considered the U.S. decade data 1750-1980 on the wholesale price index (see Batra, 1985, p. 85).

For the purpose of forecasting we estimated $\hat{E}(P_t \mid P_{t-3})$ by using (11) and the kernel function in (30). The choice of P_{t-3} was due to the fact that the inflationary peaks appeared roughly after every three decades (see Figure 4). Our calculations provided $\hat{E}(P_{1990} \mid P_{1960}) = 0.031$ and $\hat{E}(P_{2000} \mid P_{1970}) = 0.029$. These results are consistent with the cycle of inflation in Figure 4 and the conjecture of low inflation rates during 1990-1994 indicated in Batra (1985, p. 95).

The variability in inflation, $\hat{V}(P_t \mid I_{t-1})$ can be obtained by using (20). For this purpose we considered I_{t-1} as P_{t-1} and calculated $\hat{V}(P_t \mid P_{t-1})$ as well as $\hat{E}(P_t \mid P_{t-1})$. The plots of these values in Figure 5 support the hypothesis that, in the U.S. case, variability does increase with the anticipated inflation. A similar result was also found on the basis of the plot using unanticipated inflation, $\hat{P}_t = P_t - \hat{E}(P_t \mid P_{t-1})$ instead of P_t. The positive relationship between $\hat{V}()$ and $\hat{E}()$ has been referred to as absolute variability by Pagan et al. (1983).

5. Conclusion

We have considered the class of nonparametric density estimators and explored their applications in the estimation of regression functions, model specification, specification testing, and finite sample econometrics. Illustrative examples of the estimation of regression function, variability and forecasting are presented.

The list of applications, in addition to ones provided in Sections 3 and 4, is large and not all of them can be presented here. In fact one can analyze any econometric issue by nonparametric methods. We emphasize here that the examples in Section 4 are mainly for illustrative purposes, and in some cases it is difficult to claim that sample sizes are large. The potential users should be well aware of the limitations of the nonparametric methods; for example, very little is known about the small sample properties of the nonparametric estimators and their confidence intervals. The estimates may be imprecise if the number of regressors is large or the sample is small. This is because the speed of convergence of the mean squared error of, say, density estimator $\hat{f}(x)$ is slow (see, e.g., Silverman, 1986). Also not much is known about the selection of the window width in finite samples. We hope that these issues will be the subject of future research in the area of nonparametric econometrics.

* This is a revised version of the paper presented at the First Econometric Group Meeting held in Kingston, Ontario, Canada in 1984. The authors are grateful to the NSERC for support, and to Virginia Ho for excellent research assistance. They are also thankful to R. Carter, D. Poirier, and J. Mackinnon for useful comments on an earlier version of this paper.

References

Ahmad, I. A.: 1979, 'Strong Consistency of Density Estimation by Orthogonal Series Methods for Dependent Variables with Applications', *Annals of the Institute of Statistical Mathematics*, **31**, 279-288.

Amemiya, T.: 1973, 'Regression Analysis When the Dependent Variable is Truncated Normal', *Econometrica*, **41**, 997-1016.

Batra, R. N.: 1985, *Regular Cycles of Money, Inflation, Regulation and Depression*, Venus Books, Dallas, Texas, U.S.A.

Bhattacharya, P. K.: 1967, 'Estimation of a Probability Density Function', *Sankhya*, Ser. A, **29**, 373-382.

Bierens, H. J.: 1987, 'Kernel Estimators of Regression Function', in T. F. Bewley (ed.), *Advances in Econometrics*, Vol. I, Cambridge University Press, Cambridge, New York, U.S.A., pp. 19-144.

Burbea, J., and C. R. Rao: 1982, 'Entropy Differential Metric, Distance and Divergence Measures in Probability Spaces: A Unified Approach', *Journal of Multivariate Analysis*, **12**, 575-596.

Cacoullos, T.: 1966, 'Estimation of a Multivariate Density', *Annals of the Institute of Statistical Mathematics*, **18**, 176-189.

Carroll, R. J.: 1982, 'Adapting for Heteroskedasticity in Linear Models', *Annals of Statistics*, **10**, 1224-1233.

Castellana, J. V., and M. R. Leadbetter: 1986, 'On Smooth Probability Density Estimation for Stationary Processes', *Stochastic Theory and Their Applications*, **21**, 179-193.

Cohen, A. C. Jr.: 1950, 'Estimating the Mean and Variance of Normal Populations from Singly and Doubly Truncated Samples', *Annals of Mathematical Statistics*, **21**, 557-569.

Collomb, G., and W. Hardle: 1986, 'Strong Uniform Convergence Rates in Robust Nonparametric Time Series Analysis and Prediction: Kernel Regression Estimation from Dependent Observations', *Stochastic Processes and Their Applications*, **23**, 77-89.

Davidson, R., and J. G. Mackinnon: 1981, 'Several Tests for Model Specification in the Presence of Alternative Hypothesis', *Econometrica*, **49**, 781-1244.

Devroye, L., and L. Gyorfi: 1985, *Nonparametric Density Estimation*, John Wiley, New York, New York, U.S.A.

Efron, B.: 1979, 'Bootstrap Methods: Another Look at the Jackknife', *Annals of Statistics*, **7**, 1-26.

Engle, R. F., D. F. Hendry, and J. F. Richard: 1983, 'Exogeneity', *Econometrica*, **51**, 277-304.

Engle, R. F., C. W. J. Granger, J. Rice, and A. Weiss: 1986, 'Semiparametric Estimates of the Relation Between Weather and Electricity Sales', *Journal of the American Statistical Association*, **81**, 310-320.

Friedman, M.: 1977, 'Nobel Lecture: Inflation and Unemployment', *Journal of Political Economy*, **85**, 451-472.

Gallant, A. R., and G. Tauchen: 1987, 'Semi-nonparametric Estimation of Conditionally Constrained Heterogeneous Processes: Asset Pricing Applications', Research Report, North Carolina State University.

Granger, C. W. J.: 1969, 'Investigating Causal Relation by Econometric Models and Cross-spectral Methods', *Econopmetrica*, **37**, 424-438.

Hardle, W.: 1987, 'Applied Nonparametric Regression', mimeo, University of Bonn, Bonn, West Germany.

Hausman, J.: 1978, 'Specification Tests in Econometrics', *Econometrica*, **46**, 1251-1271.

Hausman, J. A., and D. A. Wise: 1976, 'Social Experimentation, Truncated Disturbances and Efficient Estimation', *Econometrica*, **45**, 319-339.

Hausman, J. A., and D. A. Wise: 1978, 'A Conditional Profit Model for Qualitative Choice: Discrete Decisions Recognizing Interdependence and Heterogeneous Preferences', *Econometrics*, **46**, 403-426.

Heckman, J.: 1976, 'Simultaneous Equations Model with Continuous and Discrete Endogenous Variables and Structural Shifts', in Goldfeld and Quant (eds.), *Studies in Non-linear Estimation*, Ballinger, Cambridge, Massachusetts, U.S.A., pp. 235-272.

Lee, L. F.: 1982, 'Specification Error in Multinormal Logit Models: Analysis of the Omitted Variable Bias', *Journal of Econometrics*, **20**, 197-210.

McFadden, D.: 1984, 'Econometric Analysis of Qualitative Response Models', *Handbook of Econometrics* Vol. II, North-Holland, New York, New York, U.S.A., pp. 1395-1467.

Nadaraya, E. A.: 1964, 'On Regression Estimators', *Theory of Probability and Applications*, **9**, 157-159.

Pagan, A. R., A. D. Hall, and P. K. Trivedi: 1983, 'Assessing the Variability of Inflation', *Review of Economic Studies*, **50**, 585-596.

Parzen, E.: 1962, 'On the Estimation of Probability Density and Model', *Annals of Mathematical Statistics*, **33**, 1065-1076.

Phillips, P. C. B.: 1983, 'Exact Small Sample Theory in the Simultaneous Equations Model', in Z. Griliches and M. D. Intriligator (eds.), *Handbook of Econometrics*, Vol. 1, North Holland, New York, New York, U.S.A., pp. 451-501.

Powell, J. L.: 1986, 'Symmetrically Trimmed Least Squares Estimation of Tobit Models', *Econometrica*, **54**, 1435-1460.

Prakasa Rao, B. L. S.: 1983, *Nonparametric Functional Estimation*, Academic Press, Orlando, Florida, U.S.A.

Robinson, P. M.: 1983, 'Nonparametric Estimators for Time Series', *Journal of Time Series Analysis*, **4**, 85-208.

Rosenblatt, M.: 1956, 'Remarks on Some Nonparametric Estimates of Density Function', *Annals of Mathematical Statistics*, **27**, 832-837.

Rosenblatt, M.: 1969, 'Conditional Probability Density and Regression Estimators', *Journal of Multivariate Analysis*, **2**, 25-31.

Silverman, B. W.: 1986, *Density Estimation for Statistics and Data Analysis*, Chapman and Hall, New York, New York, U.S.A.

Singh, R. S.: 1977, 'Applications of Estimators of a Density and its Derivatives to Certain Statistical Problems', *Journal of the Royal Statistical Society Series B*, **39**, 357-363.

Singh, R. S., and D. S. Tracy: 1977, 'Strongly Consistent Estimators of the Order Regression Curves and Rates of Convergence', *Z. Wahrsch Verw Grebiete*, **40**, 339-348.

Singh, R. S., A. Ullah, and A. L. Carter: 1987, 'Nonparametric Inference in Econometrics: New Applications, Time Series and Econometric Modelling', in MacNeill and Umphrey (eds.), D. Reidel Publishing Co., Boston, Massachusetts, U.S.A., pp. 253-278.

Tobin, J.: 1958, 'Estimation of Relationships for Limited Dependent Variables', *Econometrica*, **26**, 24-36.

Ullah, A.: 1985, 'Specification Analysis of Econometric Models', *Journal of Quantitative Economics*, **1**, 187-210.

Watson, G. S.: 1964, 'Smooth Regression Analysis', *Sankhya*, Ser. A, **51**, 175-186.

CHAPTER 5

ESTIMATION OF THE SHAPE OF THE DEMAND CURVE BY NONPARAMETRIC KERNEL METHODS

JOHN McMILLAN*
Univ. of California
Dept. of Economics
San Diego
California, U.S.A.

AMAN ULLAH
Univ. of Western Ontario
Dept. of Economics
London, Ontario
Canada

H. D. VINOD
Fordham University
Dept. of Economics
Bronx, 10458-5158
New York, U.S.A.

ABSTRACT. Nonparametric Kernel methods have been discussed by Vinod and Ullah (1988), who develop an estimator of the partial derivatives of conditional expectations. These have been applied in Econometrics for estimation of elasticities and other constructs related to partial derivatives. Applications of those ideas need not be restricted to the first partials. This paper is concerned with estimation of second partials with similar kernel methods. We attempt to empirically study Marshall's 'law' of the elasticity of demand which claims that elasticity increases with price.

1. Introduction

In *Principles of Economics*, Alfred Marshall proposed two empirical generalizations about demand curves. The best known is the law of demand: demand falls as price increases. Less well known is what Marshall called the law of the elasticity of demand: elasticity increases as price increases. "The elasticity of demand is great for high prices, and great, or at least considerable, for medium prices; but it declines as the price falls; and gradually fades away if the fall goes so far that satiety level is reached." Marshall went on to argue that this law "appears to hold with regard to nearly all commodities".[1]

The economics of consumer behavior is comprised of two kinds of propositions: deductive propositions (for example, that the Slutsky matrix is symmetric and negatively sloped) and inductive propositions (for example, demand curves are negatively sloped). Just as the law of demand, arguably the most important proposition in consumer economics, is not a deductive proposition (because of the possibility that income effects outweigh substitution effects), the law of the elasticity of demand cannot be derived theoretically. This is because the rate of change of elasticity depends upon the curvature of the demand curve, which in turn depends upon the third derivative of the utility function, about which nothing can be presumed. Thus Marshall's law of the elasticity of demand is not a deductive proposition. Does it hold empirically?

Casual empiricism suggests that it is plausible that demand elasticity is an increasing function of price: this merely says that the higher a commodity's price, the more sensitively buyers react to price changes. Indeed, Marshall's argument supporting the law of the elasticity of demand was based on casual empiricism (see Marshall, 1920, pp. 87-92). Since Marshall's hypothesis is about the functional form of the demand curve, it is most appropriately tested not by standard econometric methods which impose a particular functional form *a priori*, but by using nonparametric methods. This paper uses newly-developed techniques of nonparametric econometrics to investigate the shape of demand curves and to test the empirical validity of the law of the elasticity of demand.

The shape of the demand curve is not of interest only because of what Marshall said 65 years ago; it also has implications for a number of current questions in theoretical and applied economics. First, many empirical studies obtain tractability by assuming linear demand; others assume constant elasticity of demand. Are either of these reasonable approximations? Second, microeconomic theorists sometimes make particular assumptions about the curvature of demand curves. For example, the weakest known sufficient condition for the existence of an equilibrium in Cournot's oligopoly model is that one firm's marginal revenue is a declining function of its rivals' output (Novshek, 1985); a sufficient condition for this is concavity of the demand curve, which also ensures that the law of the elasticity of demand holds. Third, elasticity increasing with price implies marginal revenue is monotonic in price. Thus, for example, a monopolist with constant marginal cost facing an unknown demand can be sure he will find his global profit-maximizing price by experimenting with small changes in his price if the law of the elasticity of demand holds.

Let x_1 denote price and y denote quantity. Marshall's law of the elasticity of demand states

$$\frac{\partial}{\partial x_1}\left[-\frac{\partial y}{\partial x_1}\frac{x_1}{y}\right] \geq 0.$$

This is equivalent to

$$\frac{\partial^2 y}{\partial x_1^2} \leq -\frac{1}{x_1}\frac{\partial y}{\partial x_1} + \frac{1}{y}\left[\frac{\partial y}{\partial x_1}\right]^2. \tag{1}$$

If the law of demand holds, $\partial y / \partial x_1 < 0$, so that a sufficient condition for the inequality (1) to be satisfied is that the demand curve is concave.

In Section 2 nonparametric methods are extended to evaluate the partial derivatives in (1) directly at specified (average) values of y and x_1. Section 3 gives an empirical example based on demand for meat in the U.S. for 1950-1972 from Theil (1976).

2. Estimation of Partial Derivatives

Let us consider an 'amorphous' model

$$y = R(x_1, \ldots, x_p) + \varepsilon = E(y \mid x_1, \ldots, x_p) + \varepsilon \tag{2}$$

where y is an $n \times 1$ vector of observations on the dependent variable, $x_1, \ldots, x_p$ are each $n \times 1$ vectors of observations on p regressors, ε is an $n \times 1$ vector of errors and the regression function $R = R(\cdot)$ is an unspecified expectation of y conditional on x_1 to x_p. Note that when $R(x) = R(x_1, \ldots, x_p)$ is linear, as often specified in parametric econometrics, estimation of the first partials of $R(x)$ is equivalent to estimating regression coefficients. For higher order partials one usually specifies nonlinear forms of $R(x)$.

An alternative approach to this problem of specifying $R(x)$ is to estimate it nonparametrically. The partial derivatives can then be obtained by using the nonparametric estimator of $R(x)$.

Kernel nonparametric regression estimates the conditional expectation $R(x)$ by a weighted average of the observed values of y_t, where the weight of the t-th observation depends on the distance x_{jt} to $x_j, j = 1, \ldots, p$. Denoting the weight function (the kernel) by $K()$ and letting $R_n(x)$

denote the kernel estimator $R(x)$, the estimator is:

$$R_n(x) = \sum_{t=1}^{n} y_t K(w_t) \Big/ \sum_{t=1}^{n} K(w_t) \tag{3}$$

where, for $j = 1, \ldots, p$,

$$K(w_t) = K(w_{1t}, \ldots, w_{pt}); \ w_{jt} = (x_{jt} - x_j)/h_j .$$

The estimator $R_n(x)$ in (3) is the well known Nadarya-Watson type regression function estimator; see e.g., Prakasa-Rao (1983) and Singh et al. (1987). Note that in (3) the difference between x_{jt} and x_j is scaled by a scalar h_j which depends on the sample size. This scalar h_j is called the windowidth, which determines the width of the 'window' surrounding the point x_j over which the data are averaged. Both the kernel and the windowidth must be chosen to use the estimator in practice. Following Singh et al. (1987) among others, we choose:

$$h_j = s_j n^{-1/(4+p)} \tag{4}$$

where s_j is the sample standard deviation of x_j defined by

$$s_j = \left[\sum_{t=1}^{n} (x_{jt} - \bar{x}_j)^2 / n \right]^{1/2} ,$$

and for the kernel we choose a product of normal kernels:

$$K(w_1, \ldots, w_p) = \prod_{j=1}^{p} K(w_j) = (2\pi)^{-1/2} \exp \left[(-\tfrac{1}{2}) w_j^2 \right]. \tag{5}$$

This and h_j in (4) will be used in our numerical example in Section 3. We note here that the choices of h_j and K considered above are optimal in the sense of minimizing asymptotic mean squared error of the nonparametric density estimator. For technical details the reader is referred to Prakasa-Rao (1983, ch. 2).

An analytical partial derivative of $R(x)$ in (2) is denoted by

$$pd(x) = \frac{\partial R(x)}{\partial x_j}$$

and its amorphous estimate by $apd(x)$. We have

$$apd(x) = \frac{\partial R_n(x)}{\partial x_j} = \sum y_t (K_{1t} - K_{2t}) \tag{6}$$

where the summation is from $t = 1$ to $t = n$,

$$K_{1t} = K'(w_t) \left(\sum K(w_t) \right)^{-1} \tag{7}$$

$$K_{2t} = K(w_t) \left(\sum K'(w_t) \right) \left(\sum K(w_t) \right)^{-2}$$

$$K'(w_t) = \partial K(w_t)/\partial x_j .$$

For the normal kernel in (5) $K'(w_t) = h_j^{-1} w_{jt} K(w_t)$. Note that $apd(x)$ represents the jth response coefficient of y due to a unit change in x_j. The asymptotic properties of $apd(x)$ are derived in Vinod and Ullah (1988). We develop below an extension of (6) since our application requires second order partial, keeping the functional form amorphous.

A second order partial is defined by [2]

$$p^2 d(x,j,l) = \partial^2 R(x)/\partial x_j \partial x_l \tag{8}$$

and its analytical estimate, for the normal kernel in (5), is

$$ap^2 d(x,j,l) = \sum (y_t/h_j)(K_{3t} + K_{4t}) \tag{9}$$

where, writing $K(w_t)$ as K_t,

$$K_{3t} = \frac{K_t}{h_l(\sum K_t)^2} [w_{tj} w_{tl} K_t] - w_{tj} \sum w_{tl} K_t - w_{tl} \sum w_{tj} K_t]$$

$$K_{4t} = \frac{K_t}{h_l(\sum K_t)^3} [2(\sum w_{tj} K_t)(\sum w_{tl} K_t) - (\sum K_t)\sum w_{tj} w_{tl} K_t].$$

The expression (9) can be written for any kernel K by using (7). Following Vinod and Ullah (1988), an asymptotic expression for the variance of $ap^2 d(x,j,l)$ for the normal kernel of (5) can be written as:

$$Var[ap^2 d(x_j)] = \frac{3}{2h_j^2} Var[apd(x_j)] \tag{10}$$

where

$$Var[apd(x_j)] = 2^{-1} \sigma^2(x) \int_{-\infty}^{\infty} K^2(z)dz / [h_j^2 a_n f(x)$$

where $a_n = n \prod_{j=1}^{p} h_j$; and $\sigma^2(x)$ can be replaced by its consistent estimator: $\hat{\sigma}^2(x) = [\sum_{t=1}^{n} y_t^2 K(w_t) / \sum_{t=1}^{n} K(w_t)] - R_n^2(x)$. Notice that the speed of convergence of the variance in (10) is $(a_n h_j^4)^{-1}$ is much slower than the usual n^{-1}. Hence the estimate (8) may be subject to a greater sampling variability.

3. An Illustration: Demand for Meat in the U.S.

Theil (1976) developed an illustration of the Rotterdam model using demand for four meats in the U.S. for 1950 to 1972. For the purpose of illustration we use Theil's data (see his Table 7.1 on page 9) for a single meat, pork, with quantities (y) measured by per capita consumption, real prices for pork (x_1) being cents per pound, deflated by the Bureau of Labor Statistics (BLS) index given by Theil, the income variable (x_2) given by total per capita consumer expenditures in nominal dollars, and a price index x_3 of competing meats (potential substitutes in consumption) computed as a weighted average of the real prices of beef, chicken, and lamb with weights equal to the quantities of the respective meats also given by Theil.

We cannot use least-squares techniques to test Marshall's law because it would be begging the question to assume the demand function is linear. Instead, we specify the demand function amorphously by

$$y = R(x_1, x_2, x_3) + \varepsilon. \tag{11}$$

Our interest is in finding kernel estimates of R and two partial derivatives of R with respect to the price variable x_1. Hence we report the simple non-linear specification (11) for only one price, one price index, and an income variable. We omit from the specification (11) the three individual prices of other meats (combining them into one index) because simulations (not reported here) show the nonparametric estimator to be more reliable when there are few regressors.[3]

TABLE I. Estimates of Demand for Pork: Amorphous Model (evaluated at means of regressors)

FIRST PARTIALS OF $E(y \mid x)$ with respect to:

variable	coefficient	std. error	t-statistic
x_1	−44.634	16.278	−2.742
x_2	0.0001	0.0001	−0.092
x_3	11.533	9,945	1.160

SECOND PARTIALS OF $E(y \mid x)$ with respect to:

variable	coefficient	std. error
x_1	−780.03	451.187
x_2	0.000002	0.0000038
x_3	45.009	168.406

The intercept, which equals the average of y_t minus the $E(y \mid x)$ evaluated at each observation, is 0.016. Residual SS (after correcting for the intercept) = 43.717, R^2 = 1 - (Residual SS / Total SS) = 0.8636, Trimmed Residual SS = 39.905 if two observations are omitted at each end, and the Durbin-Watson Statistic = 1.863. (Tabulated upper limit 1.29 at 1% level.)

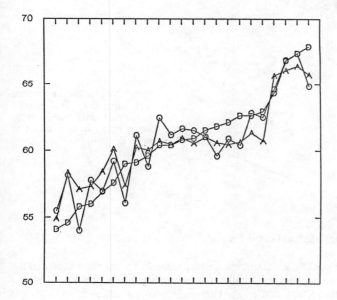

Symbols:
-D-D-=Quantity demanded for pork
-O-O-=OLS fitted quantity
-A-A-=Amorphous fitted quantity

Figure 1. Goodness of fit of amorphous versus OLS.

Our results are summarized in Table I. The coefficient of the (own real) price variable is significant and equals -44.6340: this is the slope of the demand curve evaluated at the average values of the variables. The amorphous model fits the data better than the ordinary-least-squares model (unadjusted $R^2 = 0.863$ and 0.833 respectively); and there is less serial correlation in the amorphous model than with ordinary least squares (the Durbin-Watson statistic is 1.863 as compared with 1.315 for OLS). From Figure 1 it is clear that the actual demand (-D-D- line) is closer to the -A-A- line of the amorphous model than the -O-O- line of OLS.

Although the first derivative with respect to income is not significantly different from zero, we cannot conclude that income effects are absent. This derivative is evaluated at a single point, the mean values of the variables: it may be nonzero elsewhere. Omitting the income variable from the nonparametric estimation leads to a large decline in the Durbin-Watson statistic. Furthermore, the t statistic for the income variable in OLS is 4.395, which is highly significant.

The partial derivative with respect to the price index of competing meats is also highly significant in the OLS specification (t value = 8.846). In the amorphous specification it has the expected positive sign, since the rise in the prices of competing meats leads to a rise in the demand for pork.

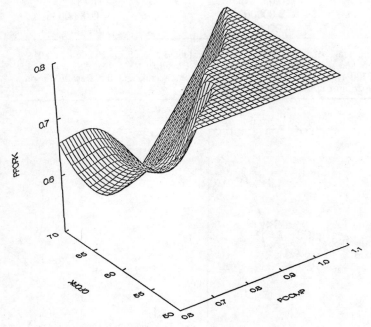

Note: Price is on the vertical axis, quantity is on the horizontal axis, and price index of competing meats is along the third (depth) axis.

Figure 2. Three dimensional demand curve for pork.

The estimates of second-order partials are also indicated in Table I. To test the validity of the Marshallian law of the elasticity of demand, in equation (1) we replace $\partial^i y / \partial x_1^i$ by $\partial^i E(y \mid x)/\partial x_1^i$ for $i = 1, 2$ and use the $R(x)$ function of (2) as $E(y \mid x)$. Our amorphous partials defined in (6) and (9) are estimated at the average real price $\bar{x}_1 = 0.680$ in Table I. We estimate the lefthand side of

(1) to be -780.03 and the righthand side to be 98.393. Since the lefthand side is much smaller we conclude that the empirical evidence does not reject the Marshallian law of elasticity of demand. However, the standard errors appear to be large so that the results from this limited data set are not definitive with respect to sampling variation.[4] Similar conclusions regarding Marshall's law hold for the other three meats in Theil's data (beef, chicken, and lamb). However, the demand equation for beef has a relatively low t value for the price of competing meats, the demand for chicken has a high t value for the income variable, and the demand for lamb has low t value for the price of competing meats.

Figure 2 is a three dimensional smoothed diagram of the data, with price along the vertical axis and quantity along the horizontal axis. The demand curve is seen to slope nonlinearly. The price index for competing meats is along the depth axis (extending away from the observer); it has positive slope because the different meats are substitutes. Moreover, nonlinearity is suggested by the fact that our nonlinear model gives a better fit than the linear model as seen in Figure 1, and has mostly removed the autocorrelated errors problem. The first order (serial) autocorrelation coefficient is 0.2085 for the residuals from the amorphous model.

4. Conclusion

We have developed a nonparametric kernel method for estimating the shape of the demand curve by extending the work on 'amorphous' partial derivative estimation to second derivatives — including a new formula for the approximate asymptotic variance of the second derivative. We find that data on demand for meats does not reject Marshall's hypotheses that the demand elasticity increases with price. Of course a single test is not enough to establish an inductive law.

Notes

* John McMillan and Aman Ullah thank the National Science Foundation and SSHRCC, respectively, for research support. This paper is an extension of a paper presented at the Third Canadian Econometric Study Group Conference in Montreal, Canada, September 1986. The authors thank Robin Carter and Preston McAfee for comments.

1. Marshall (1920), p. 87. An account of Marshall's invention of the concept of elasticity is given by Keynes (1963), who described it as one of Marshall's most important contributions to economics.

2. In an earlier paper Gasser and Müller (1984) considered the second derivative in the case of regression with fixed design variables. In the related work Rilstone (1987) and Rilstone and Ullah (1987) have considered the derivative estimation by using the finite difference method.

3. We ignore here possible simultaneity problems arising from the interaction of supply and demand. This can be given both an economic and a statistical justification. First, the existence of a production lag may mean that supply does not depend on current price; instead, it depends on a prediction about price made some time in the past. Second, Kramer (1984) has shown that there is no asymptotic simultaneous equations bias when the regressors are trended.

4. We note that the estimates of second order partial may be biased due to the normal kernel considered in this paper. This bias could however be eliminated by using kernels which are not necessarily positive; see Bartlett (1963). One such kernel is $g_3(w) = 2^{-1} K(w) (3 - w^2)$, another kernel among many in Vinod (1987) is $g_7(w) = (1/48)(105 - 105w^2 + 21w^4 - w^6)K(w)$, where $K(w)$ is the same as in (5). It can be shown that g_3 satisfies $\mu'_1 = \mu_k = 0$ for its first three moments; and similarly g_7 satisfies $\mu'_1 = \mu_k = 0$ for $k = 2,3,4,5,6,7$. These will be the subject of future study.

References

Bartlett, M. S.: 1963, 'Statistical Estimation of Density Function', *Shankhya*, Ser. A., **25**, 245-254.

Gasser, T., and H. G. Müller: 1984, 'Estimating Regression Functions and their Derivatives by the Kernel Method', *Scandinavian Journal of Statistics*, **11**, 171-185.

Keynes, J. M.: 1963, *Essays in Biography*, Norton, New York, New York, U.S.A.

Krämer, W.: 1984, 'On the Consequences of Trend for Simultaneous Equation Estimation', *Economics Letters*, **14**, 23-30.

Marshall, A.: 1920, *Principles of Economics*, 8th Ed., Macmillan, London, England.

Novshek, W.: 1985, 'On the Existence of Cournot Equilibrium', *Review of Economic Studies*, **52**, January, 85-98.

Prakasa Rao, B. L. S.: 1983, *Nonparametric Functional Estimation*, Academic Press, New York, New York, U.S.A.

Rilstone, P., and A. Ullah: 1987, 'Nonparametric Estimation of Response Coefficients', mimeo, University of Western Ontario, Canada.

Rilstone, P.: 1987, 'Nonparametric Partial Devrivative Estimation', Ph.D. Thesis, University of Western Ontario, Canada.

Rosenblatt, M.: 1956, 'Remarks on some nonparametric estimates of density', *Annals of Mathematical Statistics*, **27**, 832-837.

Singh, R., A. Ullah, and R. A. L. Carter: 1987, 'Nonparametric Inference in Econometrics: New Applications', in I. MacNeil and G. Umphrey (eds.), *Time Series and Econometric Models*, D. Reidell Publishing, Boston, Massachusetts, U.S.A.

Theil, H.: 1976, *Theory and Measurement of Consumer Demand*, Vol. 2, North Holland, New York, New York, U.S.A.

Vinod, H. D.: 1987, 'Simple New Densities with Zero Low Order Moments', Discussion Paper ES188, Department of Econometrics, University of Manchester, Manchester, U.K.

Vinod, H. D., and A. Ullah: 1988, 'Flexible Production Estimation of Nonparametric Kernel Estimators', in T. B. Fomby and G. F. Rhodes (eds.), *Advances in Econometrics: Robust and Nonparametric Statistical Inference*, JAI Press, forthcoming.

PART THREE

MODELLING DEMAND SYSTEMS

CHAPTER 6

A CLASS OF DYNAMIC DEMAND SYSTEMS*

GUOQIANG TIAN
Texas A&M University
Department of Economics
College Station
TX 77843-4228

JOHN S. CHIPMAN
University of Minnesota
Department of Economics
Minneapolis
MN 55455

ABSTRACT. This paper derives closed-form solutions for the total consumption-expenditure function (i.e., aggregate consumption function), the savings function and the demand functions from a nonstationary intertemporal utility-maximization problem under uncertainty for a class of demand systems, including the linear expenditure system (LES) from the Klein-Rubin-Samuelson (KRS) utility function, the generalized linear expenditure systems (GLES) from the CES and S-branch-tree utility functions, the Almost Ideal Demand System (AIDS) from the PIGLOG class of preferences, and the indirect addilog demand system (IADS). We do so by following Hicks' and Tintner's method of maximizing a discounted utility function subject to expected constraints rather than the more fashionable method of maximizing an expected discounted utility function subject to stochastic constraints. Furthermore, the preferences are allowed to vary with the time period. Theoretical analyses for these systems are also given in this paper.

1. Introduction

Since the linear expenditure system (LES) was first studied by Stone (1954), many analyses of demand systems have been undertaken and many models have been proposed for alternative specifications and functional forms (see, e.g., Christensen, Jorgenson, and Lau 1975, Deaton and Muellbauer 1980, Theil 1965, 1976). These models have been widely used in applications of demand theory as well as in international trade (cf. Powell 1966, Parks 1969, Pollak and Wales 1969, Goldberger and Gamaletsos 1970, Musgrove 1974, Anderson and Browning 1986, Chipman 1985). A number of generalizations of these models have been provided (Johansen 1969, Wales 1971, Brown and Heien 1972, Lluch 1973, 1974, Howe 1975, and Musgrove 1977). Estimation methods for these systems have been worked out (Barten 1969, Pollak and Wales 1969, Parks 1971, Powell 1973, Howe 1974, MacKinnon 1976, Blackorby, Boyce, and Russell 1978, Woodland 1979, Ronning 1983, Wales and Woodland 1983, and Chipman and Tian 1988a, 1988b).

Almost all of the above-mentioned studies treat total consumption expenditure as exogenously given and make no attempt to analyze the consumption-savings decision. The modern intertemporal utility-maximizing model is usually put at Ramsey's 1928 article on optimal saving (1928). Tintner (1938a, 1938b) considered formally the general intertemporal problem of faced by a consumer with given expectations about prices, income, and interest rate both in discrete time and continuous time as a theoretical tool (see also Hicks 1935, 1939). However, he did not attempt to specialize the utility function. Empirical implementation did not appear until the work of Modigliani and Brumberg (1954) (who used a one-commodity assumption) and Lluch (1973). Lluch is the first to extend the LES into an intertemporal maximization problem over continuous time, subject to an expected-wealth constraint, and to derive the expenditure equations and the aggregate consumption function. However, Lluch's approach assumes that the commodity prices and the interest rate on non-human wealth and the shift-parameters are constant over the time path. This is clearly not a suitable assumption. Also it is well known that the (dynamic) LES embodies some undesirable restrictions so that it is necessary to develop alternative dynamic demand systems (such as the dynamic GLES and the dynamic AIDS) which would be of greater interest to applied workers.

In order to avoid the assumption of perfect foresight, two quite different approaches have been followed in the literature. The first — which is the more fashionable one in the current literature (cf. Hall 1978, MaCurdy 1983, Sargent 1987) — is to maximize an *expected* utility function (i.e., the expectation of the present value of future instantaneous utilities) subject to a set of stochastic constraints. This approach is based on the axioms of von Neumann and Morgenstern (1947), and in particular on the crucial 'independence axiom' that was later brought out explicitly by Marschak (1950) and Samuelson (1953). The empirical realism of this axiom has been challenged by a number of writers, starting with Wold (1952) and Allais (1953), and more recently by Kahneman and Tversky (1979), Machina (1982), and Yaari (1987), who have proposed alternative sets of postulates. A further criticism has been raised by Ben-Tal and Ben-Israel (1987), namely that it allows realized values of decision variables to violate stochastic inequality constraints. A final, practical, drawback of the expected-utility approach is that closed-form solutions for decision functions cannot in general be obtained, unless very specific assumptions are made concerning the instantaneous utility functions and uncertainty (cf. e.g., Epstein and Wolpin 1988).

The second approach is an older one due to Hicks (1935, 1939) and Tintner (1938a, 1938b); followers are Lluch (1973, 1974), Lluch and Morishima (1973), Powell (1973, 1974), Howe (1974, 1975), and Musgrove (1974, 1977). In this approach the instantaneous utility functions are assumed to be nonstochastic in the parameters, and the intertemporal utility-maximization problem is to maximize a discounted utility function (the expectation of the present value of future instantaneous utilities) subject to *expected* constraints, i.e., subject to given expectations about prices, income, and interest rate over time. It is known (cf. Simon 1956, Theil 1954, 1957) that a sufficient condition for the von Neumann-Morgenstern approach to reduce to the Hicks-Tintner approach, i.e., for each random variable to have a 'certainty equivalent', is that the instantaneous utility functions be quadratic and the constraints be linear in the random variables and decision variables (cf. Sargent 1979, p. 346). Under these conditions the mathematical expectation can be taken 'inside' the marginal utility function, i.e., $E_t u'(x(t)) = u'(E_t x(t))$. Whether and under what circumstances this condition is also necessary appears to be an open question. Another condition that would justify the Hicks-Tintner approach is the existence of perfect markets permitting hedging and insurance; for, if the consumer's instantaneous utility function $u(x)$ is concave, $E_t u(x(t)) \leq u(E_t x(t))$ by Jensen's inequality. We do not pretend in this paper to have axiomatic foundations for the Hicks-Tintner approach, but follow it for more pragmatic reasons: (1) it permits closed-form solutions for general classes of preferences, and is thus amenable to practical application; and (2) the expected-utility approach, which does not permit closed-form solutions except for special types of preferences and constraints, does not have strong empirical support, and indeed has been increasingly called into question in empirical research.

This paper deals with the discrete intertemporal consumption-maximization problem under uncertainty using the Klein-Rubin-Samuelson (KRS) utility function, the CES utility function, the Brown-Heien S-branch-tree utility function which is a modification of Sato's two-level CES production function, from which the LES and the generalized linear expenditure systems (GLES) are derived, and further, the PIGLOG class of preferences resulting in the AIDS (see Deaton and Muellbauer 1980). The demand functions together with the savings function as well as the endogenous total consumption expenditure associated with the LES, the GLES, and the AIDS are called the dynamic linear expenditure system (DLES), the dynamic generalized linear expenditure systems (DGLES), and the dynamic AIDS (DAIDS) respectively. In addition, we also derive the dynamic indirect addilog demand system (DIADS) with b_i-parameter identical among goods.

In the context of these dynamic demand systems, we can answer questions about the responses of the consumption, savings, and demand functions to changes in the interest factor, expected labor income, the expected prices and the last-period savings. The signs of the derivatives of the minimum expenditure $-d(p(t))$ are crucial to determining the signs of the derivatives of the optimal decision functions with respect to prices. For instance, when $\dfrac{\partial d(p(t))}{\partial p_i(t)}$ is positive, an increase in the current price of the ith commodity will lead to increases in the current-period savings and to a decrease in the current total consumption expenditure; an increase in expected future prices will lead to decreases in current savings and to increases in total consumption expenditure if $\dfrac{\partial d(p(t+s))}{\partial p_i(t+s)}$ is positive $(s > 0)$. When $\dfrac{\partial d(p(t+s))}{\partial p_i(t+s)}$ is negative $(s \geq 0)$, the conclusions are reversed. Thus we can see that the assumption made by Lluch (1973), that prices of commodities are constant over the time path, may not be suitable. Also his assumption that the interest rate is constant over the time path may not be suitable because, as we shall show later, an increase in the last-period interest rate causes the current-period savings, current demands and total consumption expenditure to increase only if the consumer had been lending in the last period.

Our approach presented here has a number of advantages. We know that intertemporal analysis has been widely used in macro-economic models of the balance of payments in international trade. Owing, however, to the considerable mathematical difficulties involved, theoretical contributions (see, e.g., Lucas 1982), have adopted a one-commodity assumption and/or have neglected production. Even so, empirical applications to international trade or macro models have been rare. Our approach here offers a way to derive the consumption-savings decision functions with many commodities so that we can easily carry out the theoretical analysis and empirical applications. More realistically, we allow the model to be nonstationary in instantaneous preferences, i.e., the instantaneous preferences of the consumer vary over time periods. In fact, for any instantaneous utility function, if its indirect utility function is log-linear or is quadratic in total consumption expenditure, we can easily derive the savings-decision functions by solving the Euler equation; then we can derive the demand functions by solving the consumer's static maximization problem. Since the indirect utility functions associated with these dynamic demand systems are log-linear in the total consumption expenditure $c(t)$, the functional forms of the consumption-savings decision functions for these utilities are the same, while only the demands are different.

The plan of the paper is as follows. Section 2 sets forth a general form of the consumer's intertemporal maximization problem and derives closed-form solutions of the consumption-savings functions for a class of preferences. In Section 3, the DLES, the DGLES, the DAIDS, and the DIADS are derived. In Section 4, we carry out a theoretical analysis of the optimal decision functions. In Section 5, further assumptions are made so that we can simplify the formulas for the optimal decision functions. In Section 6, some conclusions and remarks are presented.

2. The General Intertemporal Consumer Problem

The basic variables of the model are indicated by the following notation (t denotes time):

m = the number of consumption goods;

$x(t) = (x_1(t), \ldots, x_m(t)) = m$–vector of consumption goods;

$p_i(t)$ = the price of the ith consumption good, which is assumed to be random;

$p(t) = m$–vector of the prices;

$b(t)$ = bondholdings (savings) at the end of period t;

$s(t) = b(t) - b(t-1)$ = saving during period t;

$r(t)$ = the given one-period interest rate on one-period savings;

$R(t) = 1 + r(t)$ = the interest factor on one-period savings;

$y(t)$ = labor earnings, which are assumed to be random;

β = the pure time-preference factor or subjective rate of discount;

$u(\cdot)$ = instantaneous utility function;

$v(\cdot)$ = instantaneous indirect utility function;

$c(t) = p(t) \cdot x(t)$ = the total consumption expenditure at time t.

Remark 1. *In order to avoid the assumption of perfect foresight, we assume that the distribution of the random prices and labor income are known (this is the rational-expectations hypothesis). Then at time t, the expected future prices and labor income are denoted by*

$$p(t, t+j) = E_t p(t+j)$$

$$y(t, t+j) = E_t y(t+j)$$

for $j = 1, 2, \ldots, \infty$, where E_t denotes the mathematical expectation conditional on the information set available at time t.

In the following, we adopt the Hicks-Tintner approach to the intertemporal problem of a consumer faced with given expectations about prices and income. That is, we assume that the consumer's problem at $t = 0$ is

$$\max \sum_{t=0}^{\infty} \beta^t u(x(t))$$

subject to

$$E_0[(p(t)) \cdot x(t) + b(t)] = E_0[y(t) + R(t-1)b(t-1)] \tag{1}$$

with $b(-1)$ given.[1]   Writing (1) in another way, we have

$$E_0[p(t) \cdot x(t) + s(t)] = E_0[y(t) + r(t-1)b(t-1)].$$

This states that that the expected value (conditional on the information at time 0) of consumption plus saving in period t is equal to the expected value of labor income plus property income at time t. The period utility function $u(\cdot)$ is assumed to be twice-continuously differentiable, and increasing in each argument.

In addition to the above constraint, the terminal condition (or borrowing constraint)

$$\lim_{t \to \infty} \Phi(t)^{-1}\Phi(t+j)\,b\,(t+j) = 0 \tag{2}$$

is needed to prevent the consumer from borrowing arbitrarily large amounts, where

$$\Phi(t) = \prod_{\tau=0}^{t-1} R(\tau)^{-1}.$$

The interpretation for (2) is that the present value of borrowing goes to zero, or equivalently, debt does not grow at a rate exceeding the interest rate.

Remark 2. *The terminal condition (2) and the budget constraint (1) are equivalent to a lifetime budget constraint which can be written in terms of the following stock balance:*

$$E_0 \sum_{t=0}^{\infty} \Phi(t) p(t) \cdot x(t) = E_0 \sum_{t=0}^{\infty} \Phi(t) y(t).$$

This states that the present value of planned expenditures should equal the present value of earned income (cf. Chipman and Tian 1988c).

Let the indirect utility function be defined by

$$v(p(t), c(t)) = \max\{u(x(t)): p(t) \cdot x(t) = c(t)\}.$$

Then the maximization problem at $t = 0$ becomes

$$\max \sum_{t=0}^{\infty} \beta^t v(p(0,t), c(t)) \tag{3}$$

subject to

$$E_0[(c(t)+b(t))] = E_0[y(t)+R(t-1)\,b\,(t-1)].$$

This is because after we obtain the solution for $c(t)$ and $b(t)$, we can obtain the demand functions by the Antonelli-Allen-Roy partial differential equation

$$x_i(t) = -\frac{\dfrac{\partial v(p(t), c(t))}{\partial p_i(t)}}{\dfrac{\partial v(p(t), c(t))}{\partial c(t)}}.$$

In general, it is very difficult to derive the optimal solution of (3) even though we can analyze its existence and properties by using discounted dynamic programming. Empirical applications have been rare for this reason in the discrete-time problem.

In order to discover necessary conditions for (3) it is convenient to consider the finite-horizon problem:

$$\max \sum_{t=0}^{T} \beta^t v(E_0 p(t), E_0[y(t)+R(t-1)\,b\,(t-1)-b(t)]) \tag{4}$$

with $b(-1)$ given and $\Phi(T)b(T) = 0$ (or equivalently, $b(T) = 0$). This problem matches our infinite-horizon problem when T goes to infinity. Then the Euler equation (first-order necessary condition) is obtained by differentiating (4) with respect to $b(t)$:

$$-\beta^t v_c(p(t), y(t) + R(t-1) b\,(t-1) - b(t)) +$$ (5)

$$+ \beta^{t+1} R(t) v_c(E_t p(t+1), E_t[y(t+1) + R(t)b(t) - b(t+1)]) = 0$$

for $t = 0, 1, 2, \ldots, T-2$, and

$$-\beta^{T-1} v_c(p(T-1), y(T-1) + R(T-2)b(T-2) - b(T-1)) +$$

$$+ \beta^T R(T-1) v_c(E_{T-1}p(T), E_{T-1}[y(T) + R(T-1)b(T-1)]) = 0$$

for $t = T-1$.

The latter is the terminal condition of the Euler equation (known as the transversality condition) and is a necessary condition for optimality. To obtain the terminal condition in the infinite-horizon problem, it is appropriate to take

$$\lim_{T \to \infty} \beta^{T-1} [-v_c(p(T-1), y(t-1) + R(T-2)b(T-2) - b(T-1)) +$$ (6)

$$+ \beta R(T-1) v_c(p(T), y(T) + R(T-1)b(T-1))] = 0.$$

To obtain closed-form solutions for the optimal decision functions, we assume that the instantaneous indirect utility function is of the form[2]

$$v_t(p(t), c(t)) = \log g_t(p(t)) + b \log [c(t) + d_t(p(t))],$$ (7)

where $d_t(p(t))$ is a linear homogeneous function of within-period prices. $-d_t(p(t))$ can be regarded as the cost of subsistence or minimum-required expenditure.

In the following sections, we will see that several indirect utility functions which are widely used in the demand-system literature have this form; these include the Klein-Rubin-Samuelson (KRS) utility function whose maximization leads to the LES, the CES utility and Brown-Heien S-branch utility tree which are both generalizations of the LES, the PIGLOG class preferences resulting in the AIDS, and Houthakker's (1960) indirect addilog utility function. Note that we allow the preferences of the consumer to change with time periods.

In order to guarantee the existence of the solutions, we assume $R(t) > 1$, $\beta R(t) < 1$ for $t = 0, 1, 2, \ldots, \infty$ and

$$\lim_{t \to \infty} \Phi(t)[d_t(p(t)) + y(t)] = 0.$$

Since

$$v_c(p(t), c(t)) = \frac{b}{c(t) + d_t(p(t))},$$

the Euler equation (5) becomes

$$-\frac{\beta^t b}{\xi(t) + R(t-1)b(t-1) - b(t)} + \frac{\beta^{t+1} R(t) b}{E_t[\xi(t+1) + R(t)b(t) - b(t+1)]} = 0$$

or

$$E_t b(t+1) - (1+\beta)R(t)b(t) + \beta R(t)R(t-1)b(t-1) = E_t \xi(t+1) - \beta R(t)\xi(t),$$ (8)

where

$$\xi(t) = d_t(p(t)) + y(t).$$

The transversality condition (6) becomes

$$\lim_{T \to \infty} \beta^{T-1} [-(1+\beta)R(T-1)b(T-1) + \beta R(T-1)R(t-2)b(T-2) - \tag{9}$$

$$-\xi(T) + \beta R(T-1)\xi(T-1) = 0.$$

The transversality condition holds under the given assumptions. In fact, from $\lim_{T \to \infty} \beta^T b(T) = \lim_{T \to \infty} (\prod_{\tau=0}^{T-1} \beta R(\tau))(\Phi(T)b(T)) = 0$ and $\lim_{T \to \infty} \beta^T \xi(t) = \lim_{T \to \infty} (\prod_{\tau=0}^{T-1} \beta R(\tau))(\Phi(T)\xi(T)) = 0$, we know that the limit of each term of (9) goes to zero as $t \to \infty$. This shows that the transversality condition holds. In order to solve (8) for $b(t)$, we first assume that $R(t) \equiv R$. Then (8) becomes

$$E_t b(t+1) - (1+\beta)Rb(t) + \beta R^2 b(t-1) = E_t \xi(t+1) - \beta R \xi(t). \tag{10}$$

Define the lag operator L and its inverse operator L^{-1} by

$$Lb(t) = b(t-1)$$

and

$$L^{-1}b(t) = E_t b(t+1).$$

The (10) can be written as

$$\left(L^{-1} - (1+\beta)R + \beta R^2 L \right)b(t) = E_t \xi(t+1) - \beta R \xi(t). \tag{11}$$

The characteristic equation is

$$\lambda^2 - (1+\beta)R\lambda + \beta R^2 = 0$$

whose roots are $\lambda_1 = R$ and $\lambda_2 = \beta R$. Therefore we can write (11) as

$$-\lambda_1(1 - \lambda_1^{-1}L^{-1})(1 - \lambda_2 L)b(t) = E_t \xi(t+1) - \beta R \xi(t).$$

The general solution of the above difference equation is

$$(1 - \lambda_2 L)b(t) = \frac{-\lambda_1^{-1}}{1 - \lambda_1^{-1}L^{-1}}(E_t \xi(t+1) - \beta R \xi(t)) + AR^t$$

$$= -R^{-1}\sum_{j=0}^{\infty} R^{-j}E_t(\xi(t+1+j) - \beta R \xi(t+j)) + AR^t$$

$$= -\sum_{j=0}^{\infty} R^{-(j+1)}E_t \xi(t+1+j) + \beta \sum_{j=0}^{\infty} R^{-j}E_t \xi(t+j) + AR^t$$

$$= \beta \xi(t) - (1-\beta)\sum_{j=0}^{\infty} R^{-j}E_t \xi(t+j) + AR^t$$

where A is a constant. However, since $R > 1$, we must have $A = 0$ in order to satisfy the borrowing constraint (2), for the above equation can be written as

$$A = R^{-t}b(t) - \beta R^{-(t-1)}b(t-1) - \beta R^{-t}\xi(t) + (1-\beta)\sum_{j=0}^{\infty} R^{-(t+j)}E_t \xi(t+j)$$

of which each term on the right goes to zero as t goes to infinity. Setting $A = 0$, we have

$$b(t) = \beta R b(t-1) + \beta \xi(t) - (1-\beta)\sum_{j=1}^{\infty} R^{-j} E_t \xi(t+j).$$

Now we consider the general case where $R(t)$ is not constant. We guess that the solution of (8) is of the form

$$b(t) = \beta R(t-1)b(t-1) + \beta \xi(t) - (1-\beta)\sum_{j=1}^{\infty}\prod_{\tau=0}^{j-1} R(t+\tau)^{-1} E_t \xi(t+j) \tag{12}$$

and thus

$$b(t+1) = \beta R(t)b(t) + \beta \xi(t+1) - (1-\beta)\sum_{j=1}^{\infty}\prod_{\tau=0}^{j-1} R(t+1+\tau)^{-1} E_{t+1} \xi(t+1+j) \tag{13}$$

for $t = 0, 1, 2, \ldots, \infty$. Now we verify that (12) is the solution of (8). In fact, using (12) - (13) and that fact that $E_t E_{t+1} f(t+j) = E_t f(t+j)$ for any integral function $f(\cdot)$ and $j \geq 0$, we have

$$E_t b(t+1) - (1+\beta)b(t)R(t) + \beta R(t)R(t-1)b(t-1)$$

$$= \beta R(t)b(t) + \beta E_t \xi(t+1) - (1-\beta)\sum_{j=1}^{\infty}\Phi(t+1)^{-1}\Phi(t+1+j)E_t\xi(t+1+j) -$$

$$- \beta R(t)b(t) - R(t)b(t) + \beta R(t)R(t-1)b(t-1)$$

$$= -R(t)b(t) + \beta R(t)R(t-1)b(t-1) + \beta E_t\xi(t+1) - (1-\beta)\sum_{j=1}^{\infty}\Phi(t+1)^{-1}\Phi(t+1+j)E_t\xi(t+1+j)$$

$$= -R(t)\left(\beta R(t-1)b(t-1) + \beta\xi(t) - (1-\beta)\sum_{j=1}^{\infty}\Phi(t)^{-1}\Phi(t+j)E_t\xi(t+j)\right) +$$

$$+ \beta R(t)R(t-1)b(t-1) + \beta E_t\xi(t+1) - (1-\beta)\sum_{j=1}^{\infty}\Phi(t+1)^{-1}\Phi(t+1+j)E_t\xi(t+1+j)$$

$$= \beta E_t\xi(t+1) - \beta R(t)\xi(t) + (1-\beta)\sum_{j=1}^{\infty}\Phi(t+1)^{-1}\Phi(t+j)E_t\xi(t+j) -$$

$$- (1-\beta)\sum_{j=1}^{\infty}\Phi(t+1)^{-1}\Phi(t+1+j)E_t\xi(t+1+j)$$

$$= \beta E_t\xi(t+1) - \beta R(t)\xi(t) + (1-\beta)\sum_{j=0}^{\infty}\Phi(t+1)^{-1}\Phi(t+1+j)E_t\xi(t+1+j) -$$

$$- (1-\beta)\sum_{j=1}^{\infty}\Phi(t+1)^{-1}\Phi(t+1+j)E_t\xi(t+1+j)$$

$$= \beta E_t\xi(t+1) - \beta R(t)\xi(t) + (1-\beta)E_t\xi(t+1)$$

$$= E_t\xi(t+1) - \beta R(t)\xi(t).$$

This shows that (12) is the solution of (8). Hence the total consumption function (expenditure function) is given by

$$c(t) = (1-\beta)\Phi(t)^{-1}\sum_{j=0}^{\infty}\Phi((t+j)E_t\xi(t+j)) - d_t(p(t)) \qquad (14)$$

$$= -\beta d_t(p(t)) + (1-\beta)\,[y(t) + R(t-1)b(t-1) +$$

$$+ \sum_{j=1}^{\infty}\prod_{\tau=0}^{j-1}R(t+\tau)^{-1}E_t(d_{t+j}(p(t+j)) + y(t+j))\,].$$

Let

$$w(t) = R(t-1)b(t-1) + y(t) + \sum_{j=1}^{\infty}\prod_{\tau=0}^{j-1}R(t+\tau)^{-1}E_t y(t+1),$$

$$\bar{d}(t) = d_t(p(t)) + \sum_{j=1}^{\infty}\prod_{\tau=0}^{j-1}R(t+\tau)^{-1}E_t d_{t+j}(p(t+j)).$$

$w(t)$ consists of property income plus the expected present value of nonproperty (labor) income. Thus $w(t)$ can be considered as the permanent income of the consumer. $-\bar{d}(t)$ is the expected present value of minimum-required consumption expenditure; it can be interpreted as the permanent necessary expenditure. Thus (12) and (14) can be rewritten in terms of $w(t)$ and $\bar{d}(t)$ as

$$b(t) = R(t-1)b(t-1) + y(t) + d_t(p(t)) - (1-\beta)\,[w(t) + \bar{d}(t)\,];$$

$$c(t) = -d_t(p(t)) + (1-\beta)\,[w(t) + \bar{d}(t)].$$

3. A Class of Dynamic Demand Systems

3.1 THE DYNAMIC LINEAR-EXPENDITURE SYSTEM

The Klein-Rubin-Samuelson (KRS) utility function[3] is of the form

$$u(x(t);\alpha,\gamma(t)) = \sum_{i=1}^{m}\alpha_i\log(x_i(t) + \gamma_i(t)) \quad (\alpha_i > 0 \;\&\; \sum_{i=1}^{m}\alpha_i = 1) \qquad (15)$$

where α_i and $\gamma_i(t)$ are parameters.

Since the demands for the commodities, in general, vary over time, we may assume that the $\gamma_i(t)$'s vary over time. In Chipman and Tian (1988a, 1988b) the $\gamma_i(t)$ are assumed to have the form

$$\gamma_i(t) = \sum_{l=0}^{n}\gamma_{li}\phi_{li}(t)$$

which is a very general form and covers the case of linear trend as well as those of Pollak (1970) and Chipman (1985) as special cases.

The indirect KRS utility function is given by

$$v(p(t),c(t)) = \sum_{i=1}^{m}\alpha_i\log\alpha_i/p_i(t) + \log(p(t)\cdot\gamma(t) + c(t)),$$

which has the form specified by (7) with $d_t(p(t)) = p(t)\cdot\gamma(t)$. Thus the consumption-savings functions of the DLES are given by (12) and (14) and the demand functions $x_i(t)$ of the DLES are given by

$$x_i(t) = \frac{\alpha_i}{p_i(t)} (p(t) \cdot \gamma(t) + c(t)) - \gamma_i(t)$$

$$= \frac{\alpha_i}{p_i(t)} (1 - \beta) [p(t) \cdot \gamma(t) + y(t) + R(t-1)b(t-1) +$$

$$+ \sum_{j=1}^{\infty} \prod_{\tau=0}^{j-1} R(t+\tau)^{-1} E_t(p(t+j) \cdot \gamma(t+j) + y(t+j))] - \gamma_i(t)$$

$$= (1 - \beta) \frac{\alpha_i}{p_i(t)} [w(t) + \bar{d}(t)] - \gamma_i(t).$$

Thus the expenditure equations for the DLES are

$$p_i(t)x_i(t) = \alpha_i(1 - \beta) [p(t) \cdot \gamma(t) + y(t) + R(t-1)b(t-1) +$$

$$+ \sum_{j=1}^{\infty} \prod_{\tau=0}^{j-1} R(t+\tau)^{-1} E_t(p(t+j) \cdot \gamma(t+j) + y(t+j))] - p_i(t)\gamma_i(t)$$

$$= (1 - \beta)\alpha_i[w(t) + \bar{d}(t)] - p_i(t)\gamma_i(t).$$

Remark 3. *When we let $p(t) \equiv p$, $R(t) \equiv R$ and $\gamma(t) \equiv \gamma$ over time, the functional forms (12) - (14) are the same as those in Lluch (1973), only the definitions of $w(t)$ and $\bar{d}(t)$ of Lluch are different. This is because Lluch uses a continuous time path, while we use a discrete time path.*

3.2 DYNAMIC GENERALIZED LINEAR EXPENDITURE SYSTEMS

As we know, the KRS utility function is directly additive, hence there are no specific substitution effects in the LES. We cannot deal with inferior goods (since $\alpha_i / p_i(t) > 0$) and complementary goods (since the Slutsky term $\hat{s}_{ij}(t)$ is > 0 for $i \neq j$), nor can we deal with price elasticities whose absolute values exceed unity when $-\gamma_i(t)$ is interpreted as the minimum-required quantities (i.e., we need to assume that $\gamma_i(t) < 0$). We can verify that the GLES also has the same restrictions mentioned above as the LES. Brown and Heien (1972) have modified Sato's (1967) two-level CES production to obtain the utility function which they term the 'S-branch utility tree'. The demand system associated with this utility has the following properties: Specific substitution effects do not necessarily vanish. Goods in the system can be complementary under some conditions. Own-price elasticities are free to vary in the interval $(-\infty, 0)$. Finally, the S-branch utility tree contains the LES and the CES utility function as special cases.

The CES utility function is of the form

$$u(x(t)) = \frac{1}{\rho} \log \left[\sum_{i=1}^{m} \alpha_i [x_i(t) + \gamma_i(t)]^\rho \right] \quad (-\infty < \rho < 1) \tag{16}$$

which is of course analogous to the CES production function. The utility function is a generalization of the KRS utility function because (16) tends to (15) as ρ tends to zero. The demand functions implied by (16) are also reasonably simple:

$$x_i(t) = \frac{\left(\dfrac{\alpha_i}{p_i(t)}\right)^{\alpha}}{\displaystyle\sum_{j=1}^{m}\left(\dfrac{\alpha_j}{p_j(t)}\right)^{\alpha} p_i(t)} \, p(t)\cdot\gamma(t) + c(t)) - \gamma_i(t) \tag{17}$$

when the budget constraint is given by

$$p(t)\cdot x(t) = c(t)$$

where

$$\sigma = \frac{1}{1-\rho}.$$

Brown and Heien (1972) proposed a further generalization of (15) and (16) which they called the S-branch utility tree. The consumption goods are assumed to be divided into S branches, with m_l commodities in the l-th branch where the $\displaystyle\sum_{l=1}^{S} m_l = m$, so that the utility function can be written as

$$U(x(t)) = \frac{1}{\rho}\log\left(\sum_{l=1}^{S}\alpha_l\left[\sum_{i=1}^{m_l}\alpha_{li}(x_{li}(t)+\gamma_{li}(t)^{\rho_l}\right]^{\rho/\rho_l}\right) \quad (-\infty < \rho_l, \, -\infty < \rho < 1) \tag{18}$$

which is called the Brown-Heien S-branch utility function. (16) is just the special case of (18) when $s = 1$; hence some people call the CES utility function the 1-branch utility function. The parameters α_l reflect the importance of the different branches (blocks) in generating total utility; the α_{li}, on the other hand, reflect the importance (in generating utility) of particular commodities within given branches. The α_ls and α_{li}s are all assumed to be positive. The demand functions implied by (18) which were first derived by Brown and Heien (1972) are much more complicated than those implied by (15) or (16). The demand functions are

$$x_{si}(t) = -\gamma_{si}(t) + \left(\frac{\alpha_{si}}{p_{si}(t)}\right)^{\sigma_s} [a_s^{\sigma} X_s(t)^{(\sigma-\sigma_s)/(\sigma_s-1)}] \times \tag{19}$$

$$\times\left(c(t) + \sum_{l=1}^{S}\sum_{j=1}^{m_l}p_{lj}(t)\cdot\gamma_{lj}(t)\right)\cdot\left[\sum_{l=1}^{S}a_l^{\sigma} X_l(t)^{(\sigma-1)/(\sigma_s-1)}\right]^{-1}$$

for $i = 1, 2, \ldots, m_s$ and $s = 1, 2, \ldots, S$. They satisfy the budget constraint

$$\sum_{l=1}^{S}\sum_{j=1}^{m_l}p_{lj}(t)\cdot x_{lj}(t) = c(t).$$

Here

$$\sigma_s = \frac{1}{1-\rho_s}$$

and

$$X_l(t) = \sum_{j=1}^{m_l}\left(\frac{\alpha_{lj}}{p_{lj}(t)}\right)^{\sigma_l}p_{lj}(t).$$

A simple derivation can be found in Powell (1974).

Substituting the demand functions (17) and (19) in (15) and (16) respectively, we obtain

$$v(p(t), c(t)) = \log(c(t) + p(t) \cdot \gamma(t)) + \frac{1}{\rho} \log \left(\sum_{i=1}^{m} \alpha_i (Q_i(t))^\rho \right)$$

where

$$Q_i(t) = \frac{(\alpha_i / p_i(t))^\sigma}{\sum_{j=1}^{m} (\alpha_j / p_j(t))^\sigma p_i(t)}$$

and

$$v(p(t), c(t)) = \log(c(t) + p(t) \cdot \gamma(t)) - \log \left[\sum_{l=1}^{S} a_l^\sigma X_l(t)^{(\sigma-1)/(\sigma_l-1)} \right] +$$

$$+ \frac{1}{\rho} \log \left(\sum_{l=1}^{S} a_l \left[\sum_{i=1}^{m_l} B_{li}(t) \right] \right),$$

where

$$B_{li}(t) = \left(\frac{\alpha_{li}}{p_{li}(t)} \right)^{\sigma_l} \left[a_l^\sigma X_l(t)^{(\sigma-\sigma_l)/(\sigma_l-1)} \right].$$

Thus these indirect utility functions have the form specified by (6). Therefore the consumption-savings functions of the DGLES are given by (12) and (14) and the demand functions of the DGLES with the CES utility function and S-branch utility tree are obtained by substituting (14) in (17) and (19) respectively:

$$x_i(t) = (1-\beta)(w(t) + \bar{d}(t)) \frac{(\alpha_i/p_i(t))^\sigma}{\sum_{j=1}^{m} (\alpha_j/p_j(t))^\sigma p_i(t)} - \gamma_i(t) \tag{20}$$

$$x_{si}(t) = (1-\beta)(w(t) + \bar{d}(t)) \frac{(\alpha_{si}/p_{si}(t))^{\sigma_s} a_s^\sigma X_s(t)^{(\sigma-\sigma_s)/(\sigma_s-1)}}{\sum_{l=1}^{S} a_l^\sigma X_l(t)^{(\sigma-1)/(\sigma_l-1)}} - \gamma_{si}(t). \tag{21}$$

3.3 THE DYNAMIC ALMOST IDEAL DEMAND SYSTEM

The Almost Ideal Demand System (AIDS) was introduced by Deaton and Muellbauer (1980); it has many desirable properties such as furnishing an arbitrary first-order approximation to any demand system, aggregating perfectly over consumers without invoking parallel linear Engel curves, etc. The preferences resulting in the AIDS are the so-called PIGLOG class which are represented via the cost or expenditure function

$$\log c(v(t), p(t)) = (1 - v(t)) \log a(p(t)) + v(t) \log b(p(t)), \tag{22}$$

which defines the minimum expenditure necessary to attain a specific utility level at given prices. Here $a(p(t))$ and $b(p(t))$ are linear homogeneous function of within-period prices and given by

$$\log a(p(t)) = a_0(t) + \sum_{i=1}^{m} \alpha_i \log p_i(t) + \frac{1}{2}\sum_{i=1}^{m}\sum_{j=1}^{m} \gamma_{ij}(t)\log p_i(t)p_j(t)$$

$$\log b(p(t)) = \log a(p(t)) + \theta_0 \prod_{i=1}^{m} p_i^{\theta_i}(t).$$

From (22), the indirect utility function is given by

$$v_t(p(t), c(t)) = \frac{\log c(t) - \log a(p(t))}{\log \dfrac{b(p(t))}{a(p(t))}}.$$

The demand function can be obtained by the Antonelli-Allen-Roy equation

$$x_i(t) = c(t)\left[\frac{a'_i(p(t))}{a(p(t))} + \frac{\log \dfrac{c(t)}{a(p(t))}}{\log \dfrac{b(p(t))}{a(p(t))}}\left(\frac{b'_i(p(t))}{b(p(t))} - \frac{a'_i(p(t))}{a(p(t))} \right) \right], \tag{23}$$

where $a'_i(p(t)) = \dfrac{\partial a(p(t))}{\partial p_i(t)}$ and $b'_i(p(t)) = \dfrac{\partial b(p(t))}{\partial p_i(t)}$.

In order for the indirect utility function to have the form specified by (7), we assume[4] $E_t p(t+1) = \rho p(t)$. Then $E_t p(t+1) = \rho^{t+1} p(0)$ and thus $\log \dfrac{b(E_t p(t+1))}{a(E_t p(t+1))} = \log \dfrac{b(p(0))}{a(p(0))}$ so that the indirect utility function has the form specified by (7). Thus the consumption-savings functions of the DAIDS are given by (12) and (14) and the demand functions $x_i(t)$ of the DAIDS are obtained by substituting (14) in (23).

The demand functions $x_i(t)$ for the DIADS are

$$x_i(t) = (1-\beta)w(t)\left[\frac{a'_i(p(t))}{a(p(t))} + \frac{\log \dfrac{c(t)}{a(p(t))}}{\log \dfrac{b(p(t))}{a(p(t))}}\left(\frac{b'_i(p(t))}{b(p(t))} - \frac{a'_i(p(t))}{a(p(t))} \right) \right].$$

3.4 THE DYNAMIC INDIRECT ADDILOG DEMAND SYSTEM

The indirect addilog system can be obtained from the indirect additive utility function

$$v(c(t), p(t)) = \log\left[\sum_{i=1}^{m} a_i\left(\frac{c(t)}{p_i(t)} \right)^{b_i} \right]; \quad (b_i > -1) \tag{24}$$

where the a_i and b_i are parameters which are called the preference indicators and coefficients respectively. The resulting demand function is

$$x_i(t) = \frac{a_i b_i c(t)^{b_i} p_i(t)^{-(b_i+1)}}{\sum_{j=1}^{m} a_j b_j c(t)^{b_j-1} p_j(t)^{-b_j}} \tag{25}$$

In order to obtain the closed-form solution, we consider a special case $b_i = b$ for all $i = 1, 2, \ldots, m$

so that (24) becomes

$$v(c(t), p(t)) = b \log c(t) + \log \left(\sum_{i=1}^{m} \frac{a_i}{p_i(t)^b} \right)$$

and (25) becomes

$$x_i(t) = \frac{a_i c(t) p_i(t)^{-(b+1)}}{\sum_{j=1}^{m} a_j p_j(t)^{-b}}.$$

The demand functions $x_i(t)$ for the DIADS are

$$x_i(t) = (1 - \beta) w(t) \frac{a_i p_i(t)^{-(b+1)}}{\sum_{j=1}^{m} \frac{a_j}{p_j(t)^b}}.$$

Remark 4. *From the above discussion, we know that all of the utility functions considered above can be written in the form $v_t(p(t), c(t)) = \log g_t(p(t)) + b \log [c(t) + d_t(p(t))]$, and the solutions for the consumption-savings decision are independent of $g_t(p(t))$. Furthermore, we can allow the preferences to change with time periods and the functional forms of the consumption-savings functions are the same as long as the preferences are represented by the above utility functions.*

4. Some Properties of the Dynamic Demand Systems

We know from the last section that the functional forms of the savings decision function and total consumption expenditures from the DLES, the DGLES, and the DIADS are the same. Only the demand functions for the consumption goods are different for the DLES, the DGLES, and the DIADS. In this section, we analyze responses of historical savings, interest factor, the current and future price to the optimal decision functions, and give elasticities for the DLES, the DGLES and the DIADS. Take the solution functions $b(t), c(t)$ and $x_i(t)$ as the functions of $b(t-1), R(t-1), R(t+j), E_t y(t+j), E_t p(t+j)$ $(j \geq 0)$, which are denoted $b(t) = \tilde{b}(\cdot)$, $c(t) = \tilde{c}(\cdot)$, and $x_i(t) = \tilde{x}_i(\cdot)$.

4.1 PROPERTIES OF THE CONSUMPTION-SAVINGS FUNCTIONS

We investigate the properties of the following partial derivatives:

$$\frac{\partial \tilde{b}(\cdot)}{\partial b(t-1)} = \beta R(t-1);$$

$$\frac{\partial \tilde{b}(\cdot)}{\partial R(t-1)} = \beta b(t-1);$$

$$\frac{\partial \tilde{b}(\cdot)}{\partial R(t+s)} = \frac{(1-\beta)}{R(t+s)} \sum_{j=s+1}^{\infty} \prod_{\tau=0}^{j-1} R(t+\tau)^{-1} E_t \xi(t+j) \quad (\forall s \geq 0);$$

$$\frac{\partial \tilde{b}(\cdot)}{\partial y(t)} = \beta;$$

$$\frac{\partial \tilde{b}(\cdot)}{\partial y(t, t+s)} = -(1-\beta)\prod_{\tau=0}^{s-1} R(t+\tau)^{-1} \quad (\forall s > 0);$$

$$\frac{\partial \tilde{b}(\cdot)}{\partial p_i(t)} = \beta \frac{\partial d_t(p(t))}{\partial p_i(t)};$$

$$\frac{\partial \tilde{b}(\cdot)}{\partial p_i(t, t+s)} = -(1-\beta)\prod_{\tau=0}^{s-1} R(t+\tau)^{-1} \frac{\partial d_{t+s}(p(t, t+s))}{\partial p_i(t, t+s)} \quad (\forall s > 0);$$

$$\frac{\partial \tilde{c}(\cdot)}{\partial b(t-1)} = (1-\beta)R(t-1);$$

$$\frac{\partial \tilde{c}(\cdot)}{\partial R(t-1)} = (1-\beta)b(t-1);$$

$$\frac{\partial \tilde{c}(\cdot)}{\partial R(t+s)} = -\frac{(1-\beta)}{R(t+s)} \sum_{j=s+1}^{\infty} \prod_{\tau=0}^{j-1} R(t+\tau)^{-1} E_t \xi(t+j) \quad (\forall s > 0);$$

$$\frac{\partial \tilde{c}(\cdot)}{\partial y(t)} = (1-\beta);$$

$$\frac{\partial \tilde{c}(\cdot)}{\partial y(t, t+s)} = (1-\beta)\prod_{\tau=0}^{s-1} R(t+\tau)^{-1} \quad (\forall s > o);$$

$$\frac{\partial \tilde{c}(\cdot)}{\partial p_i(t)} = -\beta \frac{\partial d_t(p(t))}{\partial p_i(t)};$$

$$\frac{\partial \tilde{c}(\cdot)}{\partial p_i(t, t+s)} = (1-\beta)\prod_{\tau=0}^{s-1} R(t+\tau)^{-1} \frac{\partial d_{t+s}(p(t, t+s))}{\partial p_i(t, t+s)} \quad (\forall s > 0).$$

The above derivatives show that an increase in the past-period bondholdings $b(t-1)$ causes the current-period bondholdings $b(t)$ and the current total consumption expenditure $c(t)$ to increase. An increase in the last-period interest factor $R(t-1)$ causes the current-period savings and the current total consumption expenditure to decrease if the consumer was borrowing the last period (i.e., $b(t-) < 0$) or to increase otherwise; an increase in a future interest factor causes the current-period savings to increase and the current total consumption expenditure to decrease. An increase in the current labor income $y(t)$ causes the current-period savings and total consumption to increase. An increase in the future expected labor income causes the current-period savings to decrease and the current total consumption expenditure to increase. An increase in the current-period price of the jth good causes the current-period savings to decrease (increase) and causes the total consumption expenditure to increase (decrease) if $\frac{\partial d_t(p(t))}{\partial p_j(t)}$ is negative (positive). An increase in the future expected price of the ith good causes the current-period savings to increase and the current total consumption expenditure to decrease if $\frac{\partial d_t(p(t))}{\partial p_i(t)}$ is negative, and causes the current-period savings to decrease and the current total consumption expenditure to increase if $\frac{\partial d_{t+s}(p(t))}{\partial p_i(t, t+s)}$ is positive.

4.2 PROPERTIES OF DEMAND FUNCTIONS OF THE DYNAMIC DEMAND SYSTEMS

Now we study the properties of the demand functions of the dynamic demand systems, and particularly the vectors of partial derivatives of the demand functions with respect to $b(t-1)$, $R(t-1)$, $R(t+j)$, $E_t y(t+j)$, $E_t p(t+j)$ $(j \geq 0)$. Here we only give the properties of the demand functions of the DLES and DGLES. The demand functions of the DAIDS and the DIADS can be similarly studied.

4.2.1 Properties of the DLES. For the DLES, we have

$$\frac{\partial \tilde{x}_i(\cdot)}{\partial b(t-1)} = (1-\beta)R(t-1)\frac{\alpha_i}{p_i(t)} > 0;$$

$$\frac{\partial \tilde{x}_i(\cdot)}{\partial R(t-1)} = (1-\beta)b(t-1)\frac{\alpha_i}{p_i(t)} \begin{cases} \geq 0 & \text{if } b(t-1) \geq 0 \\ < 0 & \text{otherwise} \end{cases};$$

$$\frac{\partial \tilde{x}_i(\cdot)}{\partial R(t+s)} = -\frac{(1-\beta)\alpha_i}{R(t+s)p_i(t)} \sum_{j=s+1}^{\infty} \prod_{\tau=0}^{j-1} R(t+\tau)^{-1} E_t \xi(t+j) < 0 \ (\forall s > 0);$$

$$\frac{\partial \tilde{x}_i(\cdot)}{\partial y(t)} = (1-\beta)\frac{\alpha_i}{p_i(t)} > 0;$$

$$\frac{\partial \tilde{x}_i(\cdot)}{\partial y(t, t+s)} = (1-\beta)\frac{\alpha_i}{p_i(t)} \prod_{\tau=0}^{s-1} R(t+\tau)^{-1} > 0;$$

$$\frac{\partial \tilde{x}_i(\cdot)}{\partial p_j(t)} = (1-\beta)\frac{\alpha_i \gamma_j(t)}{p_i(t)} \begin{cases} \geq 0 & \text{if } \gamma(t) \geq 0 \\ < 0 & \text{otherwise} \end{cases};$$

$$\frac{\partial \tilde{x}_i(\cdot)}{\partial p_i(t)} = -\frac{x_i(t)}{p_i(t)} - [1-(1-\beta)\alpha_i)]\frac{\gamma_i(t)}{p_i(t)} \begin{cases} \leq 0 & \text{if } \gamma_i(t) \geq (x_i(t))/(1-(1-\beta)\alpha_i) \\ < 0 & \text{otherwise} \end{cases};$$

$$\frac{\partial \tilde{x}_i(\cdot)}{\partial p_j(t, t+s)} = (1-\beta)\frac{\alpha_i}{p_i(t)} \prod_{\tau=0}^{s-1} T(t+\tau)^{-1} \gamma_j(t+s) \begin{cases} \geq 0 & \text{if } \gamma_j(t+s) \geq 0 \\ < 0 & \text{otherwise} \end{cases} \text{ for any } s > 0.$$

The interpretations for the above derivatives is similar to those in Section 4.1. In the following, we give some elasticity formulae for the GLES. The price elasticities are given by

$$\eta_{ii}(t) = \frac{d\log \tilde{x}_i(\cdot)}{d\log p_i(t)} = -1 - [1-(1-\beta)\alpha_i]\frac{\gamma_i(t)}{x_i(t)};$$

$$\eta_{ij}(t) = (1-\beta)\frac{\alpha_i \gamma_j(t)p_j(t)}{p_i(t)x_i(t)}$$

The total expenditure elasticity $\partial \log \tilde{x}_i(\cdot) / \partial \log c(t)$ is

$$E_c^i(t) = \frac{\alpha_i}{p_i(x)x_i(t)}[-p(t) \cdot \gamma(t) + (1-\beta)(w(t) + \bar{d}(t))].$$

The permanent income elasticity $\partial \log \tilde{x}_i(\cdot) / \partial \log w(t)$ is

$$E_w^i(t) = \frac{\alpha_i(1-\beta)w(t)}{p_i(t)x_i(t)}.$$

Denote by $\tilde{x}_i(\cdot) = h_i(p(t), c(t))$. Then, the Slutsky terms

$$\hat{s}_{ij}(t) = \frac{\partial h_i(p(t), c(t))}{\partial p_j(t)} + \frac{\partial h_i(p(t), c(t))}{\partial c(t)} h_j(p(t), c(t))$$

are given by

$$\hat{s}_{ii}(t) = -(1-\alpha_i)(x_i(t) + \gamma_i(t)) / p_i(t) < 0$$

$$\hat{s}_{ij}(t) = \frac{\alpha_i(x_j(t) + \gamma_j(t))}{p_j(t)} > 0$$

which are identically the same in the LES.

4.2.2 Properties of the DGLES. Since the CES utility function is a special case of the Brown-Heien utility function ($s = 1$), the demand function determined by (20) is the same as the one determined by (21) when $s = 1$. So we only investigate the derivatives of the demand function given by (21).

Let

$$D_{si}(t) = (1-\beta) \left(\frac{\alpha_{si}}{p_{si}(t)} \right)^{\sigma_s} \frac{a_s^{\sigma} X_s(t)^{(\sigma-\sigma_s)/(\sigma_s-1)}}{\sum\limits_{l=1}^{s} a_l^{\sigma} X_l(t)^{(\sigma-1)/(\sigma_l-1)}}.$$

Then

$$\frac{\partial \tilde{x}_{si}(\cdot)}{\partial b(t-1)} = D_{si}(t) R(t-1) > 0;$$

$$\frac{\partial \tilde{x}_{si}(\cdot)}{\partial R(t-1)} = D_{si}(t) b(t-1) \begin{cases} \geq 0 & \text{if } b(t-1) \geq 0 \\ < 0 & \text{otherwise} \end{cases};$$

$$\frac{\partial \tilde{x}_{si}(\cdot)}{\partial R(t, t+v)} = -\frac{D_{si}(t)}{R(t+v)} \sum_{v+1}^{\infty} \prod_{\tau=1}^{j-1} R(t+\tau)^{-1} \xi(t+j) < 0 \quad (\forall v > 0);$$

$$\frac{\partial \tilde{x}_{si}(\cdot)}{\partial y(t)} = D_{si}(t) > 0;$$

$$\frac{\partial \tilde{x}_{si}(\cdot)}{\partial y(t, t+v)} = D_{si}(t) \prod_{\tau=0}^{v-1} R(t+\tau)^{-1} > 0 \quad (\forall v > 0).$$

Since the $\tilde{x}_i(\cdot) = h_i(p(t), c(t))$ for the DGLES have identically the same functional forms as in the GLES, the total consumption expenditure elasticities $E_c^{si}(t)$ and Slutsky terms of the DGLES should be the same as those in the GLES. Therefore, we have

$$E_c^{si}(t) = \frac{(x_{si}(t) + \gamma_{si}(t))}{x_{si}(t)} \frac{c(t)}{(c(t) + \gamma(t))}$$

$$\hat{s}_{li,lj}(t) = \frac{(x_{si}(t) + \gamma_{si}(t))(x_{lj}(t) + \gamma_{lj}(t))}{(c(t) + \gamma(t))} \sigma$$

for $l \neq s$;

$$\hat{s}_{si,lj}(t) = \frac{(x_{si}(t) + \gamma_{si}(t))(x_{sj}(t) + \gamma_{sj}(t))}{(c(t) + \gamma(t))}\sigma -$$

$$-\frac{(x_{si}(t) + \gamma_{si}(t))(\sigma - \sigma_s)(x_{sj}(t) + \gamma_{sj}(t))}{(c_s(t) + \sum\limits_{i=1}^{m_s} p_{si}(t) \cdot \gamma_{si}(t))}$$

for $l = s$, $i \neq j$, where s, r denote the blocks, $i = 1, 2, \ldots, m_s$ and $j = 1, 2, \ldots, m_l$.

$$c_s(t) = \sum_{i=1}^{m_s} p_{si}(t)x_{si}(t).$$

The derivation for these formulas can be found in Brown and Heien (1972).

5. Simplification of the Optimal Decision Functions

To specialize the optimal decision functions, we have to be more explicit about the interest rate, the prices and labor income. For simplicity, we assume that the expected interest factor is constant over time, and that the expected prices and labor income obey

$$E_t p(t + 1) = \rho p(t)$$

$$E_t y(t + 1) = \theta(y(t) - \bar{y}) + \bar{y}$$

or

$$p(t + 1) = \rho p(t) + \varepsilon(t + 1)$$

$$y(t + 1) = \theta(y(t) - \bar{y}) + \bar{y} + u(t + 1)$$

where $\varepsilon(t + 1)$ and $u(t + 1)$ are assumed to be independently, identically distributed and $E_t\varepsilon(t + 1) = E_t u(t + 1) = 0$. Then

$$E_t p(t + j) = \rho^j p(t) \quad (j > 0);$$

$$E_t y(t + j) = \theta^j(y(t) - \bar{y}) + \bar{y} \quad (j > 0).$$

Therefore, (12) and (14) become respectively

$$b(t) = \beta R b(t - 1) + \beta\xi(t) - (1 - \beta)\sum_{j=1}^{\infty} R^{-j}(\rho^j p(t) \cdot \gamma(t) + \theta^j(y(t) - \bar{y}) + \bar{y})$$

$$= \beta R b(t - 1) + p(t) \cdot \gamma(t)\frac{\beta R - \rho}{R - \rho} + y(t)\frac{\beta R - \theta}{R - \theta} + (1 - \beta)\bar{y}\frac{R(\theta - 1)}{(R - \theta)(R - 1)}$$

$$c(t) = (1 - \beta)R b(t - 1) - p(t) \cdot \gamma(t)\frac{\beta R - \rho}{R - \rho} + y(t)\frac{R(1 - \beta)}{R - \theta} -$$

$$- (1 - \beta)\bar{y}\frac{R(\theta - 1)}{(R - \theta)(R - 1)}.$$

The demand functions of the DLES, the DGLES, the DAIDS, and the DIADS are then given by

$$x_i(t) = (1-\beta)\frac{\alpha_i R}{p_i(t)}\left(b(t-1) + \frac{1}{R-\rho}p(t)\cdot\gamma(t) + \frac{1}{R-\theta}y(t) + \frac{\theta-1)}{(R-\theta)(R-1)}\bar{y}\right) - \gamma_i(t);$$

$$x_{si}(t) = -\gamma_i(t) + (1-\beta)R\frac{(\frac{\alpha_{si}}{p_{si}(t)})^{\sigma_s}[a_s^\sigma X_s(t)^{(\sigma-\sigma_s)/(\sigma_s-1)}]}{\sum_{l=1}^{S}(\alpha_l)^\sigma(X_l(t))^{(\sigma-1)/(\sigma_l-1)}} \times$$

$$\times\left[b(t-1) + \frac{p(t)\cdot\gamma(t)}{R-p)} + \frac{y(t)}{R-\theta} + \frac{(\theta-1)\bar{y}}{(R-\theta)(R-1)}\right];$$

$$x_i(t) = \left[\frac{a_i(p(t))}{a(p(t))} + \frac{\log\frac{c(t)}{a(p(t))}}{\log\frac{b(p(t))}{a(p(t))}}\left(\frac{b_i(p(t))}{b(p(t))} - \frac{a_i(p(t))}{a(p(t))}\right)\right] \times$$

$$\times\left[b(t-1) + \frac{p(t)\cdot\gamma(t)}{R-p} + \frac{y(t)}{R-\theta} + \frac{(\theta-1)\bar{y}}{(R-\theta)(R-1)}\right];$$

$$x_i(t) = \frac{(1-\beta)Ra_ip_i(t)^{-(b+1)}\left(b(t-1) + \frac{y(t)}{(R-\theta)} + \frac{(\theta-1)\bar{y}}{(R-\theta)(R-1)}\right)}{\sum_{j=1}^{m}\frac{a_j}{p_j(t)^b}}.$$

The permanent income and permanent indispensable expenditure are given respectively by

$$w(t) = R\left[b(t-1) + \frac{1}{R-\theta}y(t) + \frac{1-\theta}{(R-1)(R-\theta)}\bar{y}\right],$$

$$\bar{d}(t) = \frac{R}{R-\rho}d_t(p(t)).$$

The theoretical analysis can be similarly studied for the simplified decision functions. We omit it here.

6. Conclusions

In this paper, we have derived the consumption-savings decision functions and demand functions from the consumer's intertemporal maximization problem over discrete time for a class of utility functions, namely the Klein-Rubin-Samuelson (KRS) utility function, the CES utility function, the Brown-Heien S-branch utility tree, the PIGLOG class of preferences, and Houthakker's indirect addilog utility function. Theoretical analysis was also provided in this paper. We generalized the Klein-Rubin linear expenditure system, Wales's generalized linear expenditure system, Brown and Heien's generalization of the linear expenditure system, the Almost Ideal

Demand System, and Houthakker's indirect addilog demand system to include the consumption-savings decisions. Since the explicit forms for the optimal decision functions were obtained, these may be easy to use in empirical applications.

Notes

* Work supported by NSF grant SES-8607652. The comments and suggestions of an anonymous referee of this Volume greatly improved the paper.

1. The inequality in the budget constraint can be removed by assuming preferences to be locally nonsatiated. Note that if the stochastic budget constraint holds with equality, so must the expected budget constraint.

2. Extension to the general case where b varies with time is possible but the exposition is simpler if attention is restricted to the case where b is constant over time.

3. We use this terminology in place of the widespread 'Stone-Geary utility function' used by Powell (1973) and which apparently derives from Brown and Heien (1972), who referred to the LES as the 'Stone-Geary linear expenditure system'. This attribution is simply not accurate and we do not wish to perpetuate it. The form (15) was first obtained by Samuelson (1948) upon integrating the LES demand functions first proposed by Klein and Rubin (1948) — who had shown that this system of demand functions was integrable. Samuelson's result was subsequently rediscovered — without reference to Samuelson — by Geary (1949), who expressed (15) in the shifted Cobb-Douglas form $\exp(u)$. Stone (1954) presented his work as an empirical implementation of the Klein-Rubin (1948) LES, and referred to Samuelson's (1948) result but not to Geary's (1949).

4. As was pointed out in footnote 2, we can still obtain closed-form solutions even if this assumption is dropped.

References

Allais, M.: 1953, 'Le comportement de l'homme devant le risque; critique des postulats et axiomes de l'école américaine', *Econometrica*, **21**, 503-546.

Anderson, G., and R. Blundell: 1985, 'Empirical Approaches to Dynamic Consumer Demand Behavior', Working Paper No. 85-23, Department of Economics, McMaster University, Hamilton, Ontario, Canada.

Anderson, G., and M. Browning: 1986, 'Allocating Expenditure: Demand Systems and the Consumption Function, an Integrated Approach', Working Paper No. 86--07, Department of Economics, McMaster University, Hamilton, Ontario, Canada.

Barten, A. P.: 1969, 'Maximum Likelihood Estimation of a Complete System of Demand Equations', *European Economic Review*, **1**, 7-73.

Ben-Tal, A., and A. Ben-Israel: 1987, 'A Recourse Certainty Equivalent for Decisions under Uncertainty', Department of Industrial Engineering, University of Michigan, Ann Arbor, Michigan, U.S.A.

Blackorby, C., R. Boyce, and R. R. Russell: 1978, 'Estimation of Demand Systems Generated by the Gorman Polar Form; A Generalization of the S-Branch Utility Tree,' *Econometrica*, **46**, 345-363.

Brown, M., and D. M. Heien: 1972, 'The S-branch Utility Tree: A Generalization of the Linear Expenditure System', *Econometrica*, **40**, 737-747.

Chipman, J. S.: 1985, 'Estimation of Net-Import Demand Functions for the Federal Republic of Germany, 1959-1982', in H. Giersch (ed.), *Probleme und Perspektiven der weltwirtschaftlichen Entwicklung*, Jahrestag des Vereins für Socialpolitik, Duncker & Humblot, Berlin, Germany, pp. 197-213.

Chipman, J. S. and G. Tian: 1988b, 'Generalized Maximum-Likelihood Estimation of the Linear Expenditure System', manuscript.

Chipman, J. S. and G. Tian: 1988c, 'A General-Equilibrium Intertemporal Model of An Open Economy', manuscript.

Chipman, J. S. and G. Tian: 1989, 'Stochastic Specification and Maximum-Likelihood Estimation of the Linear Expenditure System', in B. Raj (ed.), *Advances in Econometrics and Modelling*, Kluwer Academic Publishers, Dordrecht, the Netherlands, pp.131-142.

Christensen, L. R., D. W. Jorgenson, and L. J. Lau: 1975, 'Transcendental Logarithmic Utility Functions', *American Economic Review*, **65**, 367-383.

Epstein, Z., and K. I. Wolpin: 1988, 'Dynamic Labor Force Participation of Married Women and Endogenous Work Experience', typescript.

Deaton, A., and J. Muellbauer: 1980, 'An Almost Ideal Demand System', *American Economic Review*, **70**, 312-326.

Geary, R.C.: 1949, 'A Note on "A Constant-Utility Index of the Cost of Living"', *Review of Economic Studies*, **18**, 65-66.

Goldberger, A. S., and T. Gamaletsos: 1970, 'A Cross-Country Comparison of Consumer Expenditure Patterns', *European Economic Review*, **1**, 357-400.

Hall, R. E.: 1978, 'Stochastic Implications of the Life-Cycle Permanent-Income Hypotheses: Theory and Evidence', *Journal of Political Economy*, **86**, 971-987.

Hicks, J. R.: 1935, 'Wages and Interest: The Dynamic Problem', *Economic Journal*, **45**, 456-468.

Hicks, J. R.: 1939, *Value and Capital*, Clarendon Press, Oxford, England.

Houthakker, H. S.: 1960, 'Additive Preferences', *Econometrica*, **28**, 244-257.

Howe, H.: 1974, *Estimation of the Linear and Quadratic Expenditure Systems: A Cross-Section Case for Colombia*, Ph. D. dissertation, University of Pennsylvania, Philadelphia, Pennsylvania, U.S.A.

Howe, H.: 1975, 'Development of the Extended Linear Expenditure System from Simple Saving Assumptions', *European Economic Review*, **6**, 305-310.

Johansen, L.: 1969, 'On the Relationship between some Systems of Demand Functions', *Liiketaloudellinen Aikakauskirja*, **18**, 30-41.

Kahneman, D., and A. Tversky: 1979, 'Prospect Theory: An Analysis of Decision under Risk', *Econometrica*, **47**, 263-291.

Klein, L. R., and H. Rubin: 1948, 'A Constant-Utility Index of the Cost of Living', *Review of Economic Studies*, **15**, 84-87.

Lluch, C.: 1973, 'The Extended Linear Expenditure System', *European Economic Review*, **4**, 21-32.

Lluch, C.: 1974, 'Expenditure, Savings and Habit Formation', *International Economic Review*, **15**, 786-797.

Lluch, C., and M. Morishima: 1973, 'Demand for Commodities under Uncertain Expectation', in M. Morishima, et al., *Theory of Demand, Real and Monetary*, Clarendon Press, Oxford, England, pp. 169-183.

Lluch, C., A. A. Powell, and R. A. Williams: 1977, *Patterns in Household Demand and Saving*, Oxford University Press, New York, New York, U.S.A.

Lucas, R. E.: 1982, 'Interest Rates and Currency Prices in a Two-Country World', *Journal of Monetary Economics*, **10**, 335-359.

Machina, M. J.: 1982, '"Expected utility" Analysis without the Independence Axiom', *Econometrica*, **50**, 277-323.

MacKinnon, J. G.: 1976, 'Estimating the Linear Expenditure System and its Generalizations', in S. M. Goldfeld and R. E. Quandt (eds.), *Studies in Nonlinear Estimation*, Lippincott, Ballinger, Cambridge, Massachusetts, U.S.A., pp. 143-166.

MaCurdy, T. E.: 1983, 'A Simple Scheme for Estimating an Intertemporal Model of Labor Supply and Consumption in the Presence of Taxes and Uncertainty', *International Economic Review*, 24, 265-289.

Marschak, J.: 1950, 'Rational Behavior, Uncertain Prospects, and Measurable Utility', *Econometrica*, 18, 111-141.

Modigliani, F., and R. Brumberg: 1964, 'Utility Analysis and the Consumption Function: An Interpretation of Cross-Section Data', in *Post Keynesian Economics*, K. K. Kurihara (ed.), Rutgers University Press, New Brunswick, New Jersey, U.S.A., pp. 388-436.

Musgrove, P.: 1974, *Determination and Distribution of Permanent Household Income in Urban South America*, Ph. D. dissertation, Massachusetts Institute of Technology, Cambridge, Massachusetts, U.S.A.

Musgrove, P.: 1977, 'An Extended Linear Permanent Expenditure System (ELPES)', in A. S. Blinder and P. Friedman (eds.), *Natural Resources, Uncertainty, and General Equilibrium Systems, Essays in Memory of Rafael Lusky*, Academic Press, New York, New York, U.S.A., 241-255.

Neumann, J. von, and O. Morgenstern: 1947, *Theory of Games and Economic Behavior*, 2nd ed., Princeton University Press, Princeton, New Jersey, U.S.A.

Parks, R. W.: 1969, 'Systems of Demand Equations: An Empirical Comparison of Alternative Functional Forms', *Econometrica*, 37, 629-650.

Parks, R. W.: 1971, 'Maximum-Likelihood Estimation of the Linear Expenditure System', *Journal of the American Statistical Association*, 66, 900-903.

Pollak, R. A., and T. J. Wales: 1969, 'Estimation of the Linear Expenditure System', *Econometrica*, 37, 611-628.

Pollak, R. A.: 1970, 'Habit Formation and Dynamic Demand Functions', *Journal of Political Economy*, 78, 745-763.

Powell, A.: 1973, 'Estimation of Lluch's Extended Linear Expenditure System from Cross-Sectional Data', *Australian Journal of Statistics*, 15, 111-117.

Powell, A.: 1974, *Empirical Analytics of Demand Systems*, Heath, Lexington, Massachusetts, U.S.A.

Ronning, G.: 1983, 'A Note on Barten's Result Concerning the Estimation of Share Equations', Postfach 5560, Universität Konstanz, D-7750 Konstanz.

Ramsey, F. P.: 1928, 'A Mathematical Theory of Saving', *Economic Journal*, 38, 543-559.

Samuelson, P. A.: 1948, 'Some Implications of "Linearity"', *Review of Economic Studies*, 15, 88-90.

Samuelson, P. A.: 1953, 'Utilité, préference et probabilité, in *Econométrie*, Paris: Centre National de la Recherche Scientifique, Colloques Internationaux, XL, 141-150. English translation: 1966, 'Utility, Preference, and Probability', in J. E. Stiglitz (ed.), *The Collected Scientific Papers of P. A. Samuelson*, The MIT Press, Cambridge, Massachusetts, U.S.A., Vol. 1, 127-136.

Sargent, T. J.: 1979, *Macroeconomic Theory*, Academic Press, New York, New York, U.S.A.

Sargent, T. J.: 1987, *Dynamic Macroeconomic Theory*, Harvard University Press, Cambridge, Massachusetts, U.S.A.

Sato, K.: 1972, 'Additive Utility Functions with Double-Log Consumer Demand Functions', *Journal of Political Economy*, **80**, 102-124.

Simon, H. A.: 1956, 'Dynamic Programming under Uncertainty with a Quadratic Criterion Function', *Econometrica*, **24**, 74-81.

Stone, R.: 1954, 'Linear Expenditure Systems and Demand Analysis: An Application to the British Pattern of Demand', *Economic Journal*, **64**, 511-527.

Theil, H.: 1954, 'Econometric Models and Welfare Maximization', *Weltwirtschaftliches Archiv*, **72**, 60-83.

Theil, H.: 1957, 'A Note on Certainty Equivalence in Dynamic Programming', *Econometrica*, **25**, 346-349.

Theil, H.: 1965, 'The Information Approach to Demand Analysis', *Econometrica*, **33**, 67-87.

Theil, H.: 1986, *Theory and Measurement of Consumer Demand*, Vols. 1 and 2, North-Holland, Amsterdam, Holland.

Tintner, G.: 1938a, 'The Maximization of Utility over Time', *Econometrica*, **6**, 154-158.

Tintner, G.: 1938b, 'The Theoretical Derivation of Dynamic Demand Curves', *Econometrica*, **6**, 375-380.

Wales, T.: 1971, 'A Generalized Linear Expenditure Model of the Demand for Nondurable Goods in Canada', *Canadian Journal of Economics*, **4**, 471-484.

Wales, T. J. and A. D. Woodland: 1983, 'Estimation of Consumer Demand System with Binding Non-Negativity Constraints', *Journal of Econometrics*, **21**, 263-285.

Wold, H. O. A.: 1952, 'Ordinal Preference or Cardinal Utility?', *Econometrica*, **20**, 661-664.

Woodland, A. D.: 1979, 'Stochastic Specification and the Estimation of Share Equations', *Journal of Econometrics*, **10**, 361-383.

Yaari, M. E.: 1987, 'The Dual Theory of Choice under Risk', *Econometrica*, **55**, 95-115.

CHAPTER 7

A REINTERPRETATION OF THE ALMOST IDEAL DEMAND SYSTEM

CHRISTOPHER J. NICOL*
University of Regina
Department of Economics
Regina, Saskatchewan
Canada
S4S 0A2

ABSTRACT. In this paper, some implicit restrictions in the 'Almost Ideal Demand System' (AIDS) of Deaton and Muellbauer (1980) are pointed out. Relaxing these restrictions allows the AIDS to be interpreted as a third-order translog subject to exact aggregation. These implicit restrictions in the AIDS are tested, using Canadian cross-sectional micro-data on samples of homogeneous households. The restrictions are not rejected. Also, homogeneity and symmetry restrictions, conditional on either model, are generally supported. Some rejections do, however, occur in the context of the third-order translog model.

1. Introduction

The 'Almost Ideal Demand System' (AIDS) of Deaton and Muellbauer (1980) is the basis of many applied studies of consumer behavior which use either aggregate time-series data or cross-sectional micro-data. (See, for example, Ray, 1980, 1982, 1986; Blanciforti and Green, 1983; Anderson and Blundell, 1982, 1983). The AIDS is attractive since it can be interpreted as an arbitrary first-order approximation to the unknown demand system. It also satisfies requirements for exact aggregation and it is easier to estimate than the translog of Christensen, Jorgenson and Lau (1975), the most widely used flexible functional form.

In this paper, implicit restrictions embodied in the AIDS are pointed out. It is shown that the AIDS can be interpreted as a third-order translog embodying exact aggregation if these implicit restrictions are relaxed. Empirical results based on Canadian cross-sectional micro-data for households with homogeneous demographic characteristics are also presented. These results indicate that the implicit restrictions in the AIDS are not rejected.

Tests are also conducted of homogeneity and symmetry restrictions, conditional on the AIDS and on the above third-order translog. Most of these tests do not reject the homogeneity and symmetry hypotheses. This last finding is very interesting since so many studies (usually employing aggregate time-series data) have rejected these restrictions. (See, for example, Christensen, Jorgenson and Lau, 1975; Deaton and Muellbauer, 1980). Some subsequent residual diagnostic tests, however, suggested the possibility of heteroskedastic residuals.

A revision of the hypotheses tests, robust to heteroskedasticity, resulted in no change to the previous results. That is, there was continued support for the implicit restrictions and homogeneity plus symmetry conditional on the AIDS. However, the homogeneity plus symmetry restrictions were rejected conditional on the third-order translog. This seems to indicate some source of specification error other than heteroskedasticity was responsible for these anomalous results. Possible sources of specification error are the imposition of exact aggregation in the models considered here, and errors in the price variables used. These are potential areas for future research using the type of data employed in this study.

In Section 2, the AIDS is briefly reviewed, and the implicit restrictions embodied in it are derived. Homogeneity and symmetry restrictions are also reviewed. Section 3 describes the data used in the empirical part of this study. Results of estimation and hypotheses testing are presented in Section 4. Finally, Section 5 provides a brief summary and concluding comments.

2. Implicit Restrictions in the AIDS

The expenditure function underlying the AIDS for household h is

$$\ln E(p,U_h) = \alpha_0 + \ln p\alpha + \tfrac{1}{2}\ln pB\ln p^T + U_h\gamma_0 \prod_{n=1}^{N} p_n^{\gamma_n}, \ \forall h = 1,...,H$$

where $E(p,U_h)$ is the minimum expenditure required to attain a utility level of U_h at $p \equiv (p_1,...,p_N)$, the vector of N prices; $\ln p \equiv (\ln p_1,\ldots, \ln p_N)$; α_0, γ_0 and γ_n are unknown scalar parameters; and $\alpha^T = (\alpha_1,\ldots,\alpha_N), B = \{\beta_{ij}^*\}$ are a vector and matrix respectively of unknown parameters. Partially differentiating $\ln E(p,U_h)$ with respect to $\ln p_n$ gives $w_{nh}(p,U_h) = p_n q_n(p,U_h)/y_h$, the Hicksian budget-share of household h for the n'th good. However, assuming utility maximization by h, total expenditure (y_h) is equal to $E(p,U_h)$. U_h can therefore be solved for as a function of p and y_h. Substituting $U(p,y_h)$ in $w_{nh}(p,U_h)$ therefore yields the Marshallian budget-shares, $w_{nh}(p,y_h)$, that is

$$w_{nh} = \alpha_n + \ln p\beta_n + \gamma_n\ln (y_h/P), \ \forall n, h \tag{1}$$

The price index, P, is defined as $\ln P = \alpha_0 + \ln p\alpha + 1/2\ln pB\ln p^T$, whilst $\beta_n^T = (\beta_{1n},\ldots, \beta_{Nn})$ and $\beta_{jn} = 1/2(\beta_{jn}^* + \beta_{nj}^*)$, for all $n \neq j$. To satisfy adding up conditions, $\sum_n \beta_n = 0$, and $\iota^T\alpha = \iota^T\gamma = 0$, where ι^T is a unit vector of appropriate dimension and γ is a vector containing the elements, γ_n. Homogeneity requires that $\iota^T\beta_n = 0$, and symmetry that $\beta_{nj} = \beta_{jn}$, $n \neq j$.

Although the adding-up conditions are not empirically testable, the homogeneity and symmetry restrictions are. Furthermore, substituting for $\ln P$ in (1) yields

$$w_{nh} = (\alpha_n - \gamma_n\alpha_0) + \ln p(\beta_n - \gamma_n\alpha) + \gamma_n\ln y_h - \tfrac{1}{2}\ln p\gamma_n B\ln p^T, \ \forall n, h \tag{2}$$

This system is equivalent to

$$w_{nh} = \tilde{\alpha}_n + \ln p\tilde{\beta}_n + \gamma_n\ln y_h + \ln pC_n\ln p^T, \ \forall n, h \tag{3}$$

if the following over-identifying restrictions are imposed

$$\tilde{\alpha}_n = (\alpha_n - \gamma_n\alpha_0); \ \tilde{\beta}_n = (\beta_n - \gamma_n\alpha); \ C_n = -\tfrac{1}{2}\gamma_n B, \forall n \tag{4}$$

Equations (2) to (4) above suggest an alternative way to estimate the AIDS. First, since each equation in (3) is linear in identical regressors, this system can be estimated by single-equation ordinary least squares (after first specifying the stochastic structure of the system). Then, using (4), starting values of the underlying AIDS parameters can be recovered for nonlinear estimation of (2) as a system. This approach, however, highlights the fact that the over-identifying restrictions in (4) need not hold empirically and are testable. In effect, (4) is therefore a set of implicit restrictions embodied in the AIDS.

Equation (3) implies there could be a relationship between the AIDS and the third-order translog, since the former included quadratic terms in prices, as does the latter. To understand this relationship, recall the translog indirect utility function of Christensen, Jorgenson and Lau (1975), $\ln V_h = \Psi(\ln \bar p_1,\dots,\bar p_N) = \Psi(\ln(p_1/y_h),\dots,\ln(p_N/y_h))$. A third-order Taylor-series approximation to this indirect utility function yields

$$\ln V_h = \Psi^0 + \sum_{i=1}^{N}\Psi_i \ln \bar p_i + \tfrac{1}{2}\sum_{i=1}^{N}\sum_{j=1}^{N}\Psi_{ij}\ln \bar p_i \ln \bar p_j + \frac{1}{6}\sum_{i=1}^{N}\sum_{j=1}^{N}\sum_{m=1}^{N}\Psi_{ijm}\ln \bar p_i \ln \bar p_j \ln \bar p_m, \ \forall h = 1,\dots,H$$

where Ψ^0, Ψ_i, Ψ_{ij} and Ψ_{ijm} indicate evaluation of Ψ, its first, second and third derivatives at the point of expansion, $(p^0, y_h^0) = \iota^T$. A logarithmic form of Roy's identity yields the n'th budget-share equation for household h

$$w_{nh} = \frac{\Psi_n + \sum_{j=1}^{N}\Psi_{nj}\ln \bar p_j + \tfrac{1}{2}\sum_{j=1}^{N}\sum_{m=1}^{N}\Psi_{njm}\ln \bar p_j \ln \bar p_m}{\sum_{i=1}^{N}\{\Psi_i + \sum_{j=1}^{N}\Psi_{ij}\ln \bar p_j + \tfrac{1}{2}\sum_{j=1}^{N}\sum_{m=1}^{N}\Psi_{ijm}\ln \bar p_j \ln \bar p_m\}} \quad \forall n, h \tag{5}$$

Simmons and Weiserbs (1979) and Deaton (1986) point out that normalizing prices by y_h imposes homogeneity. This criticism also applies to (5). Relaxing homogeneity yields a homogeneity-unconstrained third-order translog, written more compactly in matrix form as

$$w_n = \frac{\alpha_n + B_n \ln p^T + \gamma_n \ln y + L_n \ln p^T \ln y + \ln p C_n \ln p^T + \mu_n (\ln y)^2}{\iota^T(\alpha + B\ln p^T + \gamma \ln y + L\ln p^T \ln y + \mu(\ln y)^2) + \sum_m \ln p\, C_m \ln p^T} \quad \forall n \tag{6}$$

with appropriate redefinition of parameters and omission of the household subscript, h, for convenience. Homogeneity of (6) would thus require that

$$\iota^T B_n = -\gamma_n;\ L_n = -2\iota^T C_n;\ \iota^T C_n \iota = \mu_n, \ \forall n$$

Symmetry, on the other hand, would require

$$B_{nj} = B_{jn}, \ \forall n \neq j \text{ and}$$
$$C_{njm} = C_{nmj} = C_{jnm} = C_{jmn} = C_{mnj} = C_{mjn}, \ \forall n \neq j \neq m$$

The relationship between the third-order translog and the AIDS can be seen when imposing exact aggregation on (6) in the form of the following restrictions

$$\iota^T \alpha = 1;\ \iota^T B = 0;\ \iota^T \gamma = 0;\ \iota^T L = 0;\ \sum_m C_m = 0;\ \iota^T \mu = 0 \tag{7}$$

The system in (6) then reduces to one which is linear in identical regressors across equations with a similar structure to (3), that is

$$w_n = \alpha_n + B_n \ln p^T + \gamma_n \ln y + L_n \ln p^T \ln y + \ln p C_n \ln p^T + \mu_n (\ln y)^2, \ \forall n \tag{8}$$

Equation (8) is observationally equivalent to (3) if the restrictions

$$L_n = 0;\ \mu_n = 0, \ \forall n \tag{9}$$

are imposed. With appropriate redefinition of parameters, the combined restrictions in (4) and (9) can be interpreted as nesting the AIDS within the third-order translog (under exact aggregation). It is therefore of interest to determine whether the restrictions in (4) and (9) are empirically supported. If they are, the immediate advantage of the AIDS is that it is more parsimonious than the third-order translog, although relatively more difficult to estimate, since the former is nonlinear in parameters.

Before proceeding, an additional point of concern should be mentioned. Exact aggregation restrictions are embodied in both the AIDS and in the third-order translog, (8), which the former will be tested against. Violation of exact aggregation could influence the outcome of hypotheses tests. One way to reduce the importance of these restrictions empirically is to condition household observations on a common set of demographic characteristics. If households are homogeneous, it is reasonable to impose exact aggregation, especially since recent evidence (Browning, 1987 and Nicol, 1988a) indicates these restrictions might not hold for heterogeneous groups of households. The approach followed in the empirical part of this paper will therefore employ households with homogeneous demographic characteristics.

3. Data

The household expenditure observations for this study were extracted from the Canadian Survey of Family Expenditures Microdata Files (Family Expenditure Survey Section, Statistics Canada). These microdata files record expenditures on many commodities by cross-sections of households in Canada, for the years 1978, 1982 and 1984. Detailed information on households' demographic characteristics are also recorded, including family size, ages of family members, region of residence, and employment status of family members, for example.

As indicated previously, it is important that the households included in the data sets studied be fairly homogeneous. The empirical importance of exact aggregation restrictions is then minimized. Probably the most important demographic characteristics influencing household behavior are family size and the ages of members. Observations were therefore extracted from the main data bases in each year for only two 'types' of households, conditioned on sets of demographic characteristics. The first household type, (1), included only married couples having both adult members under the age of sixty-five, living in Canadian cities of over 100000 persons, and having up to two children under the age of nineteen. In addition, the head of household was restricted to ages twenty-five to thirty. The second family type, (2), was identical to the first, except that the age of head was restricted to ages thirty to thirty-five. Table I reports the number of households of both types extracted from each of the microdata files. Households within either (1) or (2) were thus fairly narrowly defined. Many family types were implicitly excluded, for example, single-parent families, families with retired members and rurally located families.

TABLE I. Observations in Data Sets 1 and 2

Data Set No.	1978 Cross-Section	1982 Cross-Section	1984 Cross-Section	Total
1	296	301	183	780
2	367	411	269	1047

Having selected those households which make up data sets (1) and (2), the next step was to define appropriate expenditure categories. These were food, tobacco and alcoholic beverages. This choice allowed the available price data to be matched as closely as possible to the corresponding expenditures. Other expenditure categories in these data sets tend to be more highly aggregated, or do not correspond to the published price data. In addition, problems associated with durable goods were avoided by excluding such expenditure items.

A potential problem involves expenditures on tobacco and alcoholic beverages. Many households could include non-smokers and/or non-drinkers. As a result, changes in prices or income would not elicit any response in the consumption of tobacco and/or alcohol. To avoid this difficulty, only households with positive expenditures on all three categories were included. This reduced the number of households of each type, for each year, as reported in Table II. However, notwithstanding this censoring, the data sets (*1A*) and (*2A*) are still large.

TABLE II. Observations in Data Sets *1A* and *2A*

Data Set No.	1978 Cross-Section	1982 Cross-Section	1984 Cross-Section	Total
1A	196	174	118	488
2A	235	251	160	646

The next requirement was to match households in (*1A*) and (*2A*) to their price vectors. Inter-city indices of retail price differentials are published for these expenditure categories in *Consumer Prices and Price Indexes* (Statistics Canada, Ottawa). To preserve anonymity of respondents, public-use data from the Family Expenditure Survey Microdata Files include only 'region of residence' information on households. These regions of residence are: Atlantic Provinces (New Brunswick, Newfoundland, Nova Scotia and Prince Edward Island); Quebec; Ontario; Prairie Provinces (Alberta, Manitoba and Saskatchewan); and British Columbia. Using the inter-city indices in 1978, 1982 and 1984, regional price indices were constructed for each expenditure category. The degree of inter-regional and inter-temporal price variability is reported in Appendix A. The price vectors for each year and expenditure category exhibit sufficient variability to identify all price parameters in the models estimated. The price vectors of Appendix A were then matched to the corresponding households in data sets (*1A*) and (*2A*). This completed the construction of the data sets used for estimation and testing purposes.

4. Estimation and Results

To estimate (2) or (8), a stochastic component, ε_n, is added to each equation. This captures random errors in households' utility maximizing plans and heterogeneity across agents. Since $\sum_n w_n = 1$, $\sum_n \varepsilon_n = 0$. It is therefore assumed that $\varepsilon = (\varepsilon_1,..,\varepsilon_N)^T \sim N(0,\Omega)$, and *rank* $(\Omega) = N - 1$.

Estimation of (8), the unrestricted system, is fairly straightforward, since the equations in it are linear in identical regressors. Consequently, single-equation ordinary least squares is fully efficient (Zellner, 1962) and, given the assumed stochastic structure above, equivalent to maximum likelihood estimation of the (nonsingular) system of $N - 1 = 2$ equations.

Each equation in (8), given three expenditure categories, contains fifteen parameters. The restrictions in (7) act as adding-up conditions for (8). As a result, parameters of $N - 1 = 2$ equations can be estimated and the parameters of the third recovered via (7). There are therefore thirty estimable parameters in (8).

Since the hypotheses to be tested involve complete systems, system-wide test statistics are required. The most convenient test statistic to construct is the likelihood ratio. To compute this, the residuals from two equations estimated by single-equation ordinary least squares can be used to determine $\ln L(\hat{\theta})$, the maximized value of the unrestricted log-likelihood function of (8). This value is invariant to the equation dropped in order to form the nonsingular two equation system (Barten, 1969).

Consideration is first given to a test of the restrictions which nest the AIDS, (2), within the third-order translog, (8). The AIDS is nonlinear in parameters and contains across-equation restrictions. To simplify estimation of (2), Deaton and Muellbauer (1980) suggest the approximation, $\ln P = \sum_n \bar{w}_n \ln p_n$, where $\bar{w}_n$ are sample mean budget-shares. This approximation makes the equations in (2) linear in identical regressors and reduces the number of parameters to be estimated from eleven to ten. Conditional on this approximation, each equation can be estimated by single-equation ordinary least squares. The restricted log-likelihood, $\ln L(\tilde{\theta})$, can then be computed using residuals from two equations. Although the approximation contains one less parameter than (2), there is not a statistically significant reduction in $\ln L(\tilde{\theta})$. (A similar finding was obtained by Deaton and Muellbauer, 1980, employing this approximation). Specifically, for data set $(1A)$, $\ln L(\tilde{\theta})$ falls from 1022.400 to 1022.352 and for data set $(2A)$, from 1377.570 to 1377.218 when using this approximation.

In testing the various hypotheses considered in this paper, three sequences of dependent tests are conducted, two tests in each sequence. It is therefore necessary to 'allocate' significance levels to each test in a sequence. The sum of significance levels in any sequence of dependent tests will then give an upper bound on the overall significance level of the two tests together (Savin, 1980).

The data sets used in this study are large compared to those typically employed in applied demand research. Consequently, a lower than usual significance level should be assigned to each hypothesis test. The significance level chosen for dependent tests in any sequence is 0.001 each, so the overall significance level for any given sequence will be no more than 0.002. This is a conservative significance level, to control for Type I error. It could be argued that this increases the probability of Type II error, since the tests conducted will be composed of numerous restrictions, and χ^2 statistics often have low power in such situations. However, in other studies using data sets of this type and size, Nicol (1988a, 1988b) obtains strong rejections of hypotheses under similar test conditions.

As mentioned, three sequences of hypothesis tests are to be conducted. In the first sequence, significance levels of 0.001 are allocated to tests of the system in Equation (3) versus the third-order translog, followed by a test of the AIDS (with $\ln P = \sum_n \bar{w} \ln p_n$) versus (3). In this way, the implicit restrictions embodied in the AIDS are explicitly tested via the second test in this sequence. The results of this sequence of tests are presented in Table III. When tested against the third-order translog, the system in Equation (3) is not rejected by either data set $(1A)$ or $(2A)$ at a significance level of 0.001. A subsequent test of the AIDS versus (3) yields the same result. Given the data used in this study, the implicit restrictions embodied in the AIDS are not therefore rejected.

In the second sequence of tests, significance levels of 0.001 are assigned to tests of the AIDS versus the third-order translog, and to a test of homogeneity and symmetry of the AIDS. Results of this sequence of tests are presented in Table IV. The AIDS is not rejected for either data set $(1A)$ or $(2A)$, nor is homogeneity plus symmetry, conditional on the AIDS. These results are extremely positive for the AIDS. They imply that the homogeneity-and-symmetry-constrained AIDS is not rejected (when the third-order translog is the maintained hypothesis) at a significance level of no more than 0.002.

The final sequence of hypotheses tests is of homogeneity and of homogeneity plus symmetry, conditional on the third-order translog. Allocating significance levels of 0.001 to homogeneity and symmetry respectively gives an overall significance level again of no more than 0.002 for the combined set of restrictions. Results of this sequence of tests are presented in Table V. The findings here are somewhat mixed. Homogeneity is rejected for (*1A*), but not for (*2A*), at a significance level of 0.001. On the other hand, symmetry is not rejected for either data set at the same significance level. Finally, the joint test of homogeneity and symmetry does not reject the restrictions for (*1A*) but does for (*2A*) at a significance level of 0.002.

TABLE III. Tests of (3) versus the Third-Order Translog and of the AIDS versus (3)

Data Set No.	Third-Order $\ln L(\hat{\theta})$	System (3) $\ln L(\tilde{\theta})$	Test Statistic	Degrees of Freedom	Prob. Value
1A	1039.377	1032.346	14.062	8	0.0802
2A	1396.375	1386.838	19.074	8	0.0145

Data Set No.	System (3) $\ln L(\hat{\theta})$	AIDS $\ln L(\tilde{\theta})$	Test Statistic	Degrees of Freedom	Prob. Value
1A	1032.346	1022.352	19.988	12	0.0673
2A	1386.838	1377.218	19.240	12	0.0829

Note: The test statistic is $-2(\ln L(\tilde{\theta}) - \ln L(\hat{\theta})) \overset{\Delta}{\sim} \chi^2(q)$. Here, $\ln L(\tilde{\theta})$ and $\ln L(\hat{\theta})$ are estimates of the log-liklihood under the null and alternative hypotheses respectively. The degrees of freedom, q, of the tests are the number of restrictions imposed in each case. Critical values of the test statistic at a significance level of 0.001 for 8 and 12 degrees of freedom are 26.13 and 32.91 respectively.

TABLE IV. Tests of the AIDS versus the Third-Order Translog and of Homogeneity Plus Symmetry Conditional on the AIDS

Data Set No.	Third-Order $\ln L(\hat{\theta})$	AIDS $\ln L(\tilde{\theta})$	Test Statistic	Degrees of Freedom	Prob. Value
1A	1039.377	1022.352	34.050	20	0.0257
2A	1396.375	1377.218	38.314	20	0.0081

Data Set No.	AIDS $\ln L(\hat{\theta})$	Homogeneity and Symmety $\ln L(\tilde{\theta})$	Test Statistic	Degrees of Freedom	Prob. Value
1A	1022.352	1015.829	13.046	3	0.0045
2A	1377.218	1370.053	14.330	3	0.0025

Note: The test statistic is $-2(\ln L(\tilde{\theta}) - \ln L(\hat{\theta})) \overset{\Delta}{\sim} \chi^2(q)$. Here, $\ln L(\tilde{\theta})$ and $\ln L(\hat{\theta})$ are estimates of the log-liklihood under the null and alternative hypotheses respectively. The degrees of freedom, q, of the tests are the number of restrictions imposed in each case. Critical values of the test statistic at a significance level of 0.001 for 20 and 3 degrees of freedom are 45.3 and 16.3 respectively.

On balance, the foregoing results are encouraging for the AIDS and for the homogeneity and symmetry propositions, especially since the latter are often rejected by other researchers using different data (see, for example, Christensen, Jorgenson and Lau, 1975 and Deaton and Muellbauer, 1980). Although no rejections occur for the hypotheses tested with regard to the AIDS, some rejections do arise in the framework of the more general third-order translog model. As there are two rejections in the latter case, this suggests rejection is not purely by chance. The non-rejections in the case of the AIDS could therefore imply lack of power of those tests against some other alternative for which the final sequence of tests has relatively more power.

One reason for the apparently anomalous results is that, since the tests in Tables III-V are not robust to violations of homoskedasticity, the presence of heteroskedastic errors could have influenced their outcome. The data used in this study are from cross-sections, so heteroskedastic errors are a possibility. Indeed, when analyzing the single-equation residuals of the estimated AIDS for both data sets, some evidence of heteroskedasticity is revealed in one equation of both (*1A*) and (*2A*), using White's (1980) test for heterodskedasticity. Details of these tests for heteroskedasticity are available from the author on request.

TABLE V. Tests of Homogeneity, Symmetry and Homogeneity plus Symmetry, Conditional on the Third-Order Translog

Data Set No.	Third-Order $\ln L(\hat{\theta})$	Homogeneity $\ln L(\tilde{\theta})$	Test Statistic	Degrees of Freedom	Prob. Value
1A	1039.377	1023.811	31.132	10	0.0006
2A	1396.375	1382.759	27.232	10	0.0024

Data Set No.	Third-Order $\ln L(\hat{\theta})$	Symmetry $\ln L(\tilde{\theta})$	Test Statistic	Degrees of Freedom	Prob. Value
1A	1039.377	1028.157	22.440	13	0.0489
2A	1396.375	1385.827	21.096	13	0.0711

Data Set No.	Third-Order $\ln L(\hat{\theta})$	Homogeneity and Symmetry $\ln L(\tilde{\theta})$	Test Statistic	Degrees of Freedom	Prob. Value
1A	1039.377	1018.790	41.174	20	0.0035
2A	1396.375	1372.696	47.358	20	0.0005

Note: Critical values of the test statistic at a significance level of 0.001 for 10 and 13 degrees of freedom are 29.60 and 34.50 respectively. The critical value of the test statistic at a significance level of 0.002 with 20 degrees of freedom is 43.05.

An obvious form of heteroskedasticity which might be present, given the type of data used in this study, is $\sigma_{nh}^2 = \sigma_n^2 (\ln y_h / P)^2$. A standard test for detection of this form of heteroskedasticity is due to Goldfeld and Quandt (1965). Statistically significant evidence of heteroskedasticity was again detected for both data sets. Full details of these tests are available on request.

The foregoing results suggest that the presence of heteroskedastic errors should be allowed for in the sequences of hypothesis tests reported in Tables III-V. This can be achieved by either conducting hypothesis tests which are robust to heteroskedasticity of unknown form, or which are conditional on some prior adjustment for a specific form of heteroskedastic errors. Both approaches are applied in turn to the sequences of tests considered in this paper.

In a recent paper, Davidson and MacKinnon (1985) suggest a test procedure which can be applied when exclusion restrictions on a subset of coefficients are being tested in the presence of heteroskedasticity of unknown form. Their procedure can therefore be applied directly to a test of the AIDS versus the third-order translog. Results of these tests (on single equations) indicated that the implicit restrictions nesting the AIDS within the third-order translog are not rejected by either data set (1A) or (2A), at significance levels of 0.001. These results are available from the author on request.

An alternative approach is to permit the errors to follow a specific form of heteroskedasticity, such as $\sigma_{nh}^2 = \sigma_n^2 (\ln y_h / P)^2$. System-wide tests of the AIDS versus the third-order translog and of homogeneity and symmetry conditional on either model can then be conducted, having first transformed the model to allow for the stated heteroskedastic error structure. Results of these tests are available from the author on request. Again, the implicit restrictions embodied in the AIDS were not rejected, nor was homogeneity plus symmetry, conditional on the AIDS. However, homogeneity plus symmetry was rejected for both data sets, conditional on the third-order translog, at a significance level of 0.002. This suggests that heteroskedasticity is not necessarily the source of these anomalous rejections.

It will be recalled that exact aggregation is imposed in the models estimated in this paper, given Equation (7). Also, regional price data were constructed and matched to households, introducing some errors in variables. These two factors could be influencing the outcome of hypotheses tests, and indicate directions for future research.

5. Summary and Conclusions

In this paper, some implicit restrictions embodied in the AIDS of Deaton and Muellbauer (1980) were identified. These restrictions could be interpreted as nesting the AIDS in a third-order translog, conditional on exact aggregation.

An empirical analysis of the above restrictions in the AIDS was also conducted. This analysis utilized Canadian cross-sectional micro-data from three Family Expenditure Surveys. Two data sets containing households with homogeneous demographic characteristics were drawn from the Family Expenditure Survey data bases.

Results of the empirical analysis indicated that the implicit restrictions could not be rejected, implying that the AIDS is an adequate approximation, given the data sets used.

Subsequent tests of homogeneity and symmetry, conditional on the AIDS and the third-order translog were also conducted. These restrictions were generally supported by the data, although some rejections were observed in the context of the more general third-order translog model.

Given that cross-sectional data were being used, the anomalous test results of homogeneity and symmetry prompted some diagnostic tests of residuals for heteroskedasticity. These tests indicated that heteroskedasticity might be present. In some further analysis, it was found that the implicit restrictions embodied in the AIDS could still not be rejected, even when tests were robust to an unknown form of heteroskedasticity. Conditioning estimation and testing on an explicit form of heteroskedasticity suggested by the type of data used resulted in non-rejection of the implicit AIDS restrictions and of homogeneity plus symmetry, conditional on the AIDS. However, rejections of homogeneity plus symmetry continued to be observed, conditional on the third-order translog,

The results of this paper therefore indicate that while the AIDS appears initially to be an adequate representation of consumer demands, further specification analysis reveals some shortcomings. In the current study, perhaps the most apparent sources of misspecification lie in the imposition of exact aggregation as a maintained hypothesis, and errors in the price variables. These represent possible areas where future research might yield interesting results.

* The author acknowledges financial support from the University of Regina President's Research Fund and the Government of Canada "Challenge '87 Summer Employment Programme", which met some of the costs of data purchase and research assistance respectively. David L. Beattie, Lorraine A. Nicol and an anonymous referee provided helpful comments on an earlier version of this paper. Binyam Solomon provided capable research assistance. Any errors are the responsibility of the author.

This analysis is based on the Statistics Canada Surveys of Family Expenditures Public Use Microdata Files which contain anonymized data collected in the 1978, 1982 and 1984 Family Expenditure Surveys. All computations in this paper on these microdata were prepared by the author. Responsibility for this use and interpretation of these data is entirely that of the author.

Appendix A

TABLE A1. Aggregate Price Indices for Five Regions in Canada

1978 Prices:

Geographic Region	Food	Tobacco Products	Alcoholic Beverages
Atlantic Provinces	108.1	100.3	108.5
Quebec	98.0	103.0	103.0
Ontario	98.0	101.3	97.2
Prairie Provinces	104.2	91.2	98.4
British Columbia	108.0	99.0	101.0

1982 Prices:

Geographic Region	Food	Tobacco Products	Alcoholic Beverages
Atlantic Provinces	152.4	161.5	172.3
Quebec	151.1	157.7	171.5
Ontario	150.4	155.2	155.8
Prairie Provinces	150.9	129.2	162.2
British Columbia	158.6	150.0	160.3

1984 Prices:

Geographic Region	Food	Tobacco Products	Alcoholic Beverages
Atlantic Provinces	157.6	213.8	197.1
Quebec	156.8	190.1	188.6
Ontario	166.1	208.2	180.6
Prairie Provinces	161.0	184.2	182.3
British Columbia	172.9	196.0	190.4

Notes to Appendix A

1. The Source data from which the 1978 aggregates are constructed are contained in *Consumer Prices and Price Indexes*, Statistics Canada Catalogue No. 62-010: Volume 4, No. 4, Table 12; Volume 5, No. 1,Table 9; Volume 7, No. 4, Tables 7 & 9; Volume 9, No. 1, Table 21; and Volume 9, No. 4, Table 11. Some data from *Prices and Price Indexes*, Statistics Catalogue No. 62-002, Volume 52, No. 6, Table 14 were also used.

2. The Source data from which the 1982 aggregates are constructed are contained in *Consumer Prices and Price Indexes*, Statistics Canada Catalogue No. 62-010: Volume 5, No. 4, Table 8; Volume 7, No. 4, Table 9; Volume 8, No. 4, Tables 8 & 10; Volume 9, No. 1, Table 21; Volume 9, No. 4, Tables 9 & 11. Some data from *Prices and Price Indexes*, Statistics Catalogue No. 62-002, Volume 52, No. 6, Table 14 were also used.

3. The Source data from which the 1984 aggregates are constructed are contained in *Consumer Prices and Price Indexes*, Statistics Canada Catalogue No. 62-010: Volume 5, No. 4, Table 8; Volume 7, No. 4, Table 9; Volume 8, No. 4, Tables 8 & 10; Volume 11, No. 1, Table 24; Volume 11, No. 4, Tables 10 & 12. Some data from *Prices and Price Indexes*, Statisics Canada Catalogue No. 62-002, Volume 52, No. 6, Table 14 were also used.

4. Details of the computations required to generate the data in the above Table are available from the author on request.

5. All of the indices in the Table have bases of the respective 1978 Canada combined city average price index for the goods concerned.

References

Anderson, G. J., and R. W. Blundell: 1982, 'Estimation and Hypothesis Testing in Dynamic, Singular Equation Systems', *Econometrica*, **50**, 1559-1572.

Anderson, G. J., and R. W. Blundell: 1983, 'Testing Restrictions in a Flexible Dynamic Demand System: An Application to Consumers' Expenditure in Canada', *Review of Economic Studies*, **50**, 397-410.

Barten, A. P.: 1969, 'Maximum Likelihood Estimation of a Complete System of Demand Equations', *European Economic Review*, **1**, 7-73.

Blanciforti, L., and R. Green: 1983, 'An Almost Ideal Demand System Incorporating Habits: An Analysis of Expenditures on Food and Aggregate Commodity Groups', *Review of Economics and Statistics'*, **65**, 511-515.

Browning, M.: 1987, 'Individual Heterogeneity and Perfect Aggregation: A Study of the Canadian Microdata, 1969-1982', Department of Economics Working Paper No. 87-07, McMaster University, Hamilton, Ontario, Canada.

Christensen, L. R., D. W. Jorgenson, and L. J. Lau: 1975, 'Transcendental Logarithmic Utility Functions', *American Economic Review*, **65**, 367-383.

'*Consumer Prices and Price Indexes'*, Catalogue No. 62-010, Prices Division, Statistics Canada, Ottawa, Canada.

Davidson, R., and J. MacKinnon: 1985, 'Heteroskedasticity-Robust Tests in Regression Directions', *Annales de l'Insee*, **59/60**, 183-218.

Deaton, A.: 1986, 'Demand Analysis', in Z. Griliches and M. D. Intriligator (eds.), *Handbook of Econometrics*, Vol. 3, Ch.30, North Holland, Amsterdam, Holland.

Deaton, A. and J. Muellbauer: 1980, 'An Almost Ideal Demand System', *American Economic Review*, **70**, 312-326.

Goldfeld, S. M., and R. E. Quandt: 1965, 'Some Tests for Homoskedasticity', *Journal of the American Statistical Association*, **60**, 539-547.

Nicol, C. J.: 1988a, 'Testing a Theory of Exact Aggregation', *Journal of Business and Economic Statistics*, forthcoming.

Nicol, C. J.: 1988b, 'An Alternative Model of Aggregate Consumer Behaviour', Working Paper No.23, Department of Economics, University of Regina, Regina, Saskatchewan, Canada.

Prices and Price Indexes, Catalogue No. 62-002, Prices Division, Statistics Canada, Ottawa, Canada.

Ray, R.: 1980, 'Analysis of a Time Series of Household Expenditure Surveys for India', *Review of Economics and Statistics*, **62**, 595-602.

Ray, R.: 1982, 'The Testing and Estimation of Complete Demand Systems on Household Budget Data: An Application of the Almost Ideal Demand System', *European Economic Review*, **17**, 349-369.

Ray, R.: 1986, 'Demographic Variables and Equivalence Scales in a Flexible Demand System: The Case of AIDS', *Applied Economics*, **18**, 265-278.

Savin, N. E.: 1980, 'The Bonferroni and the Scheffé Multiple Comparison Procedures', *Review of Economic Studies*, **47**, 255-73.

Simmons, P., and D. Weiserbs: 1979, 'Translog Flexible Functional Forms and Associated Demand Systems', *American Economic Review*, **69**, 892-901.

Survey of Family Expenditures Micro Data Files (1978, 1982, 1984), Family Expenditure Surveys Section, Statistics Canada, Ottawa, Ontario, Canada.

White, H.: 1980, 'A Heteroskedasticity-Consistent Covariance Matrix Estimator and a Direct Test for Heteroskedasticity', *Econometrica*, **48**, 817-838.

Zellner, A.: 1962, 'An Efficient Method of Estimating Seemingly Unrelated Regresstions and Tests of Aggregation Bias', *Journal of the American Statistical Association*, **57**, 348-368.

CHAPTER 8

STOCHASTIC SPECIFICATION AND MAXIMUM-LIKELIHOOD ESTIMATION OF THE LINEAR EXPENDITURE SYSTEM*

JOHN S. CHIPMAN
University of Minnesota
Department of Economics
Minneapolis, MN 55455
U.S.A.

GUOQIANG TIAN
Texas A & M University
Department of Economics
College Station, TX 77843-4228
U.S.A.

ABSTRACT. From the point of view of consumer demand theory the linear expenditure system (LES) provides a convenient model for representing consumer response to price and income and its linearity is one of its most attractive features. But when estimation problems are discussed, the descriptive adjective is more notable for its irony than its accuracy. Since Stone (1954) first calculated parameter estimates for the LES, some stochastic specifications for the system have been given. These specifications, however, ignore some of the requirements implied by economic theory and these methods of estimation lack desirable properties. This paper will deal with the problems of stochastic specification and maximum-likelihood estimation of the LES making full use of the restrictions of economic theory by assuming that the minimum required quantities for the commodities have a three-parameter multivariate lognormal distribution.

1. Introduction

The linear expenditure system (LES) — first introduced by Klein and Rubin (1948) — has had great appeal in applied econometrics owing to the fact that it expresses consumer expenditures on the various commodities as linear functions of prices and income, consistently with the hypothesis of utility-maximization subject to a budget constraint. It was shown by Samuelson (1948) (and subsequently again by Geary, 1949) that the corresponding system of demand functions is generated by a utility function which is linear in the logarithms of displacements of the quantities consumed, or equivalently, by a shifted Cobb-Douglas utility function. Stone (1954) was the first to apply this concept empirically, using an ingenious heuristic computational algorithm. This was further developed in Stone (1964) and Stone et al. (1964), and the approach has been the subject of a valuable exposition and development by Deaton (1975).

The pure theory of consumer behavior makes no allowance for the random errors that must be allowed for in statistical estimation. The procedure followed by Stone's followers, such as Barten (1964, 1969), Theil (1965), Malinvaud (1966), Parks (1969, 1971), Deaton (1975) and others has been to add random terms to the expenditure functions, without considering (as in the original deterministic formulation of Klein and Rubin, 1948) whether the new stochastic demand functions could find a basis in the theory of rational behavior, except in the following limited sense: it was noted independently by Barten (1969) and Parks (1969, 1971) that if the stochastic demand functions were to obey the budget constraint exactly, then the covariance matrix of the error terms would necessarily be singular, and that this restriction should be taken into account in the development of efficient estimation procedures. However, this still leaves unanswered the question of the source of the error terms. If it is not a random error in the consumer's computation of the budget constraint it must be a random error in the consumer's utility function.

The idea that preferences themselves are stochastic was apparently first suggested by Mosteller and Nogee (1951). They noted that in experiments to test transitivity of preferences, one could always find instances in which this postulate was violated unless it were recast in stochastic form. A large literature on stochastic choice emerged, of which one may cite May (1954), Quandt (1956), Papandreou (1957), Luce (1958), Debreu (1958), Davidson and Marschak (1959), Chipman (1960), and Block and Marschak (1960). The basic idea is that an individual's preference ordering is conditional on a particular 'state of mind' which can change from time to time in response to internal or external stimuli. This approach has been generally accepted in psychology but has been slow to penetrate econometrics, except in the area of discrete-choice models, where it has very successfully been applied by McFadden (1974). In the continuous-choice setting of the theory of consumer demand the only applications we are aware of are those of Pollak and Wales (1969) and Woodland (1979), and more recently Lee and Pitt (1986a, 1987, 1986b). Pollak and Wales (1969) included a random error term in the Klein-Rubin-Samuelson-Geary utility function, but unfortunately they postulated it to have a normal distribution, which is logically impossible since the logarithm is defined only for positive numbers. Woodland (1979) suggested an alternative specification on the disturbances in the LES, namely that they have a Dirichlet distribution. However, the Dirichlet distribution requires the expenditures for the different commodities to be independent of one another, by the definition of the Dirichlet distribution (see Rao 1973, p. 125). This is clearly a very strong assumption.

The main purpose of this paper is to remove those obstacles and suggest an alternative stochastic specification. We assume that the stochastic term in the utility function has a multivariate lognormal distribution and then obtain the first-order conditions from which the maximum-likelihood (ML) estimators are derived. It will be noted that our approach satisfies all of the restrictions implied by economic theory in contrast to some more general approaches such as that of the 'Rotterdam model' (Barten 1964, 1969; Theil 1965) — which uses a quadratic approximation to the utility function — and the model of Christensen, Jorgenson, and Lau (1975) — which uses a utility function which likewise does not satisfy the global concavity and monotonicity constraints assumed in consumer theory. Though this paper considers the estimation problem only for the case of the LES model, we think it quite likely that some of the techniques developed in the paper can be profitably used in other expenditure-share models, e.g., the Rotterdam differential demand model, the Christensen-Jorgenson-Lau model, and the Deaton and Muellbauer (1980b) AIDS model. Our aim in this paper is not to strive for the utmost generality but to try to carry out an exact analysis for the simplest case, in the hope that the methods can later be applied to more general cases.

One of the noteworthy consequences of the stochastic formulation undertaken in this paper is that the error terms in the expenditure equations depend upon the prices, see equation (5) below; thus, the usual procedures — if our formulation is correct — fail to take account of the pronounced heteroskedasticity in the error term of the LES that could result from price fluctuations.

One limitation of the formulation of this paper should be mentioned: no account is taken of boundary conditions. That is, it is assumed that the first-order conditions of an interior maximum are satisfied for the consumer. For most applications, where commodity aggregation assures that there will be positive consumption in each category, this should present no problem; however, this might no longer be so in the case of highly disaggregated data sets. For treatments of these problems see Wales and Woodland (1983) and Lee and Pitt (1986a, 1987, 1986b).

The plan of the paper is as follows: Section 2 begins with the discussion of the stochastic specification by making systematic use of economic theory. Section 3 gives the first-order conditions of the ML estimator for the LES under the lognormal specification. In Section 4 we report our conclusions.

2. Stochastic Specification

Let q_{ij} be the quantity of commodity j demanded at time t $(j = 1, 2, \ldots, m; t = 1, 2, \ldots, T)$, and let it be assumed that the community acts as if it maximized a stochastic utility function

$$U(q_t; \alpha, \gamma_t, \varepsilon_t) = \sum_{i=1}^{m} \alpha_i \log (q_{ti} + \gamma_{ti} + \varepsilon_{ti}) \ (\alpha_i > 0, \sum_{i=1}^{m} \alpha_i = 1) \tag{1}$$

subject to the budget constraint

$$\sum_{i=1}^{m} p_{ti} q_{ti} \leq c_t, \tag{2}$$

where $p_t = (p_{t1}, p_{t2}, \ldots, p_{tm})'$ is the price vector with $p_{ti} > 0$ $(i = 1, 2, \ldots, m)$ at time t, c_t is income, or more properly expenditure, at time t. The term $\varepsilon_t = (\varepsilon_{t1}, \ldots, \varepsilon_{tm})'$ is a random error that allows for random variation in the minimum requirement; since (1) is undefined for $q_{ti} + \gamma_{ti} + \varepsilon_{ti} \leq 0$, ε_t must be assumed to be bounded from below (and thus we cannot assume that ε_t has a multivariate normal distribution). We may take this lower bound to be zero, since any departure from zero may be considered to be absorbed in the term $\gamma_t = (\gamma_{t1}, \gamma_{t2}, \ldots, \gamma_{tm})'$. In particular, ε_t may be postulated to have a two-parameter lognormal distribution with 0 as lower bound; equivalently, the random vector $\gamma_t + \varepsilon_t$ may be postulated to have a three-parameter multivariate lognormal distribution with the (unknown) parameter $-\gamma_t$ as lower bound. The γ_t parameter is notoriously difficult to estimate (cf. Johnson and Kotz, 1970; Cohen, 1951; Hill, 1963). However, owing to the nature of the LES we can show, as in Chipman and Tian (1988), that the function h_t defined by (11) below — which is a function of the parameters to be estimated — is bounded by probability integral functions (Lemma 1 of Chipman and Tian, 1988), and further we can show that the ML estimation of the LES with lognormal distribution is strongly consistent, asymptotically normal, and asymptotically efficient by using the theory of M-estimation recently developed by Huber (1967), Duncan (1987), and others.

The γ_t here are assumed to be of the form

$$\gamma_t = \sum_{l=0}^{n} \Phi_l(t) b_l, \tag{3}$$

where $\Phi_0 = I$ is an identity matrix (thus $b_0 = \gamma_0$), $b_l = (b_{l1}, b_{l2}, \ldots, b_{lm})'$ is an m-component vector, and $\Phi_l(t) = \text{diag}(\phi_{l1}(t), \phi_{l2}(t), \ldots, \phi_{lm}(t))$ is a diagonal matrix $(l = 1, \ldots, n)$.

(3) is a very general form for γ_t. A simple special case is that of the linear time trend

$$\gamma_t = \gamma_0 + bt,$$

which was used by Stone, Brown, and Rowe (1964, p. 205).

Pollak's (1970) dynamic specification for γ_t, which is also a special case of (3), is

$$\gamma_t = \gamma_0 + Q_{t-1}b,$$

which is called linear habit formation, as it takes into account changes in tastes. This specification was already anticipated by Stone (1954, p. 522). Here $Q_t = \text{diag}(q_{t1}, q_{t2}, \ldots, q_{tm})$.

Chipman (1985) in his empirical research on net-import demand functions for the Federal Republic of Germany using monthly German data gives another dynamic specification, one which takes both seasonality and time trend into account:

$$\gamma_t = \gamma_0 + a\cos(\frac{\pi}{6}t) + b\sin(\frac{\pi}{6}t) + ct.$$

This is also a special case of (3).

There are two interpretations for γ_t: one is that $-\gamma_t$ is interpreted as minimum-required quantities or subsistence; with this interpretation one must have $q_{ti} \geq 0$. The other is that $-\gamma_t$ is interpreted as the vector of initial endowments of a set of consumers in an open economy, and that $q_{ti} = z_{ti} - \gamma_{ti}$, where z_{ti} is the gross consumption of commodity i on the part of that economy. Accordingly, only z_{ti} is required to be nonnegative; a positive q_{ti} denotes imports and a negative q_{ti} denotes exports of commodity i. In this interpretation, c_t must be interpreted not as expenditure but as the excess of expenditure over income, or the deficit in the open economy's balance of payments on current account.

Solving the maximization problem (1) with respect to (2), we obtain the linear expenditure equations

$$p_{tj}q_{tj} = c_t\alpha_j + \sum_{i=1}^{m} p_{ti}\gamma_{ti}(\alpha_j - \delta_{ij}) + u_{tj}, \tag{4}$$

where δ_{ij} is the Kronecker delta and u_{tj} is given by

$$u_{tj} = \sum_{i=1}^{m} p_{ti}(\alpha_j - \delta_{ij})\varepsilon_{ti}. \tag{5}$$

In vector form (4) becomes

$$w_t = c_t\alpha + A_t\gamma_t + u_t,$$

where

$$w_t = P_t q_t;$$
$$u_t = A_t \varepsilon_t;$$
$$A_t = (\alpha\iota' - I)P_t,$$

and where $\alpha = (\alpha_1, \alpha_2, \ldots, \alpha_m)'$, $P_t = \text{diag}(p_{t1}, p_{t2}, \ldots, p_{tm})$ and ι is a column vector with ones in all components.

As Parks (1969, 1971) pointed out, Stone (1954) and Malinvaud (1966) overlooked the fact that $u_t'\iota = 0$ and assumed that the covariance matrix of u_t is nonsingular. This is clearly not correct. Also, Pollak and Wales (1969) assumed that ε_t has a multivariate normal distribution. However, this specification violates the condition $q_{ti} + \gamma_{ti} + \varepsilon_{ti} > 0$.

To extricate oneself from this situation one has to formulate a suitable stochastic specification for ε_t. To do so we assume that one of the minimum-required quantities, say γ_{tm}, is deterministic (i.e., we assume that $\varepsilon_{tm} = 0$) and that $\tilde{\varepsilon}_t = (\varepsilon_{t1}, \ldots, \varepsilon_{t,m-1})$ has a two-parameter multivariate lognormal distribution with 0 as lower bound. With this specification, the implied stochastic expenditure equations are of the form (4) with

$$u_{tj} = \sum_{i=1}^{m-1} p_{ti}(\alpha_j - \delta_{ij})\varepsilon_{ti}$$

for $j = 1, 2, \ldots, m$. Thus (4) can be written as

$$p_{tj}q_{tj} = c_t\alpha_j + \sum_{i=1}^{m} p_{ti}\gamma_{ti}(\alpha_j - \delta_{ij}) + \sum_{i=1}^{m-1} p_{ti}(\alpha_j - \delta_{ij})\varepsilon_{ti}, \tag{6}$$

which are symmetric for all parameters to be estimated. Thus the estimation of the parameters of the LES by (6) will not be affected by which commodity is chosen to be deleted. That is, the asymmetrical stochastic specification for ε_t does not affect the estimation for the LES.

Notice that for any stochastic specification for ε_t, the mapping from ε_t to u_t is singular (because of $\iota'u_t = 0$) and thus the probability density function of u_t cannot be expressed explicitly. However, since any expenditure equation of the LES is equal to total expenditure minus the sum of the other expenditure equations, one of the equations (4) is completely redundant in the sense that using the information contained in any $(m-1)$ of the equations we can obtain the m-th equation.[1] Thus we may as well omit the m-th equation. The system with the m-th equation deleted becomes:

$$\tilde{w}_t = c_t\tilde{\alpha} + \tilde{A}\tilde{P}_t\tilde{\gamma}_t + p_{tm}\gamma_{tm}\tilde{\alpha} + \tilde{u}_t,$$

where

$$\tilde{w} = \tilde{P}_t\tilde{q}_t;$$
$$\tilde{A} = (\tilde{\alpha}\iota' - I);$$
$$\tilde{u}_t = \tilde{A}_t\tilde{\varepsilon}_t;$$
$$\tilde{A}_t = \tilde{A}\tilde{P}_t,$$

and where vectors $\tilde{\alpha} = (\alpha_1, \alpha_2, \ldots, \alpha_{m-1})'$, $\tilde{q}_t = (q_{t1}, \ldots, q_{t,m-1})'$, $\tilde{\gamma}_t = (\gamma_{t1}, \ldots, \gamma_{t,m-1})'$, and matrix $\tilde{P}_t = \text{diag}(p_{t1}, p_{t2}, \ldots, p_{t,m-1})$.

Since

$$\det \tilde{A} = \det [\tilde{\alpha}\iota' - I]$$

$$= \begin{vmatrix} \alpha_1 - 1 & \alpha_1 & \cdots & \alpha_1 \\ \alpha_2 & \alpha_2 - 1 & \cdots & \alpha_2 \\ \cdots & \cdots & \cdots & \cdots \\ \alpha_{m-1} & \alpha_{m-1} & \cdots & \alpha_{m-1} - 1 \end{vmatrix}$$

$$= -\alpha_m \begin{vmatrix} 1 & 1 & \cdots & 1 \\ \alpha_2 & \alpha_2 - 1 & \cdots & \alpha_2 \\ \cdots & \cdots & \cdots & \cdots \\ \alpha_{m-1} & \alpha_{m-1} & \cdots & \alpha_{m-1} - 1 \end{vmatrix}$$

$$= (-1)^{m-1}\alpha_m \neq 0,$$

we know that the linear transformation

$$\tilde{u}_t = \tilde{A}_t \tilde{\varepsilon}_t$$

is nonsingular and thus we can obtain the distribution of $\tilde{u}_t$ from that of $\tilde{\varepsilon}_t$.

The assumption that $\tilde{\varepsilon}_t$ has a two-parameter multivariate lognormal distribution with 0 as lower bound implies that $x_t \equiv \log \tilde{\varepsilon}_t$ has a multivariate normal distribution with the mean a_t and the covariance matrix V_t, where $\log \tilde{\varepsilon}_t = (\log \varepsilon_{t1}, \ldots, \log \varepsilon_{t,m-1})$. Thus the density function of $\tilde{\varepsilon}_t$ is of the form

$$f(\tilde{\varepsilon}_t) = \frac{\prod_{i=1}^{m-1} \varepsilon_{ti}^{-1}}{(2\pi)^{\frac{m-1}{2}} \mid V_t \mid^{1/2}} \exp \left\{ -\tfrac{1}{2} [\log \tilde{\varepsilon}_t - a_t]' V_t^{-1} [\log \tilde{\varepsilon}_t - a_t] \right\}.$$

Note that the Jacobian matrix of the transformation from $\tilde{\varepsilon}_t$ to $\tilde{u}_t$ is

$$\frac{\partial \tilde{\varepsilon}_t}{\partial \tilde{u}_t} = \tilde{A}_t^{-1}$$

and the absolute value $\mid \det \tilde{A}_t^{-1} \mid = \alpha_m^{-1} \prod_{i=1}^{m-1} p_{ti}^{-1}$. To find the density function of $\tilde{w}_t$, we use the formula $\tilde{A}^{-1} = -(I + \tilde{\alpha}\iota' / \alpha_m)$ and the facts that

$$\tilde{A}^{-1} \tilde{\alpha} = -\frac{\tilde{\alpha}}{\alpha_m} \tag{7}$$

and

$$\tilde{A}^{-1} \tilde{w}_t = -\tilde{w}_t - \frac{1}{\alpha_m} \sum_{i=1}^{m-1} p_{ti} q_{ti} \tilde{\alpha}. \tag{8}$$

Thus by using (7), (8), and $\tilde{A}_t^{-1} = \tilde{P}^{-1} \tilde{A}^{-1}$, we have

$$\tilde{A}_t^{-1} (\tilde{w}_t - c_t \tilde{\alpha} - \tilde{A}\tilde{P}_t \tilde{\gamma}_t - p_{tm}\gamma_{tm}\tilde{\alpha}) = \frac{p_{tm}(q_{tm} + \gamma_{tm})}{\alpha_m} \tilde{P}_t^{-1} \tilde{\alpha} - \tilde{q}_t - \tilde{\gamma}_t.$$

Therefore the probability density of $\tilde{w}_t$ is

$$h(\tilde{w}_t) = \alpha_m^{-1} \prod_{i=1}^{m-1} p_{ti}^{-1} f[\tilde{A}_t^{-1} (\tilde{w}_t - c_t \tilde{\alpha} - \tilde{A}\tilde{P}_t \tilde{\gamma}_t - p_{tm}\gamma_{tm}\tilde{\alpha})]$$

$$= \alpha_m^{-1} \prod_{i=1}^{m-1} p_{ti}^{-1} \frac{\prod_{i=1}^{m-1} \left(\frac{p_{tm}(q_{tm} + \gamma_{tm})}{\alpha_m} p_{ti}^{-1} \alpha_i - q_{ti} - \gamma_{ti} \right)^{-1}}{(2\pi)^{(m-1)/2} \mid V_t^{1/2} \mid} \times$$

$$\times \exp \left\{ -\tfrac{1}{2} \left[\log \left(\frac{p_{tm}(q_{tm} + \gamma_{tm})}{\alpha_m} \tilde{P}_t^{-1} \tilde{\alpha} - \tilde{q}_t - \tilde{\gamma}_t \right) - a_t \right]' V_t^{-1} \times \right.$$

$$\left. \times \left[\log \left(\frac{p_{tm}(q_{tm} + \gamma_{tm})}{\alpha_m} \tilde{P}_t^{-1} - \tilde{\alpha} - \tilde{q}_t - \tilde{\gamma}_t \right) - a_t \right] \right\}. \tag{9}$$

3. Maximum-Likelihood Estimation

In this section we derive the ML estimator for the parameters to be estimated. For simplicity we assume that the sample observations come from the same population distribution. Distributions for different observations are assumed to be uncorrelated. Thus the logarithm of the likelihood function (9) is

$$L = -T\log \alpha_m - \sum_{t=1}^{T}\sum_{i=1}^{m-1} \log p_{ti} - \sum_{t=1}^{T}\sum_{i=1}^{m-1} \log h_{ti} - \frac{(m-1)T}{2} \log (2\pi) - \tag{10}$$

$$- \frac{T}{2} \log \mid \det V \mid -\tfrac{1}{2}\sum_{t=1}^{T} [\log h_t - a]' V^{-1} [\log h_t - a].$$

Here

$$h_t = \frac{p_{tm}(q_{tm} + \gamma_{tm})}{\alpha_m} \tilde{P}_t^{-1} \tilde{\alpha} - \tilde{q}_t - \tilde{\gamma}_t. \tag{11}$$

We will obtain the first-order derivatives of L with respect to a, V, $\tilde{\alpha}$, γ_0, $b_l (l = 1, \dots, n)$. Differentiating (10) with respect to a, we have

$$\frac{\partial L}{\partial a} = \sum_{t=1}^{T} V^{-1} [\log h_t - a].$$

Letting $\dfrac{\partial L}{\partial a} = 0$, we have

$$\hat{a} = \frac{1}{T} \sum_{t=1}^{T} \log h_t.$$

Differentiating (10) with respect to v_{ij}, we have

$$\frac{\partial L}{\partial v_{ij}} = -e_i' \{TV^{-1} - \sum_{t=1}^{T} V^{-1} [\log h_t - a] [\log h_t - a]' V^{-1} \} e_j$$

for $i \neq j$ and

$$\frac{\partial L}{\partial v_{ii}} = -\frac{1}{2} e_i' \{TV^{-1} - \sum_{t=1}^{T} V^{-1} [\log h_t - a] [\log h_t - a]' V^{-1} \} e_i,$$

where e_i is an $(m-1) \times 1$ column vector with 1 in the ith place and 0 in other places, and v_{ij} is the element in the ith row and jth column of V.

Letting $\dfrac{\partial L}{\partial V} = 0$, we have

$$\hat{V} = \frac{1}{T} \sum_{t=1}^{T} [\log h_t - a] [\log h_t - a]'.$$

Similarly, we can obtain the derivatives of L with respect to α (noting that $\alpha_m = 1 - \sum_{i=1}^{m-1} \alpha_i$), γ_0 and b_l ($l = 1, 2, \ldots, n$):

$$\frac{\partial L}{\partial \tilde{\alpha}} = \frac{T}{\alpha_m}\iota - \sum_{t=1}^{T} \frac{p_{tm}(q_{tm} + \gamma_{tm})}{\alpha_m} H_t^{-1}\tilde{P}_t^{-1}\iota -$$

$$- \sum_{t=1}^{T} p_{tm}(q_{tm} + \gamma_{tm})(\alpha_m^{-1}I + \alpha_m^{-2}\hat{\tilde{\alpha}})H_t^{-1}\tilde{P}_t^{-1}V^{-1}[\log h_t - a] - \sum_{t=1}^{T}\sum_{j=1}^{m-1} \frac{p_{tm}(q_{tm} + \gamma_{tm})\alpha_j}{\alpha_m^2 h_{tj}p_{tj}}\iota;$$

$$\frac{\partial L}{\partial \tilde{\gamma}_0} = \sum_{t=1}^{T} H_t^{-1}(\iota + V^{-1}[\log h_t - a]);$$

$$\frac{\partial L}{\partial b_l} = \sum_{t=1}^{T} H_t^{-1}\Phi_l(t)(\iota + V^{-1}[\log h_t - a]);$$

$$\frac{\partial L}{\partial \gamma_{0m}} = -\sum_{t=1}^{T}\sum_{j=1}^{m-1} \frac{p_{tm}\alpha_j}{\alpha_m h_{tj}p_{tj}} - \sum_{t=1}^{T} \frac{p_{tm}}{\alpha_m}\tilde{\alpha}'H_t^{-1}\tilde{P}_t^{-1}V^{-1}[\log h_t - a];$$

$$\frac{\partial L}{\partial b_{km}} = -\sum_{t=1}^{T}\sum_{j=1}^{m-1} \frac{p_{tm}\phi_{km}(t)\alpha_j}{\alpha_m h_{tj}p_{tj}} - \sum_{t=1}^{T} \frac{p_{tm}\phi_{km}(t)}{\alpha_m}\tilde{\alpha}'H_t^{-1}\tilde{P}_t^{-1}V^{-1}[\log h_t - a],$$

where $H_t^{-1} = \text{diag}(h_{t1}^{-1}, \ldots, h_{t,m-1}^{-1})$, $\hat{\tilde{\alpha}} = \text{diag}(\alpha_1, \ldots, \alpha_{m-1})$, and $\Phi_t = \text{diag}(\phi_{t1}, \ldots, \phi_{t,m-1})$. Note that $\gamma_0 = (\tilde{\gamma}_0, \gamma_{0m})'$ and $b_l = (b'_l, b_{lm})'$, $l = 1, \ldots, n$.

The maximum-likelihood estimators are thus obtained by solving the following equations:

$$\hat{a} = \frac{1}{T}\sum_{t=1}^{T} \log h_t;$$

$$\hat{V} = \frac{1}{T}\sum_{t=1}^{T} [\log h_t - a][\log h_t - a]';$$

$$\frac{\partial L}{\partial \tilde{\alpha}} = 0;$$

$$\frac{\partial L}{\partial \gamma_0} = 0;$$

$$\frac{\partial L}{\partial b_l} = 0 \text{ for } l = 1, 2, \ldots, n;$$

$$\alpha_m = 1 - \tilde{\alpha}'\iota.$$

Note that the system of equations to be solved is nonlinear in the parameters and we have to resort to numerical methods for solutions. The consistency, asymptotic normality, and efficiency of the ML estimator can be proved in the same way as given in Chipman and Tian (1988).

4. Conclusion

This paper has discussed the specification and estimation of the linear expenditure system. It has argued that neither the normal distribution nor the Dirichlet distribution as a specification of the LES can be strictly valid for various reasons associated with the fact that the former does not allow the utility function of the LES to be well-defined while the latter requires that the w_{ti} be mutually independent. To solve the problem we deal with the problems of stochastic specification and maximum-likelihood estimation of the LES making full use of the restrictions of economic theory by assuming that the minimum required quantities for the commodities have a three-parameter multivariate lognormal distribution.

Notes

* Work done for this paper was supported by the Stiftung Volkswagenwerk, the Riksbankens Jubileumsfond, and grant SES-8607652 of the National Science Foundation. We are very grateful to an anonymous referee of this volume for useful comments.

1. This is true if the u_t are serially independent (see Barten, 1969). However, when the u_t are autocorrelated, maximum-likelihood estimates may be conditional on the equation deleted. For a detailed argument, see Berndt and Savin (1975).

References

Barten, A. B.: 1964, 'Consumer Demand Functions Under Conditions of Almost Additive Preferences', *Econometrica*, **32**, 1-38.

Barten, A. B.: 1969, 'Maximum-Likelihood Estimation of a Complete System of Demand Equations', *European Economic Review*, 7-73.

Berndt, E. R., and N. E. Savin: 1975, 'Estimation and Hypothesis Testing in Singular Equation Systems with Autoregressive Disturbances,' *Econometrica*, **43**, 937-957.

Block, H. D., and J. Marschak: 1960, 'Random Orderings and Stochastic Theories of Response', in I. Olkin et al. (eds.), *Contributions to Probability and Statistics*, Stanford University Press, Stanford, California, U.S.A., pp. 97-132.

Chipman, J. S.: 1960, 'Stochastic Choice and Subjective Probability', in D. Willner (ed.), *Decisions, Values, and Groups*, **1**, Pergamon Press, New York, New York, U.S.A., pp. 70-95.

Chipman, J. S.: 1985, 'Estimation of Net-Import Demand Functions for the Federal Republic of Germany, 1959--1982', in H. Giersch (ed.), *Probleme und Perspektiven der Weltwirtschaftlichen Entwicklung*, Duncker & Humblot, Berlin, Germany, pp. 197-213.

Chipman, J. S., and G. Tian: 1988, 'Generalized Maximum-Likelihood Estimation of the Linear Expenditure System with Lognormal Distribution', manuscript.

Christensen, L. R., D. W. Jorgenson, and L. J. Lau: 1975, 'Transcendental Logarithmic Utility Functions', *American Economic Review*, **65**, 367-383.

Cohen, A. C.: 1951, 'Estimating Parameters of Logarithmic-Normal Distributions by Maximum Likelihood', *Journal of the American Statistical Association*, **46**, 206-212.

Davidson, D., and J. Marschak: 1959, 'Experimental Tests of a Stochastic Decision Theory', in C. W. Churchman and P. Ratoosh (eds.), *Measurement: Definitions and Theories*, John Wiley & Sons, Inc., New York, New York, U.S.A., pp. 233-269.

Deaton, A. S.: 1975, *Models and Projections of Demand in Post-War Britain*, Chapman and Hall, London, England.

Deaton, A., and J. Muellbauer: 1980a, *Economics and Consumer Behavior*, Cambridge University Press, Cambridge, England.

Deaton, A., and J. Muellbauer: 1980b, 'An Almost Ideal Demand System', *American Economic Review*, **70**, 312-326.

Debreu, G.: 1958, 'Stochastic Choice and Cardinal Utility', *Econometrica*, **26**, 440-444.

Duncan, G. M.: 1987, 'A Simple Approach to *M*-Estimation with Application to Two-Stage Estimators', *Journal of Econometrics*, **34**, 373-389.

Geary, R. C.: 1949, 'A Note on "A Constant-Utility Index of the Cost of Living" ', *Review of Economic Studies*, **18**, 65-66.

Hill, B. M.: 1963, 'The Three-Parameter Lognormal Distribution and Bayesian Analysis of a Point-Source Epidemic', *Journal of the American Statistical Association*, **58**, 72-84.

Houthakker, H. S.: 1960, 'Additive Preferences', *Econometrica*, **28**, 244-257.

Huber, P.: 1967, 'The Behavior of Maximum Likelihood Estimates under Nonstandard Conditions', *Proceedings of the Fifth Berkeley Symposium on Mathematical Statistics and Probability*, **1**, University of California Press, Berkeley and Los Angeles, California, U.S.A., pp. 221-233.

Johnson, N. L., and S. Kotz: 1970, *Continuous Univariate Distributions-1*, Houghton Mifflin Company, Boston, Massachusetts, U.S.A.

Klein, L. R., and H. Rubin: 1948, 'A Constant-Utility Index of the Cost of Living', *Review of Economic Studies*, **15**, 84-87.

Lee, L. F., and M. M. Pitt: 1986a, 'Microeconometric Demand Systems with Binding Nonnegativity Constraints: The Dual Approach', *Econometrica*, **5**, 1237-1242.

Lee, L. F., and M. M. Pitt: 1986b, 'Specification and Estimation of Consumer Demand Systems with Many Binding Non-Negativity Constraints', manuscript.

Lee, L. F., and M. M. Pitt: 1987, 'Microeconometric Models of Rationing, Imperfect Markets, and Non-Negativity Constraints', *Journal of Econometrics*, **36**, 89-110.

Luce, R. D.: 1958, 'A Probabilistic Theory of Utility', *Econometrica*, **26**, 193-224.

McFadden, D.: 1974, 'Conditional Logit Analysis of Qualitative Choice Behavior', in P. Zarembka (ed)., *Frontiers in Econometrics*, Academic Press, Inc., New York, New York, U.S.A., pp. 105-142.

Malinvaud, E.: 1966, *Statistical Methods of Econometrics*, Rand McNally and Company, Chicago, Illinois, U.S.A.

May, K. O.: 1954, 'Transitivity, Utility, and Aggregation in Preference Patterns', *Econometrica*, **22**, 1-14.

Mosteller, F., and P. Nogee: 1951, 'An Experimental Measure of Utility', *Journal of Political Economy*, **59**, 371-404.

Papandreou, A. G., with the collaboration of O. H. Sauerlender, O. H. Brownlee, L. Hurwicz, and W. Franklin: 1957, 'A Test of a Stochastic Theory of Choice', *University of California Publications in Economics*, **16**, 1-18.

Parks, R. W.: 1969, 'Systems of Demand Equations: An Empirical Comparison of Alternative Functional Forms', *Econometrica*, **37**, 629-650.

Parks, R. W.: 1971, 'Maximum-Likelihood Estimation of the Linear Expenditure System', *Journal of the American Statistical Association*, **66**, 900-903.

Pollak, R. A.: 1970, 'Habit Formation and Dynamic Demand Functions', *Journal of Political Economy*, **78**, 745-763.

Pollak, R. A., and T. J. Wales: 1969, 'Estimation of the Linear Expenditure System', *Econometrica*, **37**, 611-628.

Quandt, R. E.: 1956, 'A Probabilistic Theory of Consumer Behavior', *Quarterly Journal of Economics*, **70**, 507-536.

Rao, C. R.: 1973, *Linear Statistical Inference and Its Applications*, John Wiley & Sons, Inc., New York, New York, U.S.A.

Samuelson, P. A.: 1948, 'Some Implications of "Linearity" ', *Review of Economic Studies*, **15**, 88-90.

Stone, R.: 1954, 'Linear Expenditure Systems and Demand Analysis: An Application to the Pattern of British Demand', *Economic Journal*, **64**, 511-527.

Stone, R.: 1964, 'British Economic Balances in 1970: A Trial Run on Rocket', in P. E. Hart, G. Mills, and J. K. Whitaker (eds.), *Econometric Analysis for National Economic Planning*, Butterworths, London, England, pp. 65-95.

Stone, R., A. Brown, and D. A. Rowe: 1964, 'Demand Analysis and Projections for Britain: 1900-1970; A Study in Method', in J. Sandee (ed.), *Europe's Future Consumption*, **2**, North-Holland, Amsterdam, Holland, pp. 200-225.

Theil, H.: 1965, 'The Information Approach to Demand Analysis', *Econometrica*, **33**, 67-87.

Wales, T. J., and A. D. Woodland: 1983, 'Estimation of Consumer Demand Systems with Binding Non-Negativity Constraints', *Journal of Econometrics*, **21**, 263-285.

Woodland, A. D.: 1979, 'Stochastic Specification and the Estimation of Share Equations', *Journal of Econometrics*, **10**, 361-383.

PART FOUR

MODELLING ISSUES

CHAPTER 9

SELECTION BIAS: MORE THAN A FEMALE PHENOMENON

ALICE NAKAMURA*
University of Alberta
Faculty of Business
Edmonton, Alberta
Canada, T6G 2R6

MASAO NAKAMURA
University of Alberta
Faculty of Business
Edmonton, Alberta
Canada, T6G 2R6

ABSTRACT. When a regression model is estimated using a censored subset of observations, coefficient estimates may be biased. Censored regression models have a long history in biometrics, engineering and other areas of applied statistics. The interest of economists in these models was stimulated by Tobin's work on durable goods consumption in the late 1950s. It was Heckman's publication of a simple two-step procedure for estimating censored regression models, however, that led to their widespread usage in applied econometric studies. Although this is not necessarily the best method for estimating all censored regression models, it has certain attractive properties. An understanding of this method is vital to the proper interpretation of the wealth of applied studies based on this approach. Also, valuable insights into the basic nature of sample selection problems can be gained from the formulation of the censored regression model popularized by Heckman.

We begin by exploring the estimation problems resulting from censoring and from certain properties of Heckman's two-step estimation method. Procedures are developed for assessing the nature and extent of problems resulting from censoring; these procedures are then applied in an empirical analysis of the wage rates and hours of work of individuals in 10 different demographic groups using data from the Panel Study of Income Dynamics. One of our findings is that estimation using censored data can lead to bias and other related problems even when the degree of censoring is slight.

1. Introduction

There are many variables that are only observed in conjunction with the occurrence of some probabilistic event. In medical research, for instance, survival time can only be determined for patients who can be located. Analyses involving censored dependent variables of this sort have a long history in biometrics, engineering and other areas of applied statistics.[1] The interest of economists in censored regression models was stimulated by Tobin's (1958) pioneering work on household durable goods expenditures. The amount spent on a good can be viewed as a measure of the consumer's desire for the good, but this dollar amount is only observed if the consumer's desire is high enough that a purchase takes place. Models of this sort came to be popularly known to economists as Tobit models, a phrase coined by Goldberger (1964). Despite the growing familiarity of economists with Tobit models, however, econometric applications were infrequent prior to the 1970s.

The usage of Tobit-type models in applied econometrics has burgeoned in recent years. This development is due in part to advances in computer technology and a dramatic expansion in the availability of micro sample survey data. Papers by Gronau (1974) and Heckman (1974), which made the selection bias problems associated with censored regression models a central concern in analyses of female labor supply, also spurred applied interest in these models. It was Heckman's (1976) publication of a simple two-step procedure for estimating censored regression models, however, which led to the widespread usage of these models in applied economic research.

Heckman's two-step estimation method, sometimes called Heckit analysis in recognition of its originator as well as the use of probit analysis in its first step and its application to Tobit models, is not necessarily the best method for estimating all models involving censored dependent variables. The estimation method does have certain attractive properties, however, including computational convenience which is important to applied researchers. Moreover, a thorough understanding of the properties of this estimation method is vital if the vast accumulation of applied studies based on this estimation approach are to be properly interpreted.[2] In addition, we show in this paper that valuable insights into the basic nature of sample selection problems can be elicited from the Heckit formulation of a censored regression model, regardless of how the model is to be estimated.

In Section 2 the Heckit estimation procedure is explained in the context of a simple model of individual work behavior. In Section 3 sample selection problems (problems resulting from censoring) and certain properties of the Heckit estimator are discussed. Then the procedures developed in Section 3 for assessing sample selection problems are applied in Section 4 in an analysis of wage rates and hours of work for individuals in 10 demographic groups. One of the results emerging from Sections 3 and 4 is that estimation with censored data can result in biased coefficient estimates even when the degree of censoring is slight. Our conclusions are summarized in Section 5.

2. A Model of Work Behavior and the Heckit Estimation Procedure

Two behavioral assumptions underlie the model of work behavior formalized by Heckman (1974, 1976). The first, which constitutes a selection rule, is that an individual will work if he or she receives a wage offer (the *offered wage*) in excess of the minimum for which the individual is willing to work at least one hour (the *asking wage* evaluated at zero hours of work). The second is that those who work (the selected subpopulation) will choose their hours of work so as to equate their asking wage rates (which are assumed to increase with increased hours of work) with their offered wage rates. Sample selection problems arise because of correlations between unobservable (or omitted) factors affecting the determination of who works and unobservables affecting the offered and asking wage rates and the hours of work of those who work. The simple cross-sectional form of this model adopted in this paper is used in the original papers in which the Heckit procedure was presented (see Heckman, 1976) and is still being used, particularly in studies of work behavior for countries where panel data are not available. (See, for example, Anderson and Hill, 1983, Reimers, 1983, Franz, 1985, Ofer and Vinokur, 1985, and Mroz, 1987. Dynamic versions of this model are developed in Nakamura and Nakamura, 1985a, 1985b.)

For the i'th individual, w_i denotes the offered wage, $w_i^*(h)$ denotes the asking wage at h hours of work, Z_i and Z_i^* are vectors of exogenous explanatory variables, and u_{1i} and v_i are disturbance terms assumed to obey bivariate normal distributions with zero means for the population of all individuals (workers and nonworkers). It is assumed that

$$\ln w_i = Z_i\alpha + u_{1i} \tag{1}$$

and

$$\ln w_i^*(h) = \begin{cases} \beta_1 h_i + \beta_2 \ln w_i + Z_i^* \beta_3 + v_i & \text{for } h > 0 \\ Z_i^* \beta_3 + v_i & \text{for } h = 0 \end{cases}$$

where β_1 and β_2 are scalar parameters and α and β_3 are vectors of parameters. According to the model the i'th individual will work if $w_i \geq w_i^*(0)$, which is equivalent to the *selection rule*

$$Z_i \alpha - Z_i^* \beta_3 \geq u_{3i}$$

with $u_{3i} = v_i - u_{1i}$, where the monotonicity of the log transformation is used. Moreover, workers are assumed to choose their hours of work so that $w_i^*(h) = w_i$, or equivalently $\ln w_i^*(h) = \ln w_i$. Thus

$$h_i = (1/\beta_1)[(1-\beta_2) \ln w_i^p - Z_i^* \beta_3] + u_{2i} \tag{2}$$

where in equation (2) $\ln w_i$ has been replaced by wage predictions denoted by $\ln w_i^p$ in order to avoid suspected errors-in-variables and endogeneity problems, and using the relation $u_{2i} = (1-\beta_1)[(1-\beta_2)(\ln w_i - \ln w_i^p) - v_i]$.

Wage rates are only observed for those who work. Unfortunately, under the assumptions of the model, u_{1i} and u_{2i} have individual-specific nonzero means in the censored subpopulation of workers, and these individual-specific means may be correlated with some of the variables in Z_i and Z_i^*. In particular, $E(u_{ji} \mid Z_i \alpha - Z_i^* \beta_2 \geq u_{3i}) = \sigma_j \rho_{j3} \lambda_i$ for $j = 1,2$ where $\rho_{j3} = \sigma_{j3} / (\sigma_j \sigma_3)$ for $j = 1,2$; σ_{j3} is the covariance of u_{ji} with u_{3i} for $j = 1,2$; σ_j^2 is the variance of u_{ji} for $j = 1,2,3$; and $\lambda_i = f(\phi_i) / [1 - F(\phi_i)]$ with f and F denoting the density and distribution functions for the standard normal distribution and with

$$\phi_1 = -(1/\sigma_3)[Z_i \alpha - Z_i^* \beta_3]. \tag{3}$$

The variable λ_i is sometimes referred to as a *selection bias term*. Under the assumptions of the model, the parameters $-(1/\sigma_3)\alpha$ and $(1/\sigma_3)\beta_3$ in (3) can be consistently estimated using probit analysis, and hence estimated values can be computed for ϕ_i and λ_i. Heckman (1976, 1979) has suggested that the sample selection problems associated with the estimation of (1) and (2) can be avoided by instead estimating the parameters of

$$\ln w_i = Z_i \alpha + \sigma_1 \rho_{13} \lambda_i + U_{1i} \tag{4}$$

and

$$h_i = (1/\beta_1)[(1-\beta_2) \ln w_i^p - Z_i^* \beta_3] + \sigma_2 \rho_{23} \lambda_i + U_{2i}, \tag{5}$$

where U_{1i} and U_{2i} are random disturbance terms with zero means in the subpopulation of workers, $\ln w_i^p$ now denotes the predictions of $\ln w_i$ obtained from (4), and estimated values of λ_i are obtained as described above. Although this *two-step Heckit procedure* was proposed in the context of a model of female work behavior, it has subsequently been used in the estimation of a wide range of models involving sample selection. (For a readable introduction to the Heckit procedure, see Kmenta, 1986, pp. 563-564 and Smith, 1980, Introduction. For more advanced presentations see Judge et al., 1985, Section 18.4 and particularly Amemiya, 1985, Chapter 10 and Maddala, 1983.)

3. Sample Selection Problems

Our purpose in this section is to gain a better understanding of sample selection problems through an examination of the Heckit (HEC) formulation of the log wage equation given in (4). For now, we will assume that values for λ_i are known.

Suppose (4) is estimated using data only for those who worked, but ignoring λ_i. The resulting ordinary least squares (OLS) estimator of α can be written as

$$a_{OLS} = \alpha + \sigma_1 \rho_{13} \hat{\gamma} + (Z'Z)^{-1} Z' U_1$$

where $\hat{\gamma} = (Z'Z)^{-1} Z' \lambda$, and where, for the n workers, λ is a vector of observations on λ_i, U_1 is a vector of unobservable values of U_{1i}, and Z is a matrix of observations on Z_i. Notice that $\hat{\gamma}$ may be viewed as the OLS coefficient vector from the regression of λ on Z. Thus for any value of n we can always represent λ as

$$\lambda = Z\hat{\gamma} + e \tag{6}$$

where e is the OLS residual vector, so $Z'e = 0$. The OLS bias vector is

$$E^*(a_{OLS}) - \alpha = \sigma_1 \rho_{13} \hat{\gamma}, \tag{7}$$

where E^* denotes the expectation operator for the working subpopulation conditional on Z and λ.[3] If everyone worked, then λ would be a zero vector, and hence $\hat{\lambda}$ and the bias vector given in (7) would also be zero vectors. Otherwise some or all of the elements of the bias vector may be nonzero. This is the *selection bias problem* that has received so much attention in the literature. It should be clear from (7) that the existence and size of any selection biases will depend crucially on the explanatory variables included in the study, and hence on the properties of the unobservable (or omitted) factors left in the relevant disturbance terms.

The expected sum of squared residuals for the OLS regression ignoring λ is

$$\begin{aligned} E^*[SSE(Z)] &= E^*[(\ln w - Za_{OLS})'(\ln w - Za_{OLS})] \\ &= \sigma_1^2 \rho_{13}^2 \lambda' M \lambda + E^*[U_1' M U_1] \end{aligned} \tag{8}$$

where $\ln w$ is a vector of observations on $\ln w_i$ for those who worked and $M = I - Z(Z'Z)^{-1} Z'$. Controlling for degrees of freedom, larger values of this sum of squares generally imply less precise (that is, less efficient) coefficient estimates and predictions for the dependent variable. The expected sum of squared residuals we would have if there were no sample selection is just $E^*[U_1' M U_1]$. Thus the first term on the right-hand side of the second equal sign in (8) represents the expected excess unexplained variation due to sample selection, referred to in this study as *selection related inefficiency*. Because of this inefficiency problem, sample selection problems cannot be ignored even when interest centers on prediction rather than on structural estimation.

We have seen that there will be no selection-related bias or inefficiency problems when $\lambda_i \equiv 0$ for all individuals. This insight has led many implicitly to conclude that selection bias problems will not be serious when the probability of selection into the group of interest is generally high. Thus concerns about sample selection problems have typically been raised in studies of the work behavior and earnings of married women, the young, the old, and other groups with fairly low employment rates, but not in studies of prime-aged men.[4] Yet not all prime-aged men work, and we see from (7) and (8) that sample selection problems will not necessarily be numerically small simply because the degree of censoring is slight. It is true, however, that there will be no sample selection problems if $\rho_{13} = 0$.

For the specified model of work behavior, a priori reasoning suggests that $\rho_{13} \neq 0$.[5] Even so, there will be no selection bias problems if $\hat{\gamma} = 0$, or equivalently if $R_{\lambda \cdot Z}^2 = 0$ (that is if the R^2 for the OLS regression of λ on Z is zero). But in this case the term $\lambda' M \lambda$ on the right-hand side of the second equal sign in (8) will take on the maximum possible value, since this is the sum of squared residuals from the regression of λ on Z. Hence, in this case where none of the variation in λ_i is captured in a proxy sense by variables included in Z_i, there will be selection-related inefficiency.

At the other extreme, suppose $R^2_{\lambda \cdot Z} = 1.$[6] Now $e = M\lambda = 0$, so $\lambda' M \lambda$ in (8) is zero and there is no selection-related inefficiency. However, now some of the elements in $\hat{\gamma}$ must be nonzero and there will be selection bias problems.

Usually, the value of $R^2_{\lambda \cdot Z}$ will lie between 0 and 1. When this is the case there can be selection-related inefficiency problems that can be appraised by comparing $\bar{R}^2_{\ln w \cdot Z}$ with $\bar{R}^2_{\ln w \cdot Z, \lambda}$, where $\bar{R}^2$ is the usual R^2 corrected for degrees of freedom. The extent of these inefficiency problems can also be judged by comparing consistent estimates of the respective standard errors for the OLS and Heckit coefficient estimates. In addition, there can be selection bias problems that can be appraised by comparing the elements of a_{OLS} with the corresponding elements of the coefficient vector from the regression of $\ln w$ on Z and λ (equation (4)), denoted hereafter by a_{HEC}. However, there will be no sample selection problems if $\rho_{13} = 0$; this condition can be tested by testing the significance of the coefficient of λ_i in (4). We will turn our attention to doubts that have been raised about the reliability of this test and related concerns about the precision of the coefficient estimates for (4) when $R^2_{\lambda \cdot Z}$ is close to 1 (Smith, 1980, p. 23, and Nelson, 1984, p. 186).

Letting ξ denote the coefficient of λ in (4), the OLS estimator of this parameter is

$$\xi_{HEC} = (\lambda' M \lambda)^{-1} \lambda' M \ln w = \xi + (e'e)^{-1} e' U_1$$

where $e = M\lambda$ as in (6). Since $e'e = \lambda' M \lambda$ can be rewritten as $SST_\lambda (1 - R^2_{\lambda \cdot Z})$ where SST_λ denotes the sum of squared deviations from the mean of λ_i for those individuals who worked, the variance of ξ_{HEC} conditional on Z and λ is given by

$$V^*(\xi_{HEC}) = \left(\frac{1}{1 - R^2_{\lambda \cdot Z}} \right)^2 \left(\frac{1}{SST_\lambda} \right)^2 e' \Omega e, \tag{9}$$

where Ω is a heteroskedastic diagonal matrix with the i'th diagonal element

$$\sigma^2_i = \sigma^2_1 [(1 - \rho^2_{13}) + \rho^2_{13} (1 + \phi_i \lambda_i + \lambda^2_i)].$$

The term $[1 / (1 - R^2_{\lambda \cdot Z})]^2$ on the right-hand side of (9) can be thought of as the pure multicollinearity effect on the variance of ξ_{HEC}. If $\rho_{13} = 0$, then $\sigma^2_i = \sigma^2_1$ and (9) reduces to the standard OLS formula for the variance of ξ_{HEC}. This is why the usual OLS t-test can be used to test the null hypothesis that $\xi = \sigma_1 \rho_{13} = 0$. Even if $R^2_{\lambda \cdot Z}$ is close to 1 and the variance of ξ_{HEC} is large, the critical points for this test depend only on the degrees of freedom of the t-distribution (the null distribution). Thus multicollinearity should not reduce our confidence in the results of the test when the null hypothesis of no selection bias is rejected. However, when the null hypothesis is accepted, it is more likely that a Type II error (false acceptance of the null hypothesis) is being committed when $R^2_{\lambda \cdot Z}$ is close to 1. That is, the power of the test deteriorates as $R^2_{\lambda \cdot Z}$ approaches 1 (see also Nelson 1984, p. 187).

Next we will consider the variability of the estimator of the coefficient α_j (the coefficient of the j'th variable, z_j, in Z). This estimator is given by

$$a_{j, HEC} = \alpha_j + (z_j' M^A_j z_j)^{-1} e'_{j, HEC} U_1$$

where $M^A_j = I - Z^A_j (Z^{A'}_j Z^A_j)^{-1} Z^{A'}_j$, $Z^A = [Z, \lambda]$, Z^A_j is a matrix of observations for workers for all variables in Z^A except z_j, $e_{j, HEC} = M^A_j z_j$ is the residual vector from the OLS regression of z_j on Z^A_j, and $a_{j, HEC}$ is the j'th element of a_{HEC}. The variance of this estimator, conditional on Z and λ, is

$$V^*(a_{j, HEC}) = \left[\frac{1}{SST_j (1 - R^2_{z_j \cdot Z^A_j})} \right]^2 e'_{j, HEC} \Omega e_{j, HEC} \tag{10}$$

where SST_j denotes the sum of squared deviations from the mean of z_j.[7] There is no reason why $R^2_{z_j \cdot z_j^A}$ must be close to 1 simply because $R^2_{\lambda \cdot z}$ is close to 1. Thus even if the variance of ξ_{HEC} is large due to multicollinearity effects, this does not mean that the variances must be large for some or all of the elements of a_{HEC}.

We can judge how much of the variability of $a_{j, HEC}$ is due to λ by considering the variability of the OLS estimator of α_j ignoring λ. This estimator is given by

$$a_{j, OLS} = \alpha_j + \sigma_1 \rho_{13} \hat{\gamma}_j + (z_j' M_j z_j)^{-1} e'_{j, OLS} U_1$$

where $\hat{\gamma}_j$ is the j'th element of $\hat{\gamma}$ in (6), $M_j = I - Z_j (Z_j' Z_j)^{-1} Z_j'$, Z_j is a matrix of observations for workers for all variables in Z except z_j, $e_{j, OLS} = M_j z_j$ is the residual vector from the OLS regression of z_j on the variables in Z_j, and the term $\sigma_1 \rho_{13} \hat{\gamma}_j$ is the selection bias associated with the estimator $a_{j, OLS}$. The variance of this estimator of α_j, conditional on Z, is given by

$$V^*(a_{j, OLS}) = \left[\frac{1}{SST_j (1 - R^2_{z_j \cdot z_j})} \right]^2 e'_{j, OLS} \Omega e_{j, OLS}. \tag{11}$$

Thus the relative efficiency of $a_{j, HEC}$ to $a_{j, OLS}$ is given by

$$\frac{V(a_{j, OLS})}{V(a_{j, HEC})} = \left\{ \frac{1 - R^2_{z_j \cdot z_j, \lambda}}{1 - R^2_{z_j \cdot z_j}} \right\}^2 \left\{ \frac{e'_{j, OLS} \Omega e_{j, OLS}}{e'_{j, HEC} \Omega e_{j, HEC}} \right\}. \tag{12}$$

The terms $[1/(1 - R_{z_j \cdot z_j^A})]^2$ and $[1/(1 - R^2_{z_j \cdot z_j})]^2$ in (10) and (11), respectively, may be thought of as the pure multicollinearity effects on the variances of $a_{j, HEC}$ and $a_{j, OLS}$.[8] Moreover, the first term on the right-hand side of (12) is the pure multicollinearity effect due to λ on the relative efficiency of $a_{j, HEC}$ and $a_{j, OLS}$. This term will always be less than or equal to 1. In many cases it may be true that $(e'_{j, HEC} \Omega e_{j, HEC})$ is less than $(e'_{j, OLS} \Omega e_{j, OLS})$, and hence the multicollinearity effects due to λ on the relative efficiency of $a_{j, HEC}$ and $a_{j, OLS}$ may be counteracted, to some unknown degree, by the second term on the right-hand side of (12).

An example based on empirical results presented in Section 4 may help to clarify these points concerning multicollinearity effects. For the log wage equation for a sample of young women 14-20 years of age we find that $R^2_{\lambda \cdot z} = 0.81$. Thus, considered alone, multicollinearity is responsible for a 27.7 fold magnification of the variance of ξ_{HEC}. For this same equation, $R^2_{EDU \cdot Z_{EDU}, \lambda} = 0.21$ and $R^2_{EDU \cdot Z_{EDU}} = 0.18$, where EDU is measured as years of schooling. Thus multicollinearity is responsible for 1.6 and 1.5 fold magnifications of the variances of $a_{EDU, HEC}$ and $a_{EDU, OLS}$, respectively, and the cost of correcting for bias in $a_{EDU, OLS}$ by using $a_{EDU, HEC}$ is a reduction in efficiency by a factor of 0.93 .

Finally, we will consider comparisons between $a_{j, OLS}$ and $a_{j, HEC}$. It can easily be shown that

$$a_{j, OLS} - a_{j, HEC} = \sigma_1 \rho_{13} \hat{\gamma}_j + \left[\frac{1}{SST_j (1 - R^2_{z_j \cdot z_j})} \right] e'_{j, OLS} U_1 - \left[\frac{1}{SST_j (1 - R_{z_j \cdot z_j, \lambda})} \right] e'_{j, HEC} U_1.$$

where $z_j' M_j z_j = SST_j (1 - R^2_{z_j \cdot z_j})$ and $z_j' M_j^A z_j = SST_j (1 - R^2_{z_j \cdot z_j, \lambda})$ have been used. There is no reason why U_1 should be correlated in a population sense with either the residual vector from the OLS regression of z_j on Z_j (denoted by $e_{j, OLS}$) or the residual vector from the OLS regression of z_j on Z_j^A (denoted by $e_{j, HEC}$). In fact, under the assumptions of the model, in (4) U_1 is uncorrelated with all of the variables in Z and with λ. This means that U_1 should be uncorrelated with the residuals from the regression of any variable z_j in Z on the other variables in Z or $Z^A = [Z, \lambda]$. Thus if the bias term $(\sigma_1 \rho_{13} \hat{\gamma}_j)$ is zero, for repeated samples the values of the differences between the OLS and Heckit coefficient estimates of α_j should be randomly distributed around zero, with a probability of 0.5 of being positive (or negative) for any one sample.

Throughout this section we have assumed that the values of λ_i are known. In real applications, consistent estimates of the values of λ_i are obtained using first stage probit estimation results, as described in Section 2. Most of the arguments presented in Section 3 must simply be restated in asymptotic terms if consistent predicted values, denoted by $\hat{\lambda}_i$, are substituted for actual values of λ_i. Also, Ω, which is defined in Section 3 as the variance-covariance matrix for U_1, must be redefined as the variance-covariance matrix of $\sigma_1 \rho_{13} (\lambda_i - \hat{\lambda}_i) + U_{1i}$. Consistent estimates of the components of this matrix can be obtained.[9]

4. Empirical Results

We will now examine empirical results for ten demographic groups for the model of work behavior presented in Section 2. The data used are from the Michigan Panel Study of Income Dynamics, spanning the years 1971-1978.

In the first three columns of Table I we show employment rates, sample sizes, and mean values of $\hat{\lambda}_i$.[10] The results for the different demographic groups are listed in Table I (and in the following two tables) in ascending order according to the group employment rates. As expected from the formula for the selection bias term, the mean value of $\hat{\lambda}_i$ falls monotonically as the employment rate increases. Coefficient estimates for the selection bias term $(\hat{\lambda}_i)$ in the log wage and hours equations [equations (4) and (5)] are shown in columns 6 and 10, respectively, of Table I. There is no tendency for these coefficient estimates to decrease in magnitude as we move down the columns from groups with lower to groups with higher employment rates.

We can test the null hypothesis that ignoring sample selection will not lead to sample selection problems by testing the significance of the estimated coefficients for $\hat{\lambda}_1$. (Formally, we are testing whether ρ_{13} and ρ_{23} equal zero by testing H_0: $\sigma_1 \rho_{13} = 0$ for the log wage equation and H_0^*: $\sigma_2 \rho_{23} = 0$ for the hours equation.) Significant estimated coefficients are indicated with two stars or one star depending on whether they are significant using a critical region of 0.05 or 0.20. The null hypothesis of no selection bias problems is rejected for both the log wage and hours equations for prime-aged men 21-46, but not, for instance, for women 65+ or, in the log wage equation, for wives 21-46. There does not seem to be any relationship between group employment rates and the groups for which the null hypothesis of no sample selection problems is rejected. It should be noted, however, that in the log wage equations and, particularly, in the hours equations there is a good deal of multicollinearity between $\hat{\lambda}_i$ and other included explanatory variables. Thus the power of the t-tests for sample selection problems may be low. Because of this, we will not accept the conclusion that there are no sample selection problems for any of the demographic groups without other confirming evidence.

The R^2 values for the OLS regressions of $\hat{\lambda}_i$ on the other included explanatory variables (columns 7 and 11) lie between 0 and 1 for all of our demographic groups. Thus there can be selection-related problems of both bias and inefficiency. However, the numerical differences in the values of the adjusted R^2s for the log wage and hours equations with and without $\hat{\lambda}_i$ (columns

TABLE I. Summary Information

	Employment rate[a]	Sample size	Mean value of $\hat{\lambda}$ for workers	Log wage equation[b]				Hours equation[b]			
				$\bar{R}^2$ for equation		Estimated coefficient of $\hat{\lambda}$ [c,d]	R^2 for $\hat{\lambda}$ regressed on other explanatory variables in equation	$\bar{R}^2$ for equation		Estimated coefficient of $\hat{\lambda}$	R^2 for $\hat{\lambda}$ regressed on other explanatory variables in equation
				Without $\hat{\lambda}$	With $\hat{\lambda}$			Without $\hat{\lambda}$	With $\hat{\lambda}$		
Women 65+	0.21	758	1.07	0.104	0.104	0.03 (.23)	0.40	0.247	0.248	115 (292)	0.79
Men 65+	0.44	776	0.78	0.192	0.206	−1.04 (.37)**	0.89	0.125	0.124	−152 (501)	0.89
Married Women 47-64	0.48	1240	0.76	0.225	0.234	0.66 (.28)**	0.88	0.039	0.042	−624 (455)*	0.94
Women 14-20	0.49	1212	0.73	0.057	0.065	−0.50 (.21)**	0.81	0.195	0.196	161 (383)	0.93
Married Women 21-46	0.60	3557	0.58	0.132	0.132	−0.00 (.08)	0.33	0.070	0.073	−609 (233)**	0.93
Men 14-20	0.62	1146	0.53	0.118	0.118	0.04 (.09)	0.55	0.377	0.379	−477 (319)*	0.95
Unmarried Women 47-64	0.63	1262	0.52	0.199	0.208	−0.55 (.21)**	0.79	0.086	0.087	−392 (396)	0.95
Unmarried Women 21-46	0.74	2080	0.38	0.159	0.167	−0.35 (.11)**	0.50	0.081	0.081	−120 (448)	0.97
Men 47-64	0.90	2961	0.13	0.249	0.249	−0.13 (.16)	0.83	0.125	0.125	−88 (181)	0.84
Men 21-46	0.95	6259	0.07	0.241	0.242	−0.15 (.05)**	0.19	0.108	0.116	−584 (99)**	0.46

a. People with money earnings for the given year are counted as employed.
b. Log wage and hours equations were estimated using data of those persons who were employed.
c. Numbers in parentheses are consistent estimates of asymptotic standard errors.
d. One or two stars indicate coefficients that are significant using a two-tailed test with a critical region of .20 or .05, respectively.

4 and 5 of Table I for the log wage equation and columns 8 and 9 for the hours equation) are always small, suggesting that selection-related inefficiency problems are unimportant.

TABLE II. Coefficient Estimates and Other Related Statistics for Key Explanatory Variables in the Log Wage Equation

	Coefficient estimate[a]		R^2 for explanatory variable regressed on other explanatory variables in equation		Differences between estimates of coefficient without and and with $\hat{\lambda}$ in equation (Absolute percentage difference)[b]
	Without $\hat{\lambda}$ (OLS)	With $\hat{\lambda}$ (HECKIT)	Without $\hat{\lambda}$ (OLS)	With $\hat{\lambda}$ (HECKIT)	
			1. Race dummy (black = 1)		
Women 65+	−0.381 (.214)	−0.384 (.015)	0.03	0.04	0.003 (1%)
Men 65+	−0.450 (.162)	−0.148 (.161)	0.20	0.49	−0.302 (204%)
Married women 47-64	0.042 (.073)	0.204 (.093)	0.10	0.50	−0.162 (79%)
Women 14-20	−0.174 (.060)	−0.030 (.083)	0.19	0.61	−0.144 (480%)
Married women 21-46	−0.021 (.031)	−0.021 (.031)	0.07	0.12	0.000 (0%)
Men 14-20	−0.187 (.050)	−0.198 (.053)	0.11	0.37	0.011 (5%)
Unmarried women 47-64	−0.136 (.049)	−0.037 (.058)	0.22	0.46	−0.099 (267%)
Unmarried women 21-46	−0.132 (.031)	−0.074 (.036)	0.06	0.12	−0.058 (78%)
Men 47-64	−0.182 (.031)	−0.179 (.033)	0.09	0.10	−0.003 (2%)
Men 21-46	−0.146 (.017)	−0.136 (.016)	0.13	0.16	−0.010 (7%)
			2. Disability dummy (disabled = 1)		
Men 65+	−0.051 (.099)	0.230 (.145)	0.07	0.59	−0.281 (122%)
Men 47-64	−0.169 (.044)	−0.106 (.086)	0.02	0.79	−0.063 (59%)
Men 21-46	−0.177 (.027)	−0.172 (.027)	0.01	0.01	−0.005 (3%)
			3. Years of schooling		
Women 65+	0.023 (.024)	0.024 (.025)	0.07	0.11	−0.001 (4%)
Men 65+	0.068 (.012)	0.046 (.016)	0.10	0.43	0.022 (48%)
Married women 47-64	0.127 (.011)	0.171 (.021)	0.11	0.77	−0.044 (26%)
Women 14-20	0.035 (.013)	0.041 (.013)	0.18	0.21	−0.006 (15%)
Married women 21-46	0.116 (.007)	0.116 (.008)	0.09	0.33	0.000 (0%)
Men 14-20	0.021 (.012)	0.021 (.012)	0.11	0.11	0.000 (0%)
Unmarried women 47-64	0.095 (.010)	0.059 (.016)	0.14	0.71	0.036 (61%)
Unmarried women 21-46	0.101 (.009)	0.083 (.010)	0.08	0.37	0.018 (22%)
Men 47-64	0.087 (.004)	0.085 (.004)	0.12	0.23	0.002(2%)
Men 21-46	0.072 (.003)	0.070 (.003)	0.13	0.16	0.002 (3%)

a. Numbers in parentheses are consistent estimates of asymptotic standard errors.
b. Absolute value of (actual difference/coefficient estimate with $\hat{\lambda}$) times 100.

We now turn to the problem of judging the seriousness of potential selection bias problems. In the first two columns of Table II for the log wage equation and Table III for the hours equation we show OLS and Heckit coeffient estimates for several key explanatory variables. The R^2 values in the next two columns of these tables are for the OLS regressions of each explanatory variable on all the other explanatory variables included in the designated equation. The differences between the OLS and Heckit coefficient estimates are shown in column 5 in Tables II and III. We will first discuss the results in Table II for the log wage equation and then turn our attention to the results in Table III for the hours equation.

The coefficient estimate for a race dummy in a log wage equation containing other "control" variables (such as years of schooling) is sometimes used as a measure of labor market discrimination. Most empirical studies of this sort ignore the possibility of selection bias

TABLE III. Coefficient Estimates and Other Related Statistics for Key Explanatory Variables in the Hours Equation

	Coefficient estimate[a]		R^2 for explanatory variable regressed on other explanatory variables in equation		Difference between estimates of coefficient without and and with λ in equation (Absolute percentage difference[b])	Estimated wage elasticities of hours of work[c]	
	Without λ (OLS)	With λ (HECKIT)	Without λ (OLS)	With λ (HECKIT)		Without λ	With λ
1. Number of children younger than 18							
Women 65+	-185.5 (59.0)	-183.1 (59.3)	0.12	0.13	-2.4 (1%)		
Married women 47-64	-70.0 (24.3)	-55.9 (26.7)	0.19	0.31	-14.1 (25%)		
Married women 21-46	-64.3 (11.3)	-42.2 (14.5)	0.26	0.52	-22.1 (52%)		
Unmarried women 47-64	-124.8 (27.4)	-110.4 (33.2)	0.19	0.38	-14.4 (13%)		
Unmarried women 21-46	-96.5 (49.7)	-48.5 (32.7)	0.22	0.37	-48.0 (99%)		
Men 47-64	-4.4 (8.0)	-3.8 (8.0)	0.18	0.19	-.6 (16%)		
Men 21-46	-15.1 (6.0)	-8.0 (5.9)	0.27	0.29	-7.1 (89%)		
2. Estimated log wage							
Women 65+	-222.2 (425.8)	-141.4 (461.2)	0.79	0.83	-80.8 (57%)	-0.261	-0.166
Men 65+	549.2 (193.0)	508.1 (199.6)	0.50	0.56	41.1 (8%)	0.490	0.454
Married women 47-64	123.3 (98.2)	-194.3 (239.2)	0.22	0.87	317.6 (163%)	0.093	-0.147
Women 14-20	472.3 (374.5)	365.8 (425.4)	0.81	0.87	106.5 (29%)	0.508	0.394
Married women 21-46	130.4 (67.8)	-217.0 (143.2)	0.21	0.83	347.4 (160%)	0.103	-0.171
Men 14-20	-1096.3 (418.6)	-1286.0 (439.8)	0.93	0.94	189.7 (15%)	-0.936	-1.098
Unmarried women 47-64	52.2 (96.4)	-181.8 (252.3)	0.41	0.91	234.0 (129%)	0.003	-0.111
Unmarried women 21-46	-28.4 (88.4)	-77.4 (180.0)	0.43	0.54	49.0 (63%)	-0.018	-0.050
Men 47-64	303.3 (47.0)	294.3 (50.0)	0.41	0.48	9.0 (3%)	0.142	0.138
Men 21-46	357.1 (45.0)	258.3 (48.0)	0.61	0.64	98.8 (38%)	0.162	0.117
3. Marital status dummy (married = 1)							
Women 65+	1007.9 (354.7)	858.0 (598.0)	0.83	0.90	149.9 (17%)		
Men 65+	527.7 (133.4)	452.5 (144.8)	0.08	0.13	75.2 (17%)		
Women 14-20	-149.0 (176.7)	-144.2 (296.9)	0.83	0.94	-4.8 (3%)		
Men 14-20	279.6 (102.1)	153.4 (123.3)	0.54	0.73	126.2 (82%)		
Men 47-64	351.7 (47.2)	339.0 (49.4)	0.05	0.14	12.7 (4%)		
Men 21-46	366.4 (28.3)	261.4 (48.1)	0.32	0.47	105.0 (40%)		

a. Numbers in parentheses are consistent estimates of asymptotic standard errors.
b. Absolute value of (actual difference/coefficient estimate with λ) times 100.
c. These are uncompensated wage elasticities evaluated at mean hours of work.

problems. Yet it seems likely that there are race-related unobservable (or omitted) factors (including racial discrimination) that affect both the probability of work and the wage rates of minority group members. From columns 1 and 2 of Table II we see that for adult men ($\geq$ 21 years of age), women 14-20, and both age groups of single women (21-46 and 47-64) the OLS coefficient estimates are consistently more negative than the Heckit estimates for the coefficient of the race dummy. In all, there are 7 negative OLS-Heckit differences out of a total of 10 for the OLS and Heckit estimates for the coefficient of the race dummy. The probability of observing this many negative differences if there is no selection bias is 0.17. $(P(x \geq 7) \mid p = 0.5, n = 10) = 0.17$, where x is the number of differences with the indicated sign, p is the probability of a difference of the indicated sign under the null hypothesis of no selection bias, and n is the number of coefficient differences for the designated variable.) Thus the null hypothesis of no selection bias problems for the OLS coefficient estimates for the race dummy is rejected using a critical region of 0.20. The behavioral implication is that ignoring selection bias may lead to overestimates of negative race effects on the wage rates of those who work. From the estimated standard errors shown in parentheses in columns 1 and 2 we see that the efficiency losses resulting from the use of Heckit rather than the OLS coefficient estimates are small, despite the modest increases in multicollinearity associated with the addition of $\hat{\lambda}$ that are evident from the R^2 values shown in columns 3 and 4.

From the second panel of Table II we see that the estimated negative wage effects associated with being disabled are consistently larger for the OLS coefficient estimates. Hence we also reject the null hypothesis of no selection bias for the OLS coefficient estimates of the disability dummy $(P(x \geq 3 \mid p = 0.5, n = 3) = 0.12)$. Possible selection bias problems have not usually been controlled for in studies of disability effects. In this case, the efficiency loss associated with the use of the Heckit procedure is more substantial.

Looking now at the results in the third panel of Table II, we see that for adult men and unmarried women the OLS estimates of the coefficient of the years of schooling variable are consistently more positive. Thus we also reject the null hypothesis of no selection bias problems for these OLS coefficient estimates $(P(x \geq 7 \mid p = 0.5, n = 10) = 0.17)$. Selection bias problems have not usually been controlled for in studies estimating the returns to education for demographic groups with high employment rates. The estimated standard errors associated with the Heckit estimates of the coefficient of the years of schooling variable are the same or only slightly larger than the estimated standard errors for the OLS coefficient estimates.

Looking now at the hours equation results in the first panel of Table III, we find that the OLS estimates of the coefficient for the variable for the number of children younger than 18 are more negative for all 7 demographic groups for which this variable is included. From the second panel, we find that the OLS estimates of the coefficient for the estimated log wage variable are more positive for all 10 demographic groups. And from the third panel of Table III, we find that the OLS estimates of the coefficient for the marital status dummy are more positive for 5 of the 6 demographic groups for which this variable is included. Thus the null hypothesis of no selection bias problems is rejected for the OLS estimates of the coefficients of the child status, log wage and marital status variables $(P(x \geq 7 \mid p = 0.5, n = 7) = 0.008, P(x \geq 10 \mid P = 0.5, n = 10) = 0.001$ and $P(x \geq 5 \mid p = 0.5, n = 6) = 0.12)$. In particular, for this model we find that ignoring selection bias problems leads to overly negative estimates of the impacts of children, and to overly positive estimates of the impacts of the wage variable and of being married, on hours of work for those who work. Looking at the estimated standard errors, it would appear that, with a few exceptions, the efficiency costs of using the Heckit rather than the OLS coefficient estimates are modest.

5. Conclusions

Our main conclusions are as follows:

1. The existence and magnitudes of any selection biases will depend on the properties of the omitted factors left in the disturbance terms for the selection rule and the equation of interest. Thus the common practice in empirical articles of claiming that the selection bias results of one study confirm or controvert the findings of other studies may not be meaningful unless the studies are based on exactly the same model (including the same explanatory variables). Attention should instead be focused on how the choice of explanatory variables, or other features of model specification, affect the seriousness of selection bias problems.

2. Ignoring sample selection can lead to inefficiency in estimation of the coefficients and prediction, as well as bias problems. Thus sample selection problems cannot necessarily be ignored even when interest centers on prediction rather than on structural estimation.

3. A typical reason given for using an estimation method that takes account of censoring (sample selectivity) is that the degree of censoring is severe. Thus concerns about sample selection problems are raised in most recent studies of the work behavior of married women and other demographic groups with fairly low employment rates. On the other hand, many applied researchers seem to believe that there is no need to worry about sample selection problems when the degree of censoring is slight. For instance, sample selection problems are not usually considered in studies of the earnings of prime-aged men. However, there can be sample selection problems even when the degree of censoring is slight. Nor will sample selection problems necessarily be serious even when the degree of censoring is severe.

4. Multicollinearity between the selection bias term and other explanatory variables should not necessarily reduce our confidence in the results of the usual t-test for selection bias (the test of the null hypothesis that the coefficient of the selection bias term is zero) when the null hypothesis of no selection bias is rejected. This is not the case, however, when the null hypothesis is accepted, since the power of the test is adversely affected by multicollinearity involving the selection bias term. Selection bias problems will tend to be most serious precisely when this multicollinearity problem is most severe.

5. High multicollinearity between the selection bias term and the other explanatory variables does not necessarily mean that the coefficient estimates for the other explanatory variables will have large variances.

Notes

* The authors express their appreciation to John Ham, Baldev Raj, Thanasis Stengos and two anonymous referees for their helpful comments on earlier versions of this paper.

1. See, for instance, Buckley and James (1979), Dempster, Laird and Rubin (1977), Hartley (1958), Johnson and Kotz (1970, 1972), and Kalbfleisch and Prentice (1980) for an introduction to some of this history, including further references.

2. The empirical applications we are referring to are for models which can be classified as generalized Tobit models (Type 2 Tobit models in Amemiya, 1984, 1985), where the explanatory variables entering the regression model (to be estimated with a censored subset of observations) may differ from the explanatory variables entering the selection rule. Many problems in demography, education, marketing, finance, labor economics and other fields can be expressed using this sort of model. See Amemiya (1985, p. 365, Table 10.1) for a listing of applications covering a wide range of topics. Under various circumstances, estimation methods such as the EM algorithm, Powell's least absolute deviations estimator (LAD), and various maximum likelihood procedures may yield better parameter estimates in terms of efficiency or mean squared error. See Amemiya (1973), Arabmazar and Schmidt (1981, 1982), Bera, Jarque and Lee (1984), Dempster, Laird and Rubin (1977), Dudley and Montmarquette (1976), Goldberger (1981, 1983), Huang (1964), Hurd (1979), Lee (1982), Nelson (1984), Olsen (1978, 1980), Paarsch (1984), Powell (1981, 1983a, 1983b, 1984), Robinson (1982), Wales and Woodland (1980) and Wu (1965). See Mroz (1987), for instance, concerning some of the substantive advantages of Heckman's two-step estimation method.

3. This result is also given in Nelson (1984, p. 185, eq. 12). If predetermined variables are included in Z, then the asymptotic OLS bias vector may be defined as $(\sigma_1 \rho_{13} plim\ \hat{\gamma})$ provided that $plim\ \hat{\gamma}$ exists.

4. For instance, in his discussion of Tobit-type models Kmenta (1986, p. 561) writes: " The restriction on the observable range of the dependent variable matters if the probability of falling below the cut-off point is not negligible. In terms of our examples, if only a very small proportion of the households in the population did not purchase a durable good, or if only a very small proportion of all women were not in the labor force, the limited nature of the dependent variable could be ignored. Thus there is no problem in dealing with household expenditure on food or clothing, or with recorded wages of adult males."

5. This is because theoretically $u_{3i} = v_i - u_{1i}$, and hence u_{3i} and u_{1i} will be correlated even if there is no correlation between the structural disturbance terms u_{1i} and v_i.

6. Actually λ is a nonlinear function of Z, so $R^2_{\lambda \cdot z}$ cannot equal 1 exactly. In actual applications of the Heckit procedure, we have often found that the R^2 for the OLS regression of λ on the other explanatory variables in the equation of interest is extremely close to 1.

7. See Kmenta (1986, pp. 437-438) for the usual OLS variance formula rewritten in a form so that the impacts of multicollinearity on the magnitudes of the variances of the coefficient estimates are explicit.

8. Multicollinearity problems can be considered in a more comprehensive way in the context of a principal components formulation of the model. See, for instance, Judge et al. (1985, Ch. 22) and Judge et al. (1988, Ch. 21). The approach adopted in this paper, however, may allow applied readers more readily to understand our main points.

9. See, for example, Heckman (1979, 1980) and Amemiya (1984, 1985) for the form of the variance-covariance matrix. Heckit estimation packages such as Greene (undated, p. 49) typically include some arbitrary procedure for avoiding negative estimates of the coefficient standard errors. Alternative estimates of the coefficient standard errors may be obtained using the procedure described in White (1980), as suggested by Lee (1982) and Amemiya (1984, p. 13). The latter estimates are used in this paper.

10. For a full description of the data bases and of the probit estimation results used in calculating the values of $\hat{\lambda}_i$, see Nakamura and Nakamura (1985b, Section 2.7 and Chapter 3).

References

Amemiya, T.: 1973, 'Regression Analysis When the Dependent Variable is Truncated Normal', *Econometrica*, **42**, 999-1012.

Amemiya, T.: 1984, 'Tobit Models: A Survey', *Journal of Econometrics*, **24**, 3-61.

Amemiya, T.: 1985, *Advanced Econometrics*, Harvard University Press, Cambridge, Massachusetts, U.S.A.

Anderson, K. H., and M. A. Hill: 1983, 'Marriage and Labor Market Discrimination in Japan', *Southern Economic Journal*, **49**(4), 941-953.

Arabmazar, A., and P. Schmidt: 1981, 'Further Evidence on the Robustness of the Tobit Estimator to Heteroskedasticity', *Journal of Econometrics*, **17**, 253-258.

Arabmazar, A., and P. Schmidt: 1982, 'An Investigation of the Robustness of the Tobit Estimator to Non-Normality', *Econometrica*, **50**, 1055-1063.

Bera, A. K., C. M. Jarque, and L. F. Lee: 1984, 'Testing the Normality Assumption in Limited Dependent Variable Models', *International Economic Review*, **25**, 563-578.

Buckley, J., and I. James: 1979, 'Linear Regression with Censored Data', *Biometrika*, **66**, 429-436.

Dempster, A. P., N. M. Laird, and D. B. Rubin: 1977, 'Maximum Likelihood from Incomplete Data via the EM Algorithm', *Journal of the Royal Statistical Society*, B **39**, 1-38.

Dudley, L., and C. Montmarquette: 1976, 'A Model of the Supply of Bilateral Foreign Aid', *American Economic Review*, **66**, 132-142.

Franz, W.: 1985, 'An Economic Analysis of Female Work Participation, Education, and Fertility: Theory and Empirical Evidence for the Federal Republic of Germany', *Journal of Labor Economics*, **3**, S218-S234.

Goldberger, A. S.: 1964, *Econometric Theory*, John Wiley and Sons, New York, New York, U.S.A.

Goldberger, A. S.: 1981, 'Linear Regression After Selection', *Journal of Econometrics*, **15**, 357-366.

Goldberger, A. S.: 1983, 'Abnormal Selection Bias', in S. Karlin, T. Amemiya and L. A. Goodman (eds.), *Studies in Econometrics, Time Series, and Multivariate Statistics*, Academic Press, New York, New York, U.S.A., pp. 67-84.

Greene, W.: *LIMDEP Manual*, undated.

Gronau, R.: 1974, 'The Effects of Children on the Housewife's Value of Time', *Journal of Political Economy*, **82**, 1119-1143.

Hartley, H. O.: 1958, 'Maximum Likelihood Estimation from Incomplete Data', *Biometrica*, **14**, 174-194.

Heckman, J. J.: 1974, 'Shadow Prices, Market Wages and Labor Supply', *Econometrica*, **42**, 679-694.

Heckman, J. J.: 1976, 'The Common Structure of Statistical Models of Truncation, Sample Selection and Limited Dependent Variables and a Simple Estimator for Such Models', *Annals of Economic and Social Measurement*, **5**, 475-492.

Heckman, J. J.: 1979, 'The Sample Selection Bias as a Specification Error', *Econometrica*, **47**, 153-162.

Heckman, J. J.: 1980, 'The Selection Sample Bias as a Specification Error with an Application to the Estimation of Labor Supply Functions', in J. P. Smith.

Huang, D. S.: 1964, 'Discrete Stock Adjustment: The Case of Demand for Automobiles', *International Economic Review*, **5**, 46-62.

Hurd, M.: 1979, 'Estimation in Truncated Samples When There is Heteroskedasticity', *Journal of Econometrics*, **11**, 247-258.

Johnson, N. L., and S. Kotz: 1970 and 1972, *Distributions in Statistics*, Vols. 1 and 4, Wiley, New York, New York, U.S.A.

Judge, G. G., W. E. Griffiths, R. C. Hill, H. Lütkepohl, and T. -C. Lee: 1985, *The Theory and Practice of Econometrics* 2nd edition, John Wiley and Sons, New York, New York, U.S.A.

Judge, G. G., R. C. Hill, W. E. Griffiths, H. Lütkepohl, and T. -C. Lee: 1988, *Introduction to the Theory and Practice of Econometrics* 2nd edition, John Wiley and Sons, New York, New York, U.S.A.

Kalbfleisch, J. O., and R. L. Prentice: 1980, *Statistical Analysis of Failure Time Data*, Wiley, New York, New York, U.S.A.

Kmenta, J.: 1986, *Elements of Econometrics*, 2nd edition, Macmillan Company.

Lee, L. F.: 1982, 'Some Approaches to the Correction of Selectivity Bias', *Review of Economic Studies*, **49**, 355-372.

Maddala, G. S.: 1983, *Limited Dependent and Qualitative Variables in Econometrics*, Cambridge University Press, London, England.

Mroz, T. A.: 1987, 'The Sensitivity of an Empirical Model of Married Women's Hours of Work to Economic and Statistical Assumptions', *Econometrica*, **55**(4), 765-799.

Nakamura, A., and M. Nakamura: 1985a, 'Dynamic Models of the Labor Force Behavior of Married Women Which Can Be Estimated Using Limited Amounts of Past Information', *Journal of Econometrics*, **27**, 273-298.

Nakamura, A., and M. Nakamura: 1985b, *The Second Paycheck: A Socioeconomic Analysis of Earnings*, Academic Press, Orlando, Florida, U.S.A.

Nelson, F.: 1984, 'Efficiency of the Two-Step Estimator for Models with Endogenous Sample Selection', *Journal of Econometrics*, **24**, 181-196.

Ofer, G., and A. Vinokur: 1985, 'Work and Family Roles of Soviet Women: Historical Trends and Cross-Section Analysis', *Journal of Labor Economics*, **3**, S328-S354.

Olsen, R. J.: 1978, 'Note on the Uniqueness of the Maximum Likelihood Estimator for the Tobit Model', *Econometrica*, **46**, 1211-1215.

Olsen, R. J.: 1980, 'A Least Squares Correction for Selectivity Bias', *Econometrica*, **48**, 1815-1820.

Paarsch, H. J.: 1984, 'A Monte Carlo Comparison of Estimators for Censored Regression Models', *Journal of Econometrics*, **24**, 197-214.

Powell, J. L.: 1981, 'Least Absolute Deviations Estimation for Censored and Truncated Regression Models', Technical Report No. 356, Institute for Mathematical Studies in the Social Sciences, Stanford University, California, U.S.A.

Powell, J. L.: 1983a, 'Asymptotic Normality of the Censored and Truncated Least Absolute Deviations Estimators', Technical Report No. 395, Institute for Mathematical Studies in the Social Sciences, Stanford University, California, U.S.A.

Powell, J. L.: 1983b, 'The Asymptotic Normality of Two-Stage Least Absolute Deviations Estimators', *Econometrica*, **51**, 1569-1575.

Powell, J. L.: 1984, 'Least Absolute Deviations Estimation for the Censored Regression Model', *Journal of Econometrics*, **25**, 303-325.

Reimers, C. W.: 1983, 'Labor Market Discrimination against Hispanic and Black Men', *Review of Economics and Statistics*, **65**, 570-579.

Robinson, P. M.: 1982, 'On the Asymptotic Properties of Estimators of Models Containing Limited Dependent Variables', *Econometrica*, **50**, 27-41.

Smith, J .P.: 1980, *Female Labor Supply: Theory and Estimation*, Princeton University Press, Princeton, New Jersey, U.S.A.

Tobin, J.: 1958, 'Estimation of Relationships for Limited Dependent Variables', *Econometrica*, **26**, 24-36.

Wales, T. J., and A. D. Woodland: 1980, 'Sample Selectivity and the Estimation of Labor Supply Functions', *International Economic Review*, **21**, 437-468.

White, H.: 1980, 'A Heteroskedasticity-consistent Covariance Estimator and a Direct Test for Heteroskedasticity', *Econometrica*, **48**, 817-838.

Wu, D. M.: 1965, 'An Empirical Analysis of Household Durable Goods Expenditure', *Econometrica*, **33**, 761-780.

CHAPTER 10

A COMPARISON OF TWO SIGNIFICANCE TESTS FOR STRUCTURAL STABILITY IN THE LINEAR REGRESSION MODEL

W. KRÄMER*
University of Dortmund
Department of Statistics
D-4600 Dortmund 50
West Germany

W. PLOBERGER
Technische Universität Wien
Institut für Ökonometrie
A-1040 Wien
Austria

K. KONTRUS
Institute for Advanced Studies
A-1060 Wien
Austria

ABSTRACT. We test for structural change in the linear regression model when both the number and the timing of possible structural shifts are unknown. We compare the Ploberger-Krämer-Kontrus (1987) 'Fluctuation Test' to the Brown-Durbin-Evans (1975) CUSUM test and find that the former does better for many alternatives.

1. Introduction

The problem of structural change in linear regression has concerned econometricians for quite some time. Statistical tests for the existence of structural change can be distinguished according to whether or not they have a particular alternative in mind.

The well known Chow test assumes that there is just one structural change at a known point in time. It can easily be generalized to several structural shifts, whose timing must however still be known. The Farley-Hinich test (1970) assumes that the timing of the shift follows a certain probability distribution. Watson and Engle (1985), among others, test against the alternative that the regression coefficients follow an AR(1) process. For a bibliography of this literature, see Hackl and Westlund (1988).

Below we focus on tests which do not assume any knowledge about the possible type of structural shifts. Such tests are often called pure significance tests. We discuss in detail the Ploberger-Krämer-Kontrus (1987) Fluctuation test, and compare it to the Brown-Durbin-Evans (1975) CUSUM test. We also comment on the CUSUM of squares tests, but do not, for reasons given later, include it in the detailed comparison.

The model and notation are given in Section 2. Section 3 discusses the local and finite sample power of the tests, and Section 4 applies the tests to real data from the economic literature.

2. The Model and Notation

We consider the linear regression model

$$y_t = x_t'\beta_t + u_t \qquad (t=1,...,T)$$

where y_t is the dependent variable, x_t is a (Kx1) vector of observations on the independent variables, β_t is a (Kx1) vector of unknown regression coefficients, and u_t is an unobservable disturbance term. The null hypothesis under test is that $\beta_t = \beta_0$ is the same for all periods $t = 1,...,T$.

Below we assume fixed regressors and iid $(0,\sigma^2)$ disturbances (not necessarily normal). We also require that

$$\lim_{T\to\infty} \frac{1}{T} R(T) = R(\textit{nonsingular}), \qquad (1)$$

where $R(T) = \sum_{t=1}^{T} x_t x'_t$, and that

$$\lim_{T\to\infty} \frac{1}{T} \sum_{t=1}^{T} x_t = c.$$

This follows from (1) whenever there is a constant in the regression, and for other models is imposed as an extra requirement. We call the vector c the 'mean regressor'.

These assumptions can be relaxed in different ways for the different tests below, without affecting the limiting distribution of the tests under H_0.

Let

$$\hat{\beta}^{(t)} = R(t)^{-1} \sum_{s=1}^{t} x_s y_s \qquad (t \geq K)$$

be the OLS estimate for β_0 based on the first t observations, and let

$$\tilde{u}_t = \frac{y_t - x_t' \hat{\beta}^{(t-1)}}{(1 + x_t' R(t-1)^{-1} x_t)^{1/2}} \qquad (t > K)$$

be the familiar t 'th recursive residual.

The CUSUM test rejects the hypothesis H_0: $\beta_t = \beta_0$ for large values of

$$\frac{1}{\hat{\sigma}} \max_{t=K+1,...,T} \left| \frac{W_t}{\sqrt{T-K}} \Big/ (1 + 2\frac{t-K}{T-K}) \right|,$$

where

$$W_t = \sum_{s=K+1}^{t} \tilde{u}_s \qquad (2)$$

is the cumulated sum of the first $t-K$ recursive residuals, and where $\hat{\sigma}$ is some consistent estimate for the disturbance standard deviation σ.

The proper choice of $\hat{\sigma}$ is a matter of some importance for the power of the test (Alt and Krämer, 1985), but shall not concern us here. We use $\hat{\sigma} = [\sum \tilde{u}_t^2 / (T-K)]^{1/2}$ throughout.

The CUSUM of squares test rejects the hypothesis H_0: $\beta_t = \beta_0$ for large values of

$$\max_{t=K+1,...,T} \left| \frac{\sum_{s=K+1}^{t} \tilde{u}_s^2}{\sum_{s=K+1}^{T} \tilde{u}_s^2} - \frac{t-K}{T-K} \right|.$$

Both are only asymptotic tests. Sen (1982) gives the limiting null distribution of the CUSUM test, and the limiting null distribution of the CUSUM of squares test is in Ploberger and Krämer (1986). When the disturbances are normal, such asymptotic approximations can be improved upon, along the lines of the seminal paper by Brown et al. (1975).

Both the CUSUM and CUSUM of squares tests are well established. Our main concern is therefore with the more recent Fluctuation test, as first suggested by Ploberger (1983).

Contrary to the CUSUM and CUSUM of squares tests, the Fluctuation test is more directly based on the successive parameter estimates $\hat{\beta}^{(t)}$. The basic idea is that these should cluster around the true β_0 when there is no structural change. The test therefore rejects for large fluctuations in $\hat{\beta}^{(t)}$. The test statistic is

$$S^{(T)} = \max_{t=K,\ldots,T} \frac{t}{\hat{\sigma}T} \| R(T)^{1/2} (\hat{\beta}^{(t)} - \hat{\beta}^{(T)}) \|_\infty, \tag{3}$$

where $\| \cdot \|_\infty$ denotes the maximum norm.

The main rationale for this particular test statistic is that we can derive its (limiting) null distribution. Ploberger, Krämer and Kontrus (1987) show that

$$B^{(T)}(z) = \frac{K + z(T-K)}{\hat{\sigma}T} R(T)^{1/2} \left(\hat{\beta}^{[K+z(T-K)]} - \hat{\beta}^{(T)} \right) \tag{4}$$

tends in distribution to a K-dimensional Brownian Bridge B(z) as $T \to \infty$, where $z \in [0,1]$. This implies the following limiting distribution of $S^{(T)}$ (see, e.g., Billingsley, 1968, p. 85):

$$F(x) = \begin{cases} 0 & x < 0 \\ [1 + 2\sum_{i=1}^{\infty} (-1)^i \exp(2i^2 x^2)]^K & x \geq 0 \end{cases}.$$

Some useful critical values for an asymptotic significance level at $\alpha = 5\%$ are 1.48($K=2$), 1.54($K=3$), 1.59($K=4$) and 1.62($K=5$). A more detailed table is in Ploberger et al. (1987).

We do not claim that the test statistic (3) uses the successive parameter estimates most efficiently. Alternatively, one might maximize quadratic forms or other functions of $\hat{\beta}^{(t)} - \hat{\beta}^{(T-t)}$, where $\hat{\beta}^{(T-t)}$ is the OLS estimate for β_0 from the last $T-t$ observations. This is equivalent to successive applications of the Analysis of Covariance test. Unfortunately, the null distribution of the resulting maximum is unknown except for very special cases. If it could be found, we would have yet another and perhaps more powerful test.

A related issue concerns the particular function of the Brownian Bridge on which our decision is based. It is not at all clear whether the maximum distance from the time axis is the most efficient way of assessing possible structural changes. Again, we have chosen the particular functional (3) mainly for ease of deriving its distribution under H_0. The power of the test can almost certainly be increased if the critical line were some other curve rather than a straight line, which is closer to zero at the edges of the (0,1)-interval. However, we were not able to derive the null distribution of the resulting test statistics.

3. Local Power

Below we consider the power of the tests when the regression coefficients change according to the following pattern:

$$\beta_{t,T} = \beta_0 + \frac{1}{\sqrt{T}} g(t/T) \qquad (t = 1,\ldots,T; \ T = 1,2,\ldots). \tag{5}$$

The function g is defined on the $[0,1]$ interval and takes values in R^K. We only require that it can be expressed as a uniform limit of step functions. Otherwise it is arbitrary. If for instance $g(z) = 0$ for $z < z_0$ and $g(z) = \Delta\beta$ for $z \geq z_0$, we have a single shift in β at time $t = z_0 T$. This shift occurs always at the same quantile of the observations (at mid-sample, say) as sample size increases. The intensity of the shift however decreases as $T \to \infty$.

The local power of the tests is the limit, as $T \to \infty$ and as coefficients change according to the pattern (5), of the power of the tests. For the CUSUM of squares test, this equals the size of the test regardless of the function g (Ploberger and Krämer, 1985). Thus, the CUSUM of squares test has only trivial local power against structural change alternatives. This is in line with Deshayes and Picard (1986), who obtained poor power of the CUSUM of squares test also in the Bahadur sense. Therefore, we exclude the CUSUM of squares test from our Monte Carlo experiments below.

The local power of the CUSUM test follows from the fact that

$$W^T(z) \equiv \frac{1}{\hat{\sigma}\sqrt{T-K}} \sum_{t=K+1}^{Tz} \tilde{u}_t \tag{6}$$

$$\xrightarrow{d} W(z) + \frac{c'}{\sigma}\int_0^z g(v)dv - \frac{c'}{\sigma}\int_0^z(\frac{1}{v}\int_0^v g(w)\,dw\,)dv,$$

where $W(z)$ is the standard Wiener process, c is the mean regressor and $\xrightarrow{d}$ denotes convergence in distribution (Ploberger and Krämer, 1985).

The local power of the Fluctuation test follows from a similar limit result. Ploberger et al. (1987) show that for alternatives (5),

$$B^{(T)}(z) \xrightarrow{d} B(z) + \frac{1}{\sigma}R^{1/2}(\int_0^z g(v)\,dv - z\int_0^1 g(v)\,dv)\ . \tag{7}$$

Expressions (6) and (7) allow to exactly compute the local power of the tests, by computing the crossing probabilities of the respective underlying stochastic processes. This however turned out to be extremely difficult even for very simple g–functions. So far, we have not been able to derive any analytical results, and resort to Monte Carlo instead.

Our Monte Carlo experiments were designed to investigate the finite sample significance of an obvious consequence of (6): the CUSUM test has trivial local power whenever structural changes are orthogonal to the mean regressor c. This follows from the fact that $W^{(T)}$ has the same limiting distribution under H_0 and under local alternatives if $c'g(z) = 0$ for all z.

To save computer time, we confine ourselves to the case $K=2$ (a bivariate regression with a constant), where

$$x_t = [1, (-1)^t]'\qquad (t=1,...,T).$$

This particular sequence of independent variables was chosen to ensure that (1) holds, with mean regressor $c = [1,0]'$. It can be viewed as the prototype of a bounded regressor with seasonal variation. Regression coefficients were set to zero, and the disturbances u_t were generated as standard normal variates, using NAG library subroutines GO5CCF and GO5ODF. All simulations were performed on the Vienna Institute for Advanced Studies' Sperry Univac 1100 mainframe computer, and used up about 100 hours of CPU time.

Table I gives the empirical rejection probabilities under H_0, as estimated from $N=10000$ replications (runs), for nominal significance levels $\alpha = 5\%$ and 10%, respectively.

TABLE I. Monte Carlo Estimates of True Rejection Probabilities under H_0

	α	
	5%	10%
	a) CUSUM test	
$T = 120$	3.3%	8.2%
$T = 1000$	4.7%	9.3%
	b) Fluctuation test	
$T = 120$	2.3%	5.9%
$T = 1000$	4.1%	9.1%

These results, which were corroborated by other experiments and which agree with conventional wisdom in case of the CUSUM test, show that nominal α-levels consistently overstate the true size of the tests. This follows from the fact that both the W_t's from (2) and the $B^{(T)}(z)$'s from (4) are discrete readings from a continuous time stochastic process. Even if the crossing probabilities of the underlying continuous time process were correct (which they never are in finite samples), the crossing probabilities for discrete readings would still be less. As sample size increases, discrete readings get more densely packed, and the two probabilities coincide.

Next we investigate the power of tests. For ease of comparison with previous work, we confine ourselves to single shifts in the regression coefficients. We systematically vary (i) the timing, (ii) the intensity, and (iii) the angle of the structural shift. The shift occurs at time $T^* = dT$, where d takes the values 0.3, 0.5, and 0.7, respectively. This corresponds to a shift early, midway and late in the sample period. The shift itself is given by (5), where

$$g(z) = \begin{cases} [0,0]' & z < d \\ \Delta\beta = b[\cos \Psi, \sin \Psi]' & z \geq d \end{cases} .$$

Sample sizes were $T = 30, 60,$ and 120, and the number of replications per parameter combination is now $N = 5000$.

The parameter Ψ measures the angle between $\Delta\beta$ and the mean regressor c. If $\Psi = 0°$, the shift is only in the intercept, and only the slope is affected for $\Psi = 90°$. The intensity of the shift is $\|\Delta\beta\| = |b| / \sqrt{T}$. This varies with the parameter b. Given b, it goes down with increasing sample size so that the empirical rejection probabilities approximate the local power of the tests as T increases.

Table II reports the respective empirical rejection probabilities for various Ψ's and b's, given $\alpha = 5\%$, $T = 120$, and $d = 0.5$.

As expected, the CUSUM test deteriorates as Ψ increases. It is worst, with power even below nominal size, when the structural shift is orthogonal to the mean regressor c ($\Psi = 90°$).

By contrast, the Fluctuation test is only marginally affected by the angle Ψ. *Ceteris paribus*, its power is lowest when Ψ is around 45°, which is a consequence of the maximum norm employed in (3). For a given intensity of the shift, as measured by the Euclidean norm, the maximum norm is smallest for $\Psi = 45°$.

Ceteris paribus, both tests perform better as the intensity of the structural shift increases, except for high values of Ψ, where the CUSUM test deteriorates as b increases. This is due to the particular estimate (i.e., the standard OLS-based estimate) for the disturbance standard deviation used for the CUSUM test. We found that this is blown up for large Ψ, and as b increases, thus shrinking the CUSUM trajectories toward the horizontal axis. Additional experiments in Alt and Krämer (1985) show that this side effect can be avoided by alternative estimates for σ.

TABLE II. Empirical Rejection Probabilities under the Alternative

b	\psi (degrees)															
	0	6	12	18	24	30	36	42	48	54	60	66	72	78	84	90
a) CUSUM test																
4.8	16.5	14.7	14.6	14.2	13.1	11.2	10.4	8.9	7.6	6.1	5.1	4.7	3.9	3.4	3.4	2.7
6.0	25.2	24.7	24.4	23.2	20.0	17.8	15.4	13.5	10.5	8.3	5.9	5.2	4.3	3.6	2.6	3.0
7.2	37.6	37.0	36.1	33.3	30.2	26.6	23.3	18.2	14.1	10.5	8.2	5.7	4.7	3.2	2.5	2.5
8.4	52.1	51.5	48.1	46.5	41.3	37.0	30.9	25.0	19.1	13.8	9.9	6.0	4.8	3.1	2.3	2.5
9.6	66.2	66.0	64.4	60.4	55.1	47.6	41.9	32.9	24.5	18.2	11.7	7.8	4.5	3.2	2.4	1.5
10.8	78.7	78.1	74.6	72.2	66.2	58.7	50.6	41.4	32.9	23.7	14.3	9.7	5.0	2.4	2.1	1.6
12.0	86.6	87.3	84.9	82.6	77.2	70.5	62.4	51.9	38.6	26.7	16.6	9.2	4.9	2.7	1.8	1.4
b) Fluctuation test																
4.8	36.4	37.3	34.0	32.9	31.8	29.2	28.2	27.4	27.7	28.1	30.2	31.9	32.2	34.8	36.4	36.9
6.0	59.0	57.6	57.1	54.9	50.6	48.0	47.2	43.9	43.9	46.4	48.8	49.8	53.3	55.6	57.3	59.5
7.2	79.2	78.3	76.2	73.7	69.6	67.7	65.9	62.1	63.0	64.4	67.2	70.7	72.9	76.2	76.6	79.0
8.4	90.6	90.6	89.4	87.8	85.8	82.3	79.9	78.1	78.4	79.2	82.5	85.8	87.4	90.4	90.4	90.2
9.6	97.2	97.6	96.3	95.7	93.9	91.8	91.4	90.2	90.3	91.8	91.9	93.9	95.8	96.7	97.2	97.0
10.8	99.3	99.4	98.7	98.6	98.0	97.1	96.1	96.6	96.0	96.9	97.4	98.3	98.6	98.9	99.3	99.2
12.0	99.9	99.9	99.9	99.7	99.5	99.3	99.0	98.9	98.9	98.8	99.2	99.7	99.6	99.8	99.8	99.9

The above patterns repeated themselves for other sample sizes, significance levels, and shift-points d, and are therefore not explicitly reported here. For $T = 30$ and $T = 60$, both tests fared somewhat worse, due to smaller actual size. The CUSUM test performs best when the shift occurs early ($d = 0.3$) and worst when the shift is rather late ($d = 0.7$). This is no surprise, since a shift towards the end of the sample implies that the CUSUM test does not have much time to pick this up. Table II above, where $d = 0.5$, therefore gives a fair example of its overall performance.

The most important outcome of our experiments concerns the relative performance of the tests. As evidenced by Table II, the Fluctuation test wins most of the time. This superiority appears even more striking in view of its smaller actual size, as shown in Table I. If there were a correction for this, the Fluctuation test would perform even better. The only instances, not reported here, where the CUSUM test outperformed the Fluctuation test, occurred for small d and Ψ. For the remaining parameter combinations, the Fluctuation test has superior power, with a margin that is at times substantial.

However, some caveats apply. First, Monte Carlo simulations are only imperfect substitutes for analytical results, which in our case are only available for infinite samples. Second, the limiting distribution of the Fluctuation test, both under H_0 and under local alternatives, depends crucially on assumption (2), which excludes trending data. So far, we have not been able to demonstrate that the Fluctuation test covers such data as well.

4. A Numerical Example

For illustration, we apply the Fluctuation, CUSUM and CUSUM of squares tests to eq. (10) from Klein (1977, table 1, p. 703). This equation expresses the demand for money ($\log M$, Klein's notation) in terms of income ($\log y_p$), the short term commercial paper rate (r_s), yield on long term corporate bonds (r_L), the rate of return on money (r_M), and $\log S(\dot{p}/p)$, some measure of price uncertainty. It is estimated with OLS, using annual data from 1880 to 1972. We have selected this equation because the data were available, and because it is a prime candidate for structural change in view of the time range covered.

Reestimating the equation produced the following result:

$$\log M = -13.74 + 1.35 \log y_p - 0.28\, r_s - 0.08\, r_L + 0.32\, r_M + 0.06 \log S(\dot{p}/p). \tag{8}$$

This differs slightly from Klein's result, but can be attributed to subsequent revisions of the data.

Figures 1 to 3 give the sample trajectories of $t / (\hat{\sigma}T) \parallel R(T)^{1/2} (\hat{\beta}^{(t)} - \hat{\beta}^{(T)}) \parallel_\infty$ (Fluctuation test), of the cumulated and standardized recursive residuals (CUSUM test), and of the cumulated and standardized squares of the recursive residuals (CUSUM of squares test). The dotted lines indicate the respective critical 5% limits. The figures show that the CUSUM of squares and Fluctuation tests reject the null hypothesis of parameter constancy, whereas the CUSUM test does not.

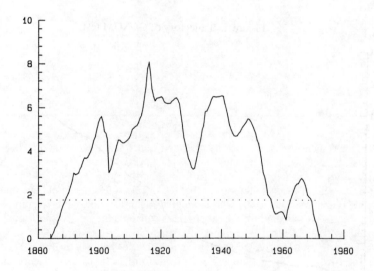

Figure 1. Trajectory of Fluctuation test.

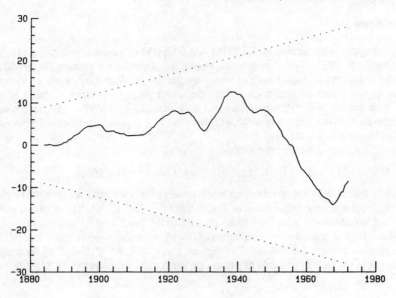

Figure 2. Trajectory of CUSUM test.

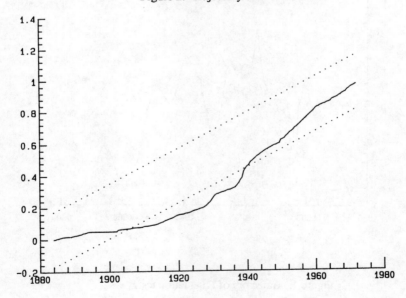

Figure 3. Trajectory of CUSUM of squares test.

These results should be viewed strictly as an illustration. Since we do not know with certainty what (if anything) is wrong with (8), we cannot tell which type of error (I or II) is made. Various diagnostic checks in Krämer and Sonnberger (1986, pp. 126-127) indicate that (8) suffers from many defects on top of structural change, so the rejection by the CUSUM of squares test, which is a bit surprising in view of its poor local power, might well be due to other reasons. Such issues are however beyond the scope of the present paper.

* Research supported by Deutsche Forschungsgemeinschaft (DFG). We are grateful to the Canadian Econometric Study Group, in particular Robin Carter and Lonnie Magee, for many helpful suggestions and comments. The paper has also benefited a lot from a very thorough refereeing process. Remaining errors are our own. All computations were done with the Institute for Advanced Studies' IAS-SYSTEM econometric software package.

References

Alt, R., and W. Krämer: 1985, 'A Modification of the CUSUM Test', *Research Memorandum No. 225*, Institute for Advanced Studies, Vienna, Austria.

Billingsley, P.: 1968, *Convergence of Probability Measures*, Wiley, New York, U.S.A.

Brown, R. L., J. Durbin, and I. M. Evans: 1975, 'Techniques for Testing the Constancy of Regression Relationships over Time (with discussion)', *Journal of the Royal Statistical Society B*, **37**, 149-192.

Deshayes, J., and D. Picard: 1986, 'Off-line Statistical Analysis of Change Point Models using Non-parametric and Likelihood Methods', in M. Basseville and A. Beneviste (eds.), *Detection of Abrupt Changes in Signals and Dynamical Systems*, Springer, Berlin, West Germany.

Farley, I. I., and M. Hinich: 1970, 'Testing for a Shifting Slope Coefficient in a Linear Model', *Journal of the American Statistical Association*, **65**, 1320-1329.

Hackl, P. and A. Westlund: 1988, 'Statistical Analysis of Structural Change: An Annotated Bibliography', *Empirical Economics*, forthcoming.

Klein, B.: 1977, 'The Demand for Quality-adjusted Cash Balances: Price Uncertainty in the U.S. Demand for Money Function', *Journal of Political Economy*, **85**, 691-715.

Krämer, W., and H. Sonnberger: 1986, *The Linear Regression Model under Test*, Physica-Verlag, Heidelberg, West Germany.

Ploberger, W.: 1983, 'Testing the Constancy of Parameters in Linear Models', paper given at the Econometric Society European meeting, Pisa, Italy.

Ploberger, W., and W. Krämer: 1985, 'The Local Power of the CUSUM and CUSUM of Squares Tests', mimeo.

Ploberger, W., W. Krämer, and K. Kontrus: 1987, 'A New Test for Structural Stability in the Linear Regression Model', *Journal of Econometrics*, forthcoming.

Sen, P. K.: 1982, 'Invariance Principles for Recursive Residuals', *The Annals of Statistics*, **10**, 307-312.

Watson, M., and R. Engle: 1985, 'Testing for Regression Coefficient Stability with a Stationary AR (1) Alternative', *Review of Economics and Statistics*, **67**, 341-346.

CHAPTER 11

RATES OF RETURN ON PHYSICAL AND R&D CAPITAL AND STRUCTURE OF THE PRODUCTION PROCESS: CROSS SECTION AND TIME SERIES EVIDENCE

JEFFREY I. BERNSTEIN*
Carleton University
Dept. of Economics
Ottawa, Ontario, Canada
and NBER, U.S.A.

M. ISHAQ NADIRI
New York University
Dept. of Economics
New York, New York
and NBER, U.S.A.

ABSTRACT. R&D investment is an outcome of a corporate plan and is influenced by the existing technology, by prices, by product demand characteristics, and by the legacy of past capital stock decisions. In this paper we focus on the determinants and interaction of labor, physical capital, and R&D capital. In particular, we investigate three major issues. The first issue relates to the nature of the factor substitution possibilities between the three inputs in response to changes in input prices in order to estimate the own and cross price elasticities of the factors of production. The second problem pertains to the magnitude by which output expansion increases labor, physical, and R&D capital. Lastly, we address the extent to which adjustment costs affect factor demands, and measure the marginal adjustment costs for physical and R&D capital.

1. Introduction

It is now a well established empirical result that research and development (R&D) is a significant element in productivity growth (see Nadiri, 1980, Griliches, 1980, Terleckyj, 1974, and Mansfield, 1968). However, R&D investment is itself an outcome of a corporate plan. This investment is influenced by the existing technology, by prices, by product demand characteristics, and by the legacy of past capital accumulation decisions. In this paper we want to investigate the influences on R&D investment, and how these effects elicit an interaction with the other factors of production. In particular, we focus on the determinants and interaction of labor, physical and R&D capital.

There are essentially three major problems which are dealt with in this paper. The first relates to the nature of the factor substitution possibilities between the three inputs. Specifically, we want to know how labor and physical capital respond to changes in the factor price of R&D capital, and how, in turn, R&D capital is affected by changes in its own price, as well as the wage rate and rental rate on physical capital. The second problem pertains to the output expansion possibilities. In particular, we investigate the magnitude by which output expansion (or product demand growth) increases labor, physical and R&D capital.

The last general problem relates directly to the dynamics of the model. Certain factors of production are costly to adjust, and therefore it takes time for the firm to adopt its long run factor requirements. It is these costs of adjustment which render the model dynamic. Generally, it is acknowledged that increases in the level of physical capital involve adjustment costs, so that it is quasi-fixed, while labor may be considered a variable input (sometimes labor is disaggregated into skilled and unskilled; the latter is variable and the former is quasi-fixed). In the present context

R&D capital is also modeled as a quasi-fixed factor because of the significant development costs incurred in this investment process. We estimate the extent to which adjustment costs affect factor demands and measure the magnitude of these costs for physical and R&D capital.

An important but unresolved issue addressed relates to the substantial difference between the rates of return on physical and R&D capital reported in the literature. Previous empirical work (see Griliches, 1980, Minasian, 1969, and Mansfield, 1965) has found, and left unexplained, the result that the marginal value of R&D (measured for example by its marginal product) exceeds both the marginal value of physical capital and the interest rate. In this paper, we show that these conclusions are the outcome of the existence of adjustment costs. The marginal value of R&D is greater than the opportunity cost of funds (i.e., the interest rate) because the former must be sufficiently large to cover the marginal costs of adjustment. Moreover, the reason that the marginal value of R&D exceeds the value for physical capital is due to the fact that the marginal adjustment costs associated with R&D are greater than the costs for physical capital. This implies that the deviation between the marginal value of R&D and the interest rate is greater than the difference between the marginal value of physical capital and the interest rate.

Sections 2 and 3 of the paper detail the theoretical model and its specification for estimation. The data, industry characteristics and estimates are discussed in Sections 4 and 5. The results concerning factor substitution, output expansion, and costs of adjustment are analyzed in Sections 6, 7, and 8. A summary of our findings is contained in the last section.

2. The Theoretical Model

Consider the production process of a firm which can be described by

$$y(t) = F(K_p(t-1), K_r(t-1), L(t), \Delta K_p(t), \Delta K_r(t)) \tag{1}$$

where $y(t)$ is output in period t, F is the twice continuously differentiable concave production function, $K_p(t-1)$ is the physical capital input at the beginning of period t, $K_r(t-1)$ is the R&D or knowledge capital input at the beginning of period t, $L(t)$ is the labor input in period t, $\Delta K_p(t) = K_p(t) - K_p(t-1)$, $\Delta K_r(t) = K_r(t) - K_r(t-1)$. The marginal products are positive and diminishing, $F_i > 0$, $F_{ii} < 0$ for $i = p, r, l$ and adjustment costs associated with $\Delta K_p(t)$ and $\Delta K_r(t)$ are internal with $F_j < 0$, $F_{jj} < 0$ $j = e, d$. Following Treadway (1971, 1974), Mortenson (1973), Meese (1980), and Morrison and Berndt (1981) we assume that the quasi-fixed factors ($K_p(t)$ and $K_r(t)$ are subject to increasing internal costs of adjustment. In other words, as purchases of additional units of each quasi-fixed input occur, the quantity of foregone output rises. This implies that the average cost of investment increases in response to physical and knowledge capital accumulation.

The two quasi-fixed factors accumulate by

$$K_i(t) = I_i(t) + (1 - \delta_i)K_i(t-1), \quad i = p, r \tag{2}$$

where $I_i(t)$ is gross investment in period t and δ_i is the fixed depreciation rate. The work of Pakes and Schankerman (1978) has shown that knowledge capital depreciates like physical capital. Moreover, they found that the depreciation rate on the former is the higher of the two rates.

We assume that the firm is a price taker in all markets, so that the flow of funds can be written as

$$V(t) = p(t)y(t) - w(t)L(t) - p_p(t)I_p(t) - p_r(t)I_r(t), \tag{3}$$

where $V(t)$ is the flow of funds, $p(t)$ is the product price, $w(t)$ is the wage, $p_p(t)$ is the physical investment price, and $p_r(t)$ is the R&D investment price in period t.

In order for a firm to maximize its expected present value of the flow of funds, it must minimize the expected discounted value of its costs. Thus at time t a plan is chosen which minimizes

$$J(t) = E(t)\sum_{\psi=t}^{\infty}\alpha(t,\psi)\,[\,w(\psi)L(\psi)+p_p(\psi)I_p(\psi)+p_r(\psi)I(\psi)\,] \tag{4}$$

where E is the conditional expectation operator and $\alpha(t,\psi)$ is the discount factor applied at date t for cost incurred at date ψ. The program can be summarized in the following manner. A firm minimizes the expected discounted costs by selecting the labor requirements, investment in R&D and physical capital subject to the production technology, capital accumulation conditions, and expectations regarding prices and the quantity of output. The conditional expectation operator is taken over all future values of the wage rate, the prices of R&D and physical capital investment, and output.

The optimizing program can be solved by inverting the production function to obtain the labor requirements function,

$$L(t) = G(K_p(t-1), K_r(t-1), \Delta K_p(t), \Delta K_r(t), y(t)) \tag{5}$$

with $G_i < 0$ $i = p,r$, $G_j > 0$ $j = e,d$ and $G_y > 0$. By substituting (2) and (5) into (4), we can observe that the intertemporal expected cost minimization problem involves the optimal selection of knowledge and physical capital. The first order conditions are,

$$E(t)[\,w(t)G_e + p_p(t) + \alpha(t,t+1)\,(w(t+1)\,(G_p - G_e) - p_p(t+1)\,(1-\delta_p))\,] = 0 \tag{6.1}$$

$$E(t)[\,w(t)G_d + p_r(t) + \alpha(t,t+1)\,(w(t+1)\,(G_r - G_d) - p_r(t+1)\,(1-\delta_r))\,] = 0. \tag{6.2}$$

These equations illustrate that the net change in expected discounted costs, from purchasing an additional unit of a stock at date t, is zero. The net change consists of the marginal adjustment cost plus the purchase price, minus the future savings in adjustment cost, purchase cost, and variable cost (i.e., labor) from having larger stocks of physical capital and R&D capital in the present.

3. Model Specification

The estimating equations consist of the inverted production function as well as the first order conditions (6.1) and (6.2). Since (6.1) and (6.2) are derived relations, in order to render the model estimable we only have to specify the labor requirements function and the nature of the error terms. The former is assumed to be

$$L(t)/y(t) = \alpha_o + \alpha_y y(t) + \sum_{i=p}^{r}\alpha_i(K_i(t-1)/y(t)) + \frac{1}{2}\alpha_{yy}y^2(t) + \tag{7}$$

$$+ \frac{1}{2}\sum_{i=p}^{r}\alpha_{ii}(K_i(t-1)/y(t))^2 + + \frac{1}{2}\alpha_{ee}(\Delta K_p(t)/y(t))^2 + \frac{1}{2}\alpha_{dd}(\Delta K_r(t)/y(t))^2 +$$

$$+ \sum_{i=p}^{r}\alpha_{yi}K_i(t-1) + \alpha_{pr}K_p(t-1)K_r(t-1)/y^2(t).$$

We have selected a linear-quadratic labor-output requirements function, which is a second order approximation to any arbitrary labor-output function. Note that we have not imposed any restrictions on the degree of returns to scale. In addition, because there is only a single variable factor of production, equation (7) is equivalent to specifying the average variable cost function for the firm. Lastly, incorporated into (7) is the reasonable condition that marginal costs of adjustment are zero at $\Delta K_p(t) = \Delta K_r(t) = 0$. This has the effect of making the adjustment costs internal but separable from the output production process.[1]

Given equation (7), the first order conditions (6.1) and (6.2) become

$$w(t)[\alpha_{ee}\Delta(K_p(t)/y(t))]+p_p(t)+E(t)\alpha(t,t+1)[w(t+1)(\alpha_p+\alpha_{pp}(K_p(t)/y(t+1))- \quad (8.1)$$

$$-\alpha_{ee}(\Delta K_p(t+1)/y(t+1))+\alpha_{yp}y(t+1)+\alpha_{pr}(K_r(t)/y(t+1))-p_p(t+1)(1-\delta_p)]=0$$

$$w(t)[\alpha_{dd}(\Delta K_r(t)/y(t))]+p_r(t)+E(t)\alpha(t,t+1)[w(t+1)(\alpha_r+\alpha_{rr}(K_r(t)/y(t+1))- \quad (8.2)$$

$$-\alpha_{dd}(\Delta K_r(t+1)/y(t+1))+\alpha_{yr}y(t+1)+\alpha_{pr}(K_p(t)/y(t+1))-p_r(t+1)(1-\delta_r))]=0.$$

Our basic model consists of equations (7), (8.1), and (8.2). We can observe that equations (8.1) and (8.2) are simultaneous, and that the overall system is nonlinear in the variables.

To obtain parameter values for equation set (7), (8.1), and (8.2), we must consider the nature of the error terms in each of these equations. The first order conditions describe the expected effects on cost from adding physical and R&D capital stocks. Moreover, these expectations are conditional on all information available to the firm at the date the investment decisions are made. Thus the errors in (8.1) and (8.2) represent unanticipated information (i.e., surprises) which become available at date t, and therefore their conditional expected values are zero. The error associated with the labor requirements function represents technological shocks which illustrate the randomness in the production process.[2] The conditional expectation of the labor requirements function is viewed as holding on a conditioning set of instrumental variables which only contain lagged variables. In this context, it is possible to employ the results of Hansen and Singleton (1982) and Hansen (1982), who developed a generalized method of moments estimator. Moreover, as shown by Pindyck and Rotemberg (1982a), when the error terms are conditionally homoskedastic the estimator is equivalent to the nonlinear three-stage estimator as developed by Jorgenson and Laffont (1974) and Amemiya (1977).

4. The Data and Industry Characteristics

The sample consists of a set of firms grouped into four two-digit SIC industry classifications. Within SIC 20 (foods) there are five firms, there are nine firms within SIC 28 (chemicals), for SIC 33 (primary metals) we have seven firms, and finally for SIC 35 (nonelectrical machinery) there are fourteen firms. The word 'industry' in this paper refers to a specific set of firms in each classification. The selection of firms was dictated by the availability of consistent time series data on R&D and physical capital (or plant and equipment) expenditures. The time period ranges from 1959-1966. Thus we have a sample of time series and cross section data which were pooled in order to provide a richer set of information in which to estimate the model under consideration.

The list of variables and their construction are: Physical or plant and equipment (P&E) capital input (K_p) is the measure of net stock generated by the declining balance depreciation formula

$$K_p(t)=I_p(t)+(1-\delta_p)K_p(t-1)$$

where $I_p(t)$ equals actual expenditures on P&E deflated by its price. Investment in P&E was obtained from the Standard & Poors tape. The investment deflator (p_p) is obtained from the *(U.S.) President's Economic Report*, 1980. The depreciation rate for each firm was calculated by summing over time depreciation allowances divided by the gross plant and equipment and then dividing this sum by the number of time periods. The R&D capital input (K_r) was obtained from a similar procedure,

$$K_r(t) = I_r(t) + (1 - \delta_r)K_r(t-1).$$

Investment in R&D (I_r) and its associated price (p_r) were obtained from Standard & Poors data series and we arbitrarily chose $\delta_r = 0.1$ to measure the depreciation rate for the stock of knowledge. The labor input (L) is defined as the labor expense, from the Standard & Poors tape, divided by the wage rate (w). The latter variable was obtained from the Bureau of Labor Statistics. Output (y) is defined as sales, obtained from the Standard & Poors data, divided by the producer price index (p). The price variable comes from the Bureau of Labor Statistics. Finally, the one period discount rate $(\alpha(t, t+1) = 1/(1 + r(t))$ is measured as the corporate bond rate (Aaa). This variable was obtained from the (U.S.) President's Economic Report, 1980.

TABLE I. Main Variable Magnitudes by Industry *

Main Variable	SIC			
	20	28	33	35
Physical Capital Stock per Unit of Output	0.27 (0.08)	0.83 (0.16)	0.83 (0.41)	0.38 (0.15)
R&D Capital Stock per Unit of Output	0.10 (0.06)	0.52 (0.18)	0.16 (0.13)	0.27 (0.11)
Labor Services per Unit of Output	0.07 (0.01)	0.16 (0.04)	0.13 (0.02)	0.13 (0.02)
Physical Capital Stock	204.16 (106.89)	487.83 (194.88)	610.71 (583.26)	22.32 (10.48)
R&D Capital Stock	82.67 (71.34)	298.65 (131.76)	86.46 (86.18)	13.98 (3.48)

* Standard deviations in parentheses

Table I presents the means and standard deviations of the main variables for each industry used in the model between 1959 and 1966. Defining variable intensities in terms of output, we see an interesting set of cross-industry patterns emerging. The food industry has the lowest intensity in all three input variables, while the chemical industry has the highest. Although primary metals and chemicals exhibit the same physical capital to output ratio, the standard deviation for the latter is substantially smaller. Primary metals exhibits a physical capital intensity which is slightly more than twice that for nonelectrical machinery. Moreover, the R&D intensity for the latter industry is about double that for primary metals. Since the labor intensities (and their standard deviations) are the same, it will be of interest to compare the results obtained for each of these two industries.

The physical capital intensity illustrates that there are two classes of 'industries', the 'highs' (chemicals and primary metals) and the 'lows' (food and nonelectrical machinery). However, the R&D intensity variable shows that there is roughly an equal spread among the four industries.

The R&D intensity of primary metals is approximately twice that for foods. Nonelectrical machinery is nearly double the value of primary metals, while chemicals is almost twice the magnitude for nonelectrical machinery. Finally, the labor intensity illustrates that three out of the four industries exhibit the same magnitude while foods is substantially smaller.

5. The Estimates

In this section we describe the empirical estimates obtained from equations (7), (8.1), and (8.2). First, we pooled all four industries to obtain the aggregate results presented in Table II. In estimating the pooled data we introduced industry dummy variables in the constant and first order terms. Therefore, the constants in the derived equations (8.1) and (8.2) are also industry specific. Overall the fit is good, as the R^2's are high in all three equations. Most of the estimates are significant, and all have the correct sign. In particular, as output increases, according to the first and second order parameters, labor intensity (or average variable cost) increases ($\alpha_y > 0$, $\alpha_{yy} > 0$). Holding output fixed, the first order terms show that as physical and R&D capital intensity rise the labor intensity falls ($\alpha_p < 0$, $\alpha_r < 0$).

The second order conditions are satisfied as $\alpha_{pp} > 0$, $\alpha_{rr} > 0$ and $\alpha_{pp}\alpha_{rr} - \alpha_{pr}^2 > 0$. Finally the cost of adjustment parameters are positive ($\alpha_{ee} > 0$, $\alpha_{dd} > 0$) and the physical capital parameter is significant. Thus physical capital is in fact a quasi-fixed factor of production. The troublesome aspect is that the adjustment parameter for R&D is insignificant.[3] This result can arise because either on average for the four industries, and over the period 1959-1966, R&D capital is a variable factor of production, or else there are more industry-specific variations than have been presently allowed for in the model. In other words, not only are the zero and first order parameters different across industries, but the second order parameters also vary. Adopting this second view, we estimate the model for each industry.

TABLE II. Industry Pooled Estimates with Dummy Variables in Zero and First Order Terms

Parameter	Estimate	t-Statistic	Parameter	Estimate	t-Statistic
α_0^{20}	0.1366	2.9283	α_r^{20}	−0.1647	− 170.8200
α_0^{28}	0.2258	8.4791	α_r^{28}	−0.1447	− 110.9200
α_0^{33}	0.1141	7.3363	α_r^{33}	−0.1279	− 122.9900
α_0^{35}	0.0289	1.7019	α_r^{35}	−0.1388	−169.2900
α_y^{20}	0.2894 E-03	2.5413	α_{yy}	0.3131 E-06	2.4916
α_y^{28}	0.4909 E-03	6.4900	α_{pp}	0.1895 E-01	3.3051
α_y^{33}	0.2658 E-03	3.6463	α_{rr}	0.5498 E-02	2.8193
α_y^{35}	0.1735 E-03	0.7121	α_{ee}	0.2001	2.1087
α_p^{20}	−0.1159	−32.527	α_{dd}	0.1358	1.2239
α_p^{28}	−0.1170	−29.659	α_{yp}	−0.2092 E-04	−4.1129
α_p^{33}	−0.0964	−24.059	α_{yr}	−0.4156 E-05	−3.0837
α_p^{35}	−0.1280	−47.408	α_{pr}	−0.5067 E-02	−3.4005
R^2 Labor Equation		0.945	SEE Labor Equation		0.0300
R^2 P&E Equation		0.994	SEE P&E Equation		0.0090
R^2 R&D Equation		0.997	SEE R&D Equation		0.0020

TABLE III. Food Industry Estimates

Parameter	Estimate	t-Statistic
α_0	0.0612	2.3640
α_y	0.8384 E-04	1.2935
α_p	−0.1044	−32.5900
α_r	−0.1288	−55.9630
α_{yy}	0.8733 E-07	1.2166
α_{pp}	0.0770	7.1015
α_{rr}	0.0485	3.0217
α_{ee}	1.3342	1.5590
α_{dd}	1.3879	1.7540
α_{yp}	−0.2111 E-04	−6.1508
α_{yr}	−0.4203 E-05	−2.0418
α_{pr}	−0.0428	−4.3744

R^2 Labor Equation	0.954	SEE Labor Equation	0.0135
R^2 P&E Equation	0.998	SEE P&E Equation	0.0037
R^2 R&D Equation	0.999	SEE R&D Equation	0.0020

TABLE IV. Chemical Industry Estimates

Parameter	Estimate	t-Statistic
α_0	0.5192	16.6690
α_y	0.6551 E-03	11.0290
α_p	−0.1336	−22.7040
α_r	−0.1268	−28.3650
α_{yy}	0.1089	13.6660
α_{pp}	0.0236	4.5452
α_{rr}	0.0214	16.7470
α_{ee}	1.8271	3.8026
α_{dd}	1.6898	3.9908
α_{yp}	−0.1922 E-04	−2.4974
α_{yr}	−0.6651 E-05	−0.9845
α_{pr}	−0.5555 E-02	−2.8038

R^2 Labor Equation	0.949	SEE Labor Equation	0.0372
R^2 P&E Equation	0.997	SEE P&E Equation	0.0057
R^2 R&D Equation	0.998	SEE R&D Equation	0.0053

Tables III-VI illustrate the estimates for foods, chemicals, primary metals, and nonelectrical machinery. In all of the industries the model fits the data quite well, most of the variables are significant, all of them have the correct sign, and, in particular, the second order conditions are satisfied.[4] The cost of adjustment estimate of physical capital is significantly different from zero at the 99 percent level of confidence for three out of the four industries. Only for the food industry is the coefficient marginally insignificant at the 90 percent level of confidence.

TABLE V. Primary Metals Industry Estimates

Parameter	Estimate	t-Statistic
α_0	0.1531	7.5820
α_y	0.3455 E-03	3.1828
α_p	−0.0986	−77.2850
α_r	−0.1433	−87.1730
α_{yy}	0.5350 E-06	2.8315
α_{pp}	0.9829 E-02	4.5640
α_{rr}	0.0227	6.1326
α_{ee}	0.8968	3.1825
α_{dd}	0.5271	1.8201
α_{yp}	−0.1254 E-04	−5.1134
α_{yr}	−0.8964 E-05	−2.9201
α_{pr}	−0.9846 E-02	−3.8210

R^2 Labor Equation	0.933	SEE Labor Equation	0.0348
R^2 P&E Equation	0.999	SEE P&E Equation	0.0026
R^2 R&D Equation	0.999	SEE R&D Equation	0.0036

TABLE VI. Nonelectrical Machinery Industry Estimates

Parameter	Estimate	t-Statistic
α_0	0.1136	4.8087
α_y	0.2152 E-02	2.4606
α_p	−0.1154	−12.6940
α_r	−0.1609	−51.3020
α_{yy}	0.3251 E-04	2.3866
α_{pp}	0.0478	2.7145
α_{rr}	0.0758	16.2430
α_{ee}	0.1018	2.2737
α_{dd}	0.3106	4.2636
α_{yp}	−0.2829 E-03	−2.7295
α_{yr}	−0.2492 E-03	−7.2832
α_{pr}	−0.0266	−4.9256

R^2 Labor Equation	0.991	SEE Labor Equation	0.0125
R^2 P&E Equation	0.989	SEE P&E Equation	0.0126
R^2 R&D Equation	0.999	SEE R&D Equation	0.0037

Since the R&D cost of adjustment estimate was insignificant in the industry-pooled model, it is of interest to see if the industry-specific estimates are different from the former. This test is one way of determining whether or not there was sufficient allowance for industry variation in the industry-pooled model. These results are presented in Table VII. Clearly, the industry-specific estimates of the cost of adjustment parameter are significantly different from the industry-pooled magnitude. In three out of the four industries the estimate of α_{dd} is significantly different from the industry-pooled estimate at the 99 percent level of confidence, while in the last industry (nonelectrical machinery) the test is marginally rejected at the 90 percent level. However, in this latter industry, although the coefficient is small, it is significantly different from zero at the 99 percent level of confidence. Hence R&D capital is a quasi-fixed factor of production, which implies that there are significant costs to develop knowledge.

TABLE VII. Test of the Equality of α_{dd} Between Industry-Pooled and Industry-Specific Estimates *

SIC 20 (Foods and Kindred Products)	$t = 11.28$
SIC 28 (Chemicals and Allied Products)	$t = 14.00$
SIC 33 (Primary Industrial Metals)	$t = 3.51$
SIC 35 (Machinery, except Electrical)	$t = 1.64$

* $\dfrac{0.1358 - \alpha_{dd}^i}{0.111}$, $i = 20, 28, 33, 35$

6. Price Elasticities of Factor Demands

There are two sets of price elasticities which are relevant to the present model. The first group relates to the situation when both quasi-fixed factors have adjusted to their long run magnitudes. Under these circumstances $\Delta K_p(t) = \Delta K_r(t) = 0$, and all prices, output, and the interest rate have adjusted to their stationary values. Consequently equations (8.1) and (8.2) become

$$\alpha_{ii} K_i / y + \alpha_i + \omega_i + \alpha_{yi} + \alpha_{pr} K_j / y = 0 \quad i = p, r \quad i \neq j , \tag{9}$$

where $\omega_i = p_i(r + \delta_i)/w$ $i = p, r$ is the wage normalized rental price for the ith quasi-fixed factor. From equation set (9), which is a simultaneous system, equation (7) (with $\Delta K_p(t) = \Delta K_r(t) = 0$) and using the estimates from Tables III to VI, all the long run price elasticities can be computed. These results are presented in Table VIII.

We can observe from this table that for the various industries there is a great deal of similarity with respect to the signs and magnitudes of the factor price elasticities. The own price elasticities of both quasi-fixed factors are negative and similar in value to each other, and across the four industries. Roughly an increase of 1 percent in the rental price of one of the quasi-fixed factors leads to a 0.5 percent decrease in its demand. Next we see that physical and knowledge capital are complements in each industry. However, the cross price elasticities differ across industries. In foods and chemicals, changes in the R&D rental price exerts greater downward pressure on the demand for physical capital, relative to a change in the physical capital rental rate on the demand for R&D capital. The converse is true for primary metals and nonelectrical machinery products. Our interest in emphasizing the demand for R&D capital as an endogenous input decision, which entails substantial development costs, has enabled us to show that there are significant own and cross price elasticity effects. These are usually neglected in treatments of R&D.[5]

Changes in the wage rate illustrate that both quasi-fixed factors are substitutes for labor, with the degree of substitution roughly the same order of magnitude for P&E and R&D capital. Only in the food industry, with the physical capital intensity of output more than twice as high as the R&D intensity and with the lowest labor-output ratio, is physical capital a significantly greater substitute for labor compared to R&D.

JEFFREY I. BERNSTEIN and M. ISHAQ NADIRI

TABLE VIII. Long-Run Elasticities of Factor Demands

Elasticity *	SIC			
	20	28	33	35
e_{pp}^{L}	–0.4784	–0.4325	–0.4738	–0.4538
e_{pr}^{L}	–0.5566	–0.1423	–0.2820	–0.1782
e_{pl}^{L}	1.0350	0.5748	0.7559	0.6320
e_{rp}^{L}	–0.2089	–0.0924	–0.3435	–0.2136
e_{rr}^{L}	–0.4965	–0.4980	–0.4696	–0.4276
e_{rl}^{L}	0.7054	0.5904	0.8131	0.6411
e_{lp}^{L}	0.2778	0.2307	0.1758	0.2945
e_{lr}^{L}	0.5045	0.3649	0.1553	0.2493
e_{ll}^{L}	–0.7822	–0.5956	–0.3311	–0.5438

* e_{ij}^{L} means long run factor j proce elasticity of factor i, with the subscript l representing labor, p means P&E capital, r stands for R&D capital, and the superscript L means the long run. All values of exogenous variables are equal to their mean.

Finally, we can observe that for each industry, and for each factor demand, changes in the wage rate elicit (in absolute value) the greatest response. This, of course, occurs because physical and R&D capital are complements, while each type of capital is a substitute for labor. Therefore, the results point out the importance of unit labor costs in the production process, and that changes in these costs cause significant modifications in the factor demands, both in absolute and relative terms.

TABLE IX. Intermediate-Run Elasticities of Factor Demands

Price Elasticities	SIC			
	20	28	33	35
	Elasticity Without Physical Capital Adjustment *			
e_{rr}^{J}	–0.4908	–0.5046	–0.4619	–0.4222
e_{rl}^{J}	0.4908	0.5046	0.4619	0.4222
e_{lr}^{J}	0.2328	0.2277	0.1986	0.2272
e_{ll}^{J}	–0.2328	–0.2277	–0.1986	–0.2272
	Elasticity Without R&D Capital Adjustment **			
e_{pp}^{I}	–0.4565	–0.4243	–0.4821	–0.4674
e_{pl}^{I}	0.4565	0.4243	0.4821	0.4674
e_{lp}^{I}	0.2172	0.1594	0.2251	0.2272
e_{ll}^{I}	–0.2172	–0.1594	–0.2251	–0.2272

* Superscript J means intermediate run with P&E not adjusted to its long run level.

** Superscript I means intermediate run with R&D not adjusted to its long run level. All values of the exogenous variables are equal to their mean.

It is often difficult to relate particular estimates to other research because of differences in model specification and data. However, if we look at the cost of adjustment models using aggregate data with at least two quasi-fixed factors (where labor was decomposed into skilled and unskilled labor), the own price elasticity of physical capital tends to be around -0.5 (see, for example, Morrison and Berndt, 1981 and Pindyck and Rotemberg, 1982b). This result is similar to our findings at the industry level.[6] In other models where there is a single quasi-fixed factor, the elasticity was approximately -0.2 (besides the previously cited two papers see Epstein and Denny, 1983).

Finally with respect to the own price elasticity of labor demand, the estimates seem to vary (see Hamermesh, 1976 for a survey of the pre-cost of adjustment literature). What appears to be consistent, though, is that the wage elasticity of labor demand is greater in absolute value to the own price elasticity of physical capital.[7]

Up to this juncture, we have calculated the factor price elasticities when both quasi-fixed factors have adjusted to their long run magnitudes. Now let us suppose only one of the quasi-fixed factors has adjusted. This second set of experiments recognizes that there may be differential speeds of adjustment in the quasi-fixed factors. These elasticities may be termed intermediate run.[8]

The intermediate run elasticities are presented in Table IX. The most striking conclusions are that the intermediate run own price elasticities for each type of capital are similar to the long run magnitudes, and the own and cross wage elasticities are significantly smaller (in absolute value) compared to the long run. The first conclusion strengthens the fact that factor prices influence R&D, as well as P&E capital. In particular, even if physical capital has not adjusted to its long run level, a 1 percent increase in the R&D rental price decreases its demand by 0.5 percent. The same is true for physical capital. The second conclusion appears to arise from the fact that in the long run both quasi-fixed factors are substitutes for labor. In the intermediate run only one of these inputs is able to adjust to the higher wage, so the degree of substitution for labor is smaller, and consequently the intermediate run own price elasticity of labor demand is smaller in absolute value.

7. Output Elasticities and the Returns of Scale

Since output is exogenous, we can calculate short, intermediate and long run output elasticities of factor demands. Table X contains these elasticities. With respect to labor, we can observe that for each industry there is a decline in output elasticity from the short to the long run. In the short run only labor is variable. Hence in response to an increase in demand for its product the firm must produce the additional output by increasing more than proportionately its demand for labor. As R&D and physical capital adjust, given the higher level of product demand, the firm increases its demand for the quasi-fixed factors and reduces the use of the variable factor of production. This result occurs because as each quasi-fixed factor increases, the demand for labor decreases. This is just another way of stating that P&E and R&D capital are substitutes for labor. Therefore in each industry we find that overshooting occurs for labor.

This finding is consistent with Morrison and Berndt (1981), where unskilled labor is a variable factor of production whose short run output elasticity is 1.349, and because they impose constant returns to scale, the long run elasticity is 1. This long run output elasticity is roughly consistent with those surveyed in Hamermesh (1976), and in Pindyck and Rotemberg (1982a, 1982b), although our short run elasticities for labor demand are quite different. Another result from the model is that the output elasticity of labor is affected when at least one of the quasi-fixed factors (but not necessarily both) adjusts to its long run level. In other words, for each industry there is virtually no difference between the intermediate and long run output elasticities of labor. All that is needed to dissipate labor overshooting is the adjustment of at least one of the quasi-fixed factors.

TABLE X. Output Elasticities of Factor Demands

Elasticities *	SIC			
	20	28	33	35
e_{ly}^S	1.8125	1.3592	1.6208	1.7024
e_{ly}^J	0.9459	0.9544	0.9436	0.9519
e_{ly}^I	0.9776	0.9864	0.9996	0.9759
e_{ly}^L	0.9754	1.0024	1.0074	0.9668
e_{ry}^J	1.0111	1.0138	1.0169	1.0462
e_{ry}^L	1.0425	1.0229	1.0412	1.0764
e_{py}^I	1.0684	1.0426	1.0337	1.0649
e_{py}^L	1.0842	1.0473	1.0435	1.0825

* The superscripts represent S - short run, J - intermediate run (P&E not adjusted), I - intermediate run (R&D not adjusted), L - long run. The values of the exogenous variables are equal to their mean.

The output elasticities of the physical and R&D capital stocks are quite similar both for the different industries and for the intermediate and long runs. It is also interesting to compare Tables VIII and IX to X. We see that output increases (or product demand growth) exert a larger effect on input demands compared to any individual price change (in absolute value). This suggests, in particular, that policies which spur product demand growth may cause more R&D and physical capital investment to be initiated than policies (such as specific tax allowances) which lower the rental rates.

Although we have not restricted the technologies to exhibit constant returns to scale, we can observe, from the long run output elasticities, that the returns to scale is not significantly different from unity.[9] In fact we can compute the returns to scale for each industry. In order to undertake this calculation, consider a general specification of the technology (adjustment costs are separable),

$$T(\ln L, \ln K_p, \ln K_r, \ln y) = 1, \tag{10}$$

where T is the transformation function defined over the natural logarithms of the inputs and output. The definition of returns to scale, which is the proportional increase in output resulting from the common proportional increase in all inputs, means that we need

$$T_L d\ln L + T_p D\ln K_p + T_r d\ln K_r + T_y d\ln y = 0. \tag{11}$$

Assuming $d\ln L = d\ln K_p = d\ln K_r = d\ln v$ then (11) becomes

$$\frac{d\ln y}{d\ln v} = -[T_L + T_p + T_r]/T_y \tag{12}$$

which is the measure of returns to scale.

We can represent the technology from (10) in terms of a labor requirements function defined over the natural logarithms of the inputs and output. Since the firm minimizes costs, and because there is a single variable factor of production, the labor requirements function is equivalent to the variable cost function. Let,

$$\ln L = H(\ln K_p, \ln K_r, \ln y) \tag{13}$$

and then the right side of (12) becomes

$$\frac{d\ln y}{d\ln v} = [\,1 - (H_p + H_r)\,]/H_y . \tag{14}$$

Equation (14) permits us to compute the returns to scale in terms of the specified labor requirements function, upon which our estimates are based.

TABLE XI. Short-Run Elasticities of Labor Demand and Returns to Scale

	SIC			
Elasticities *	20	28	33	35
e_{ly}^S	1.8125	1.3592	1.6208	1.7024
e_{lp}^S	−0.4219	−0.2106	−0.5576	−0.3680
e_{lr}^S	−0.2341	−0.1281	−0.1290	−0.3138
Returns to Scale	0.9137	0.9849	1.0406	0.9879

* The values of the exogenous variables are equal to their mean.

The results are presented in Table XI. For each industry, we show the three short run elasticities for labor demand, which are necessary for the calculation [which correspond to H_y, H_p and H_r in equation (14)]. The first row repeats the output elasticity found in the first row of Table X. The second and third rows represent respectively the short run elasticity of labor demand with respect to the physical and R&D capital inputs. There are some interesting features of these measures. First, as expected, they are all negative, so labor and the quasi-fixed factors are short run substitutes. Second, in each case labor and physical capital are stronger substitutes in the short run than labor and R&D capital, although in the nonelectrical machinery industry there is only a minor difference. The only other study we are aware of which has looked at elasticities between factor demands is Nadiri-Bitros (1980). They found, for the largest firms in their sample, a ranking of the degrees of substitution which is similar to ours, with $e_{lp}^S = -0.3430$ and $e_{lr}^S = -0.0386$. Indeed the physical capital elasticity of labor demand is strikingly close to the average of our industry measures, but our elasticity for R&D capital is substantially greater in absolute value.

The third result from Table XI is that for the industry with the lowest factor intensities of output (SIC 20, foods) and the industry with the highest intensities (SIC 28, chemicals) the P&E elasticity is nearly twice as large as the R&D elasticity. It seems that it is not the absolute magnitude of the input intensities which matters, but rather the relative difference between the capital intensities of output. This can be seen from the fact that the greatest difference between the physical and R&D capital intensities of output is found in SIC 33 (primary metals). Table XI shows that this industry exhibits the greatest difference in quasi-fixed factor short run elasticities of labor. Moreover, the industry with the smaller difference in the capital input intensities of output is SIC 35 (nonelectrical machinery), and here we observe very little difference in the degree of substitution between physical capital and R&D for labor.

The final row in Table XI shows the returns to scale. Each industry does not significantly depart from constant returns to scale, but there is some evidence of slightly decreasing returns to scale in the food industry.

8. Costs of Adjustment and Rates of Return

The model that has been estimated for the different industries is dynamic because of the presence of internal adjustment costs. This implies that for the quasi-fixed factors at each time period there is a wedge between the rental price and the marginal value for each type of capital. This wedge is represented by the marginal cost of adjustment. Hence the importance of adjustment costs can be understood by comparing the marginal cost of adjustment to the rental price. This ratio may be thought of as a 'coefficient of variability.' If the ratio is zero then the input is perfectly variable, because marginal adjustment costs are zero and the rental price equals the marginal value. Moreover, the higher the ratio the lower the degree of quasi-fixed factor variability.

For physical capital we compute,

$$\alpha_{ee}[w(t)\Delta K_p(t)/y(t)p_p(t)(r(t)+\delta_p)] \tag{15}$$

and for R&D capital the ratio is

$$\alpha_{dd}[w(t)\Delta K_r(t)/y(t)p_r(t)(r(t)+\delta_r)]. \tag{16}$$

The results are presented in Table XII. The first point to notice is that there is no consistent pattern across industries; for two (SIC 20 and 33) physical capital is relatively less variable than R&D, while the converse is true for the other two industries. Second, for foods, which exhibits the lowest input intensities of output, and for chemicals, which exhibits the highest (see Table I), we find the smallest difference (in absolute value) between the ratios; 0.044 for SIC 20 and 0.058 for SIC 28.

TABLE XII. Marginal Adjustment Costs Relative to the Rental Rate

Quasi-Fixed Factor	SIC			
	20	28	33	35
Physical Capital	0.268	0.589	0.363	0.197
R&D Capital	0.224	0.647	0.234	0.470

The third conclusion is that there is a great deal of variation across industries for each set of ratios. For both physical and knowledge capital the relative difference between the largest and smallest magnitude represents more than 200 percent. In addition, the industry with the most variability for physical capital (nonelectrical machinery) illustrates that almost 50 percent of its rental rate for knowledge capital consists of marginal adjustment costs.

There are no equivalent numbers to compare for R&D, but with respect to physical capital Pindyck and Rotemberg (1982b) found for U.S. manufacturing that equipment had a ratio of 0.23 and structures 0.34. These magnitudes seem to be in line with our findings for physical capital, across the four different industries.

The importance of marginal adjustment costs can shed some light on the nature of the rate of return to R&D capital (and to physical capital). There has been a great deal of interest in the result that the derived marginal value of R&D (for example, as measured by the marginal product) has been substantially above long-term interest rates in the economy. No clear explanation has been provided for this conclusion.

Let us step back for a moment to interpret the relationship in this model between the marginal values and the interest rate. Consider the long run situation. In this case equations (8.1) and (8.2) become

$$r = -\frac{w}{p_i}[\alpha_i + \alpha_{ii}\frac{K_i}{y} + \alpha_{yi}y + \alpha_{pr}\frac{K_j}{y}] - \delta_i \quad i, j = p, r \quad i \neq j .$$ (17)

Equation (17) states that the firm equates the interest rate (i.e., the opportunity cost of funds) to the marginal rate of return on each quasi-fixed factor. The latter consists of the per dollar decline in variable (i.e., labor) cost attributable to the specific type of capital net of depreciation. We can call the right side of equation (17) the net marginal value of either physical or knowledge capital.

The opportunity cost of funds is equated to the marginal rate of return on physical and R&D capital. However, in the short run the marginal rate of return consists of the net marginal value minus the marginal cost of adjustment. The net marginal value of capital must be sufficiently greater than the opportunity cost of funds to cover the marginal adjustment cost. Therefore, although the firm equates the marginal rate of return on each type of capital to the opportunity cost of funds, in each time period, the composition of the marginal rate of return differs between the long and short run.

The implication is that it is meaningful to investigate the relationship between the net marginal value and the interest rate. As long as marginal adjustment costs are positive, the net marginal value must be greater than the long run opportunity cost of funds. Thus the explanation, for the differences between the interest rate, the net marginal value of R&D, and physical capital, is that there are marginal costs of adjustment for each type of capital, and these costs are not equal.

TABLE XIII. Net Marginal Values and Marginal Adjustment Costs

	SIC			
	20	28	33	35
Net Marginal Values				
Physical Capital	0.080	0.133	0.091	0.047
R&D Capital	0.093	0.198	0.100	0.160
Marginal Costs of Adjustment				
Physical Capital	0.036	0.089	0.047	0.003
R&D Capital	0.049	0.154	0.056	0.116

$r = 0.044$ (mean value)

We compute the net marginal value for R&D and physical capital, for each of our four industries. The results are presented in the first two rows of Table XIII. We see that the net marginal value for physical capital is less than the magnitude for R&D in each industry. The highest value for both physical and R&D capital is found in the chemical industry (see Griliches, 1980 for a similar result). The difference between the net marginal values in the food and primary metal industries is not very large. The net marginal value for physical capital is 86 percent of that for R&D in foods, and 91 percent in primary metals. The differences are more significant in the other two industries; with 67 percent in chemicals and only 30 percent in nonelectrical machinery. These results are consistent with those presented in Table XI. For example for nonelectrical machinery, the proportion of marginal adjustment cost to the rental rate for physical capital was very small both in absolute terms and relative to the proportion for R&D. Thus we would expect that the net marginal value of physical capital would be substantially smaller than the value for R&D, and also not very different from the interest rate (which is 0.044 for the period under consideration). These conclusions are borne out in Table XIII.

In the long run (when marginal adjustment costs are zero) the net marginal value for each type of capital is the marginal rate of return, and equal to the interest rate. Hence, by subtracting the interest rate from the net marginal value we can determine the marginal cost of adjustment. These figures are given by the last two rows in Table XIII.

We see that the marginal costs of adjustment are consistently larger for R&D than for physical capital for each industry. The largest costs are found in the chemical industry, and the greatest difference between the costs for physical and knowledge capital is in the nonelectrical machinery products industry.

From Table XIII it can be observed that there are substantial differences between the short and long run net marginal value of R&D. Taking the interest rate to be the long run net marginal value for both types of capital, for chemicals the long run net marginal value is about 22 percent of the value in the short run (i.e., 0.044/0.198), for nonelectrical machinery 27 percent, for primary metals 44 percent, and for foods 47 percent. The situation is somewhat different for physical capital. As a percentage of the long run net marginal value, the long run value for chemicals is 33 percent, for primary metals 48 percent, for foods 55 percent, and for nonelectrical machinery 98 percent. We see that the ranking has changed and the percentages have increased slightly for physical capital. Consequently, our findings illustrate that the net marginal value, for both types of capital in the short run and for each industry, exceeds the interest rate, while the value for R&D is greater than the value for physical capital.

9. Conclusion

In this paper we have examined the price and output effects on factor demands and the role of adjustment costs in a dynamic cost minimizing model relating to labor, R&D, and physical capital requirements. With respect to factor substitution possibilities, we found a consistent pattern emerging for the different industries. R&D capital is quite responsive to the different factor price changes, and generally R&D and physical capital are complements, while the quasi-fixed factors are substitutes for labor.

Output growth exerts a significant impact on factor requirements across the various industries. Indeed in absolute value terms output elasticities exceed factor price elasticities. We also found that in the short run, when the capital inputs are fixed, overshooting occurs in the demand for labor. However, because the quasi-fixed factors are substitutes for labor, as they adjust the overshooting dissipates.

Finally we have detailed the importance of adjustment costs. In fact, we found for R&D that marginal adjustment costs represent anywhere from 22 percent to 65 percent of the rental rate, while for physical capital the range is from 20 percent to 60 percent. These adjustment costs enable us to explain the large differences between the marginal value of R&D and physical capital, and between the marginal values and the interest rate.

Important avenues for future research remain open. Two crucial ones relate to the problems of financing and spillovers. First, in this paper we have assumed that all the benefits from R&D can be fully appropriated. We know, of course, that in general this is not true and that the accumulation of knowledge is affected by the R&D (both present and past) decisions of other firms. By admitting less than full appropriation, we could develop a model that would permit the estimation of spillover effects. In addition, it would then be possible to see how the private rate of return on R&D differs both from the industry-specific rate of return and the social rate of return.

Conventional wisdom holds that R&D investment is generally financed out of internal funds to a greater degree than physical investment. In order to investigate and test this view it would be of interest to develop and estimate a model integrating the decisions on real capital accumulation and financial capital structure. A byproduct of this analysis would be the testing of whether financial costs or adjustment costs exert the greater influence on R&D and physical capital investment decisions.

Notes

* The authors are greatly indebted to Graham Corke for his programming assistance and would like to thank Ernst Berndt and Zvi Griliches for helpful comments on this topic. Financial support was provided by NSF grant 810635 and by the C. V. Starr Center for Applied Economics' Focal Program for Capital Formation, Technological Change, Financial Structure and Tax Policy.

1. In other words, $\partial(L(t)/y(t))/\partial\Delta K_p(t) = \partial(L(t)/y(t))/\partial\Delta K_r(t) = 0$ at $\Delta K_p(t) = \Delta K_r(t) = 0$, which is easily seen to be the case in equation (7). We have also imposed the usual assumption that the adjustment costs of the two quasi-fixed factors (in this case P&E and R&D) are independent. See Morrison and Berndt (1981) and Pindyck and Rotemberg (1982b).

2. Clearly, the disturbances in the labor-output equation could also arise through measurement errors.

3. The one-tailed test of H_0: $\alpha_{dd} = 0$, H_A: $\alpha_{dd} > 0$ at the 90% level of confidence is 1.645.

4. The second order conditions were initially imposed by the procedure described in Lau (1974). With these estimates as initial conditions, we re-estimated the models without the imposition of the second order conditions. The convergence criteria we used was 0.001. In all cases convergence was achieved.

5. This point has been previously emphasized by Nadiri (1982).

6. The focus on two quasi-fixed factors and the decomposition of labor or physical capital seems appropriate in our context, since we have two quasi-fixed factors with R&D essentially being an aggregate of a particular class of labor and physical capital.

7. Comparison of cross price elasticities is even more difficult, given the diversity of the factors involved in the different models.

8. Pindyck and Rotemberg (1982a) calculate intermediate run elasticities when labor adjusts but physical capital does not. In the present paper we calculate these elasticities under the assumption that first R&D adjusts but P&E does not, and then for the converse case.

9. A property of constant returns to scale is that the long run output elasticity of each factor demand is unity. Clearly from Table X these elasticities are close to one.

References

Amemiya, T.: 1977, 'The Maximum Likelihood and Nonlinear Three Stage Least Squares Estimator in the General Nonlinear Simultaneous Equations Model', *Econometrica*, **45**, 265-296.

Epstein, L. G., and M. G. S. Denny: 1983, 'The Multivariate Flexible Accelerator Model: Its Empirical Restrictions and an Application to U.S. Manufacturing', *Econometrica*, **51**, 647-674.

Griliches, Z.: 1980, 'Returns to Research and Development Expenditures in the Private Sector', in J. W. Kendrick and B. N. Vaccara (eds.), *New Developments in Productivity Measurement and Analysis*, The University of Chicago Press, Chicago, Illinois, U.S.A..

Hamermesh, D. S.: 1976, 'Econometric Studies of Labor Demand and Their Application to Policy Analysis', *Journal of Human Resources*, **11**, 507-525.

Hansen, L. P.: 1982, 'Large Sample Properties of Generalized Method of Movements Estimators', *Econometrica*, **50**, 1029-1054.

Hansen, L. P., and K. J. Singleton: 1982, 'Generalized Instrumental Variables Estimation of Nonlinear Rational Expectations Models', *Econometrica*, **50**, 1269-1286.

Jorgenson, D. W., and J. Laffont: 1974, 'Efficient Estimation of Nonlinear Simultaneous Equations with Additive Disturbances', *Annals of Economic and Social Measurement*, **3**, 615-640.

Lau, L.: 1974, 'The Econometrics of Monotonicity, Convexity and Quasi-Concavity', IMSS Report No. 123, Stanford University, Stanford, California, U.S.A.

Mansfield, E.: 1965, 'Rates of Return from Industrial Research and Development', *American Economic Review*, **55**, 310-322.

Mansfield, E.: 1968, *The Economics of Technical Change*, Norton, New York, New York, U.S.A.

Meese R.: 1980, 'Dynamic Factor Demand Schedules for Labor and Capital Under Rational Expectations', *Journal of Econometrics*, **14**, 141-158.

Minasian, J.: 1969, 'Research and Development, Production Functions, and Rates of Return', *American Economic Review*, **59**, 80-85.

Morrison, C. J., and E. R. Berndt: 1981, 'Short Run Labor Productivity in a Dynamic Model', *Journal of Econometrics*, **16**, 339-365.

Mortenson, D. T.: 1973, 'Generalized Costs of Adjustment and Dynamic Factor Demand Theory', *Econometrica*, **41**, 657-666.

Nadiri, M. I.: 1980, 'Sectoral Productivity Slowdown', *American Economic Review*, **70**, 349-352.

Nadiri, M. I.: 1982, 'Tax Incentives and Innovation Expenditures', in E.Collins (ed.), *Tax Policy and Investment in Innovation*, National Science Foundation, Washington, D.C., U.S.A.

Nadiri, M. I., and G. C. Bitros: 1980, 'Research and Development Expenditures and Labor Productivity at the Firm Level', in J. W. Kendrick and B. N. Vaccara (eds.), *New Developments in Productivity Measurement and Analysis*, The University of Chicago Press, Chicago, Illinois, U.S.A.

Pakes, A., and M. Schankerman: 1978, 'The Rate of Obsolescence of Knowledge, Research Gestation Lags, and the Private Rate of Return to Research Resources', Discussion Paper No. 659, Harvard Institute of Economic Research, Cambridge, Massachusetts, U.S.A.

Pindyck, R. S., and J. J. Rotemberg; 1982a, 'Dynamic Factor Demands, Energy Use and the Effects of Energy Price Shocks', Working Paper No. 82-024, M.I.T. Energy Laboratory, Cambridge, Massachusetts, U.S.A.

Pindyck, R. S., and J. J. Rotemberg: 1982b, 'Dynamic Factor Demands Under Rational Expectations', Working Paper No. 1015, NBER.

Terleckyj, N.: 1974, 'Effects of R&D on the Productivity Growth of Industries', National Planning Association, Washington, D.C., U.S.A.

Treadway, A. B.: 1971, 'On the Multivariate Flexible Accelerator', *Econometrica*, **39**, 845-855.

Treadway, A. B.: 1974, 'The Globally Optimal Flexible Accelerator', *Journal of Economic Theory*, **7**, 17-39.

INDEX

ADVANCED STUDIES IN THEORETICAL AND APPLIED ECONOMETRICS

1. Paelinck J.H.P. (ed.): Qualitative and Quantitative Mathematical Economics, 1982.
   ISBN 90 247 2623 9.
2. Ancot J.P. (ed.): Analysing the Structure of Econometric Models, 1984.
   ISBN 90 247 2894 0.
3. Hughes Hallet A.J. (ed.): Applied Decision Analysis and Economic Behaviour, 1984.
   ISBN 90 247 2968 8.
4. Sengupta J.K.: Information and Efficiency in Economic Decision, 1985.
   ISBN 90 247 3072 4.
5. Artus P. and Guvenen O. (eds.), in collaboration with Gagey F.: International Macroeconomic Modelling for Policy Decisions, 1986.
   ISBN 90 247 3201 8.
6. Vilares M.J.: Structural Change in Macroeconomic Models, Theory and Estimation, 1986.
   ISBN 90 247 3277 8.
7. Carraro C. and Sartore D. (eds.): Development of Control Theory for Economic Analysis, 1987.
   ISBN 90 247 3345 6.
8. Broer D.P. (ed.): Neoclassical Theory and Empirical Models of Aggregate Firm Behaviour, 1987.
   ISBN 90 247 3412 6.
9. Italianer A.: Theory and Practice of International Trade Linkage Models, 1986.
   ISBN 90 247 3407 X.
10. Kendrick D.A.: Feedback, A New Framework for Macroeconomic Policy, 1988.
    ISBN 90 247 3593 9 (HB). ISBN 90 247 3650 1 (PB).
11. Sengupta J.K. and Kadekodi G.K. (eds.): Econometrics of Planning and Efficiency, 1988.
    ISBN 90 247 3602 1.
12. Griffith D.A.: Advanced Spatial Statistics. Special Topics in the Exploration of Quantitative Spatial Data Series, 1988.
    ISBN 90 247 3627 7.
13. Guvenen O.: International Commodity Market Models and Policy Analysis, 1988.
    ISBN 90 247 3768 0.
14. Arbia G.: Spatial Data Configuration in Statistical Analysis of Regional Economic and Related Problems, 1989.
    ISBN 0 7923 0284 2.
15. Raj B.: Advances in Econometrics and Modelling, 1989.
    ISBN 0 7923 0299 0.
16. Aznar Grasa A.: Econometric Model Selection: A New Approach, 1989.
    ISBN 0 7923 0321 0.